"Wemigwans' concept of the digital bundle is an integral and effective intellectual intervention, [one that] I can see as the cornerstone of a much greater theoretical work about the epistemic facets of digitized Indigenous Knowledge. . . . The more documentation that we have of "digital bundles," the more that policy-makers, librarians, archivists, museum specialists, and technologists can prepare spaces for these kinds of projects. . . . Therefore, this is an important book not only to an Indigenous studies audience, but also within the field of library and information science, archival and museum studies, Internet studies, cultural studies, and society and technology studies." —MARISA DUARTE, author of *Network Sovereignty: Building the Internet across Indian Country*

"Jennifer Wemigwans' work is timely and will spark a dialogue about the cultural shift in how we share Indigenous Knowledge online. The movement promises reconciliatory and resurgent possibilities for global Indigenous collaboration and organization, so long as we ground the movement in Indigenous cultural perspectives, ethics, and care." —JEAN-PAUL RESTOULE, co-editor of *Indigenous Research: Theories, Practices, and Relationships*

"*A Digital Bundle* highlights the Internet and its role in the transmission of Indigenous Knowledge from Elders and established Indigenous academics. . . . Jennifer Wemigwans has clearly emerged as an exemplary model of a new generation of Indigenous scholar who is ethically responsible and equally knowledgeable about the generational transference of knowledge in Indigenous communities. This work is not only about the interstices of Indigenous Knowledge and technology but, based on Wemigwans' example, a new standard for practicing it." —JOLENE RICKARD, director of the American Indian and Indigenous Studies Program, Cornell University

A Digital Bundle

Protecting and Promoting Indigenous Knowledge Online

JENNIFER WEMIGWANS

University of Regina Press

Printed and bound in Canada at Marquis. The text of this book is printed on 100% post-consumer recycled paper with earth-friendly vegetable-based inks.

Cover art: Courtesy the author
Cover and text design: Duncan Campbell, University of Regina Press
Copy editor: Dallas Harrison
Proofreader: Rhonda Kronyk
Indexer: Sergey Lobchev, Brookfield Indexing Services

Library and Archives Canada Cataloguing in Publication

Wemigwans, Jennifer, author
      A digital bundle : protecting and promoting Indigenous knowledge online / Jennifer Wemigwans. Includes bibliographical references and index.
Issued in print and electronic formats. ISBN 978-0-88977-551-0 (SOFTCOVER).
—ISBN 978-0-88977-552-7 (PDF).—ISBN 978-0-88977-553-4 (HTML).

1. Internet and native peoples--Canada. 2. Internet and indigenous peoples.
3. Computer network resources. 4. Ethnoscience—Computer network resources.
5. Native peoples—Canada—Computer network resources. 6. Indigenous peoples—Computer network resources. 7. Native peoples—Canada—Communication.
8. Indigenous peoples—Communication. I. Title.

E98.C73W46 2018   302.23'108997071   C2018-903901-9   C2018-903902-7

10 9 8 7 6 5 4 3 2 1

University of Regina Press, University of Regina
Regina, Saskatchewan, Canada, S4S 0A2
TEL: (306) 585-4758 FAX: (306) 585-4699
WEB: www.uofrpress.ca

U OF R PRESS

We acknowledge the support of the Canada Council for the Arts for our publishing program. We acknowledge the financial support of the Government of Canada. / Nous reconnaissons l'appui financier du gouvernement du Canada. This publication was made possible with support from Creative Saskatchewan's Creative Industries Production Grant Program and with the help of a grant from the Federation for the Humanities and Social Sciences, through the Awards to Scholarly Publications Program, using funds provided by the Social Sciences and Humanities Research Council of Canada.

 Canada Council   Conseil des arts
for the Arts   du Canada
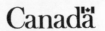 Canada
 creative SASKATCHEWAN

For those of us who are actively
searching for our ways of knowing.

CONTENTS

Jeff Thomas website
　　　https://jeff.thomas.ca

Jeff addresses the issue of "what is the valve of archival collection in addressing indigenous self-determination"?

ACKNOWLEDGEMENTS

This book comes from sharing many cups of tea with family, friends and community. Chi miigwetch to my partner Doug Anderson and my son Nigel, and to my colleagues and friends Dr. Kari Delhi, Dr. Jean-Paul Restoule, Dr. Rinaldo Walcott, Dr. Sandy Grande, Prof. Myriam Rafla, Tracy Pryce, and Dr. Susan Dion. I also want to deeply thank all the research participants who shared their insights on this project: Dr. John Borrows, Donna Bourque, Prof. Larry Chartrand, Brenda Dubois, Dr. Rainey Gaywish, Cheryl L'Hirondelle, Priscilla Lepine, Monique Mojica, Émilie Monnet, Dr. Angela Nardozi, and Janetta Soup.

I also want to acknowledge all the people who made FourDirectionsTeachings.com a reality, including Winston Bromley, a friend and ally committed to respectful representations of Indigenous Knowledge and ways of being, and to the Elders who shared their teachings: Stephen Augustine, Dr. Reg Crowshoe and Geoff Crow Eagle, Mary Lee, the late Lillian Pitawanakwat, and Tom Porter.

Thanks to the University of Regina Press, in particular Karen Clark, whose generosity of spirit and time was greatly appreciated, and to editors Kelly Laycock and Dallas Harrison, whose attention to detail pulled all the pieces together. Also a huge thanks to the anonymous reviewers, whose guidance and questions made this work better.

CHAPTER 1

INDIGENOUS RESURGENCE
AND THE INTERNET

→ Philosophical study of being (handwritten)

I ndigenous ontologies and cosmologies are regenerating communities across Turtle Island and reconnecting Indigenous
Peoples with their spiritual and cultural power. This book
looks at how Indigenous Knowledge online has had socio-cul-
tural effects and how information communication technology (ICT)
affects relationships among diverse Indigenous Peoples and the flow
of power between Indigenous Peoples and the state. Within an Indigenous framework, this work supports the notion that power residing
in media networks is stronger than that residing in government (Castells, 2010). A series of interviews with Indigenous activists, artists,
educators, and front-line workers demonstrates a vast network of cultural exchange based upon the flow of local Indigenous Knowledge
from specific community contexts to the national stage and even the
global stage. Indigenous Knowledge online is instrumental to the
success of Indigenous community resurgence and radical application
of knowledge in all fields, including education, health, law, and social
well-being. The interviews conducted across Canada reveal not only
the dialectical relationship between online and offline political action
and engagement but also how activists, educators, and front-line

workers use Indigenous Knowledge online to create, develop, and enhance their own work. Indigenous Knowledge online speaks back to dominant colonial systems of knowledge in Canada by representing an active presence rooted in the local soils of diverse Elders and Knowledge Keepers.

[handwritten: revitalization is important]

The revitalization of Indigenous Knowledge systems and practices is key to the movement of Indigenous resurgence and ultimately the transformation and sustainability of Indigenous communities. Indigenous resurgence is connected to Indigenous Knowledge and is acknowledged by writers such as Leanne Simpson who are bringing forward "fourth world theory—theories, strategies and analysis strongly rooted in the values, knowledge and philosophies of Indigenous Nations" (Corntassel & Spak, 2010, 135). However, such work is often not connected with the field of new technologies and Internet studies.

For example, scholars such as Kate Hennessy (Hennessy & Moore, 2007) and Linc Kesler,[1] who have done extensive work on online projects for Indigenous communities, are concerned with the role of digital technology in the documentation and safeguarding of cultural heritage. The notion of safeguarding is also of great interest to many Indigenous communities, which have come to see information technology as an important tool for preserving their traditional cultures for the future (Dyson, Hendriks, & Grant, 2007). In fact, early writings on the relationship between the Internet and Indigenous Peoples stressed that computer technologies can be used as tools for self-determination and that "we can determine our use of new technologies to support, strengthen and enrich our cultural communities" (L'Hirondelle, 1994). These statements speak directly to the field of Indigenous resurgence, and they have inspired this work. Beyond safeguarding cultural heritage, how do we protect the flow of communication and access to Indigenous Knowledge for the next seven generations? Knowing that net neutrality is not a given and that access to the Internet and ICTs is not a government guarantee, how do Indigenous Peoples safeguard freedom of expression and access to Indigenous Knowledge online for future generations?

[handwritten margin notes: Issues; limitation issues; information communication technology]

[handwritten bottom note: Principle that the internet service providers should enable access to all content and applications regardless of the source, and without favoring or blocking particular products or websites. — Net neutrality]

This book investigates the role of knowledge production in the construction and use of the online Indigenous Knowledge site FourDirectionsTeachings.com. The term "knowledge production" is used in an academic context, and I use it here, but it has different implications when used in the context of "producing" Indigenous Knowledge online. What I am talking about here is not the "production of knowledge" in the sense of "creating" new knowledge, at least not in the sense of being part of the "progress" of knowledge usually assumed in modern Eurocentric thought (which would be a problematic concept from many if not all traditional Indigenous perspectives). "Knowledge production" here refers to the technical production, or really the reproduction, of *aspects of long-existing Indigenous Knowledge in new formats and in relation to new contexts*—in the sense of assembling, representing, and creatively configuring this pre-existing knowledge but certainly not of creating it.

Indigenous Knowledge is a complex epistemological paradigm. To better comprehend it, I have pulled the definitions below from my readings of Marlene Brant Castellano, Taiaiake Alfred, Leanne Simpson, and John Borrows. For example, I perceive Indigenous Knowledge in two distinct forms: sacred teachings and personal knowledge.

Sacred teachings consist of Traditional Knowledge passed on through *ceremonial protocols*. Only Elders and Traditional Teachers who have been *gifted* the Indigenous Knowledge and teachings in this way can share those teachings publicly and transfer them. This type of Indigenous Knowledge is often considered as belonging to the community and held in trust by Knowledge Keepers and Elders expected to abide by the cultural protocols entrusted to that knowledge.

Personal knowledge is acquired through individual educational pursuits, empirical processes, or the gifts that one is born with or has received through revealed knowledge, which includes spiritual knowledge gained through dreams, visions, intuitions, and meditations. Personal knowledge is not bounded by the cultural protocols of the community in the way that Traditional Knowledge is. An Elder or Traditional Knowledge Keeper also acquires knowledge through

[Handwritten margin notes: "Knowledge reproduction in new formats"; "Does Birdman Rising fall under reproduction and possibly new info?"; "Sacred teaching"; "vs."; "Personal Knowledge"; "Jeff Thomas has personal knowledge and dreams visions"; "Inspired by"]

empirical observation as well as the gifts that he or she is born with or has received through revealed knowledge. However, the role of an Elder or Traditional Knowledge Keeper is very different from the role of an Indigenous artist or academic who has acquired personal knowledge. Although an Elder might choose to claim the role of an artist, it is highly unlikely that an Indigenous artist or academic or politician would claim the role of an Elder or Traditional Knowledge Keeper unless she or he is acknowledged as one and conferred with the title by the community. This distinction is important because it is a concept understood instinctively by Indigenous communities even though not always articulated or discussed.

As a producer of Indigenous Knowledge media projects and as an academic, I make it a part of my practice to articulate this distinction so as not to assume or usurp the role of a Knowledge Keeper or to disrespect Indigenous protocols held by Elders who carry the Indigenous Knowledge of their communities. In clearly articulating my knowledge as acquired knowledge, and in recognizing Indigenous Knowledge Keepers and Elders as representing the Indigenous Knowledge protocols of their communities, I hope to convey the importance and significance of locating how Indigenous Knowledge is respectfully represented in my media and academic work. I hope that this is a way of demonstrating Indigenous ethics and of reinforcing a type of Indigenous copyright on the cultivation and dissemination of Indigenous Knowledge for public consumption.

This book also explores the potential of the Internet and digital technology to serve Indigenous resurgence agendas by contributing to the efforts and goals of Indigenous nation building, and it aims to bridge the fields of Indigenous resurgence and Internet studies (Benkler, 2006), thus contributing to new understandings of the role of Indigenous Knowledge and education in a networked world.

The phenomenon of Internet users searching for Indigenous Knowledge online demonstrates the need for access to Indigenous Knowledge and reveals the intentions, experiences, and perceptions of Indigenous Internet users, who intuitively navigate the Internet within a complex understanding of Indigenous epistemology.

This book discusses knowledge production in relation to the community, using the example of how FourDirectionsTeachings.com is taken up by visitors who use the site and how the site came to be accepted as a legitimate source of Indigenous Knowledge online by many Indigenous artists and educators and Canadian institutions and organizations that work with Indigenous Peoples. It is important to note that FourDirectionsTeachings.com was created and produced within Indigenous protocols, demonstrating Indigenous practice and applied Indigenous ethics in the construction of a digital site.

In *Networks of Outrage and Hope: Social Movements in the Internet Age*, Manuel Castells (2012, 11) looks at how mass self-communication supports the ability of the social actor to be autonomous via networks of the Internet: "This is why governments are afraid of the Internet, and this is why corporations have a love-hate relationship with it and are trying to extract profits while limiting its potential for freedom (for instance, by controlling file sharing or open source networks)." In a podcast, Castells defines the networks of the Internet as a new social structure that has transformed communication networks and socialization.[2] These networks can be broadly defined as two competing streams on the Internet: the consumption model, which privileges features that support commercial transactions and advertisements, such as Facebook, Google, and Amazon; and the community model, which relies on communication features that support online community and public life (Foshay, 2016). The community model represents an inversion of mass media broadcasting and publication by allowing a bottom-up alternative through the self-produced communication features of the Internet. For Internet theorist Andrew Feenberg, "the future of the Internet depends on which actors prevail in determining its technical code" (see Foshay, 2016, 39).

To better comprehend the meaning of the technical code, it is helpful to look at Tim Berners-Lee (2014, 181), "widely acclaimed as the inventor of the Web because he wrote many of the fundamental protocols and created the original prototypes." In an interview, Berners-Lee described web science as the design of two things: a social protocol and a technological protocol (184). Using email as an example, he identified the technical code created to send and receive email. This transaction, according to him, was designed as a microscopic system with the intent of person-to-person communication. However, spam occurred. He stated that "one of our social assumptions was wrong, namely, that everybody is friendly and will only send e-mail to another person when the other person wants to read it. So the academic assumption is broken, and we have to redesign e-mail" (184). For Berners-Lee, spam is the macroscopic phenomenon that emerged from email and produced a social and technological problem now in need of redesign and reconfiguration. Spam also demonstrates the ongoing tension between business interests and community/person-to-person relational networks.

As of 2018, the World Wide Web is twenty-nine years old, a young adult, yet it is now the most ubiquitous medium of communication for business, community, and education. Be that as it may, the Truth and Reconciliation Commission of Canada, in the "Media and Reconciliation" section of its report (Sinclair, Wilson, & Littlechild, 2015, 335), completely missed any discussion of the Internet. This omission is a significant oversight, since the Internet is the main channel of communication for many Indigenous communities dispersed across North and South America and has become the main tool of dissemination of information and knowledge from the grassroots level. There has also been extensive lobbying in Canada to provide broadband services to geographically disparate Indigenous Nations, and there have been ongoing efforts to link Indigenous communities to services for e-health, education, and various online government services. For Indigenous transmedia producers like me, interested in Indigenous Knowledge on the web, a discussion of web science and its meaning in terms of social and technological protocols is necessary for what Gerald Vizenor (2008) calls our *"survivance,"* which represents our efforts at both survival of and resistance to colonization.

Autonomous social actors now have access to one of the most powerful tools of communication in society. This transformation of access to communication technology is a great threat to the dominant hegemony because it circumvents the ability of those in power

↳ leadership or dominance

to control communication.[3] In writing about social movements, Castells (2012) notes that they seek to resist economic and political oppression and reject the political arrogance of elites. The ability to shape minds is the greatest power that one can have because, for Castells, it is harder to control through fear and violence when a large number of people are independently changing how they think. The loss of persuasive influence over people's minds is what arrogant governments and elite institutions fear the most; much centralized institutional control is lost when alternative notions of social change arise independently.

Ideas related to recognizing and valuing Indigenous Knowledge in education and community building arise not from Canadian governments at any level but from Indigenous Peoples who have been disconnected from one another historically. Although of course such people have always striven (against great odds and often at great personal costs) to maintain contact with one another—and nothing can replace the need for real human interaction and knowledge transmission, especially when it comes to Indigenous Knowledge—the Internet contributes to broader cultural movements such as Indigenous resurgence by serving as a tool that (ideally) helps disseminate important ideas to act on and connect the minds of many more people than was previously possible. Castells is right when he notes that the most important thing about a movement is not the impact that it has on institutions but what it does in people's minds.[4] This book demonstrates how Indigenous Knowledge online contributes in significant ways to the movement of Indigenous resurgence and thereby represents a new social movement, a new Internet activism propelled and shaped by Indigenous perspectives and values.

It is good, I chose to title my project "Through the perspective" of... that way it distinguishes itself from Elder and traditional teachings.

Returning to Ourselves

So that we can better understand Indigenous Knowledge and perspectives, I have drawn from the work of Doug Anderson, who invited me to read the draft of *Natural Curiosity 2nd Edition: A Resource for*

the authority given by

Educators: The Importance of Indigenous Perspectives in Children's Environmental Inquiry (Anderson, Chiarotto, & Comay, 2017). He writes that "reducing Indigenous perspectives to simplistic terms is problematic. . . . However, . . . most, if not all, Indigenous perspectives include" the following:

- a strong sense of spirituality
- a deeply rooted sense of place
- a recognition that everything is related
- an emphasis on reciprocity. (6–7)

He states that "the four qualities listed above are not a comprehensive summary of Indigenous perspectives" (7), yet they are key to many Indigenous worldviews. For example, in thinking about spirituality, Anderson notes that "Indigenous perspectives ultimately see Spirit as the greater reality, preceding matter in the creative order. This creative order transcends time, so Spirit and matter co-exist constantly in the process of Creation. Everything is always *coming into being* from a spiritual source" (58).

Place is rooted in the land, and the deep connection that Indigenous Peoples have to their lands is reflected and represented in their community stories, traditions, and languages. For the Anishinaabek, the word *Aki* is understood to mean "everything," though it often gets translated into "the land" or "earth." Understanding the land as "everything in our place" and realizing that "everything has spirit" are foundational concepts in recognizing how everything is related. Anderson summarizes this notion beautifully: "Because everything is alive with Spirit, we are related to everything, and our relatives include animals, plants, the elements, past and future beings, subtle levels of being, and the spiritual world beyond time and space" (Anderson, Chiarotto, & Comay, 2017, 104). In this way, we are all part of the greater sacred hoop, which encompasses all of Creation. For this connection and our small place in this greater sacred hoop, we are grateful, and hence we emphasize reciprocity. Anderson clarifies that this value is expressed through cultural practices of giving when we need to receive something. In many Indigenous cultures, people offer tobacco or some other "gift" for what they seek, whether that gift be food or medicine from the land, or help with a ceremony. . . . [Offerings] are a way to give thanks for everything that is given to us, including our own lives and the Spirit that flows through everything around us. Ultimately, these offerings are a way to recognize our affiliation with all the gifts of Creation. (134)

Keeping these concepts in mind while reading this book will give you a greater understanding of the discussions on Indigenous Knowledge and protocols, decolonization, articulations of Indigeneity, and respect for the cultural diversity of Indigenous Peoples.

So to begin I will share some personal information as a way of introducing myself and practising *Biskaabiiyang*, what Wendy Geniusz (2009) refers to as a methodology for "returning to ourselves."

Ahnii. Anishinaabekwe endau. Makwa ndodem. Wikwemikong minowa Toronto ndobinjoba. Hello. I am an Anishinaabe (Ojibwe-Potawatomi) woman and a member of the Bear Clan. My mother is from Wikwemikong Unceded Indian Reserve in Ontario, Canada. My father is unknown to me. I have been told that he is of Irish ancestry and from the Maritimes. Genetically I am mixed, but culturally I am Anishinaabe because I was raised with my mother and her extended family. Each year was spent living in Toronto during the school year and living on the reserve during the summer and winter holidays. We would stay at my grandparents' house on Murray Hill. My grandfather was Potawatomi. His family came up from the Wisconsin area. My grandmother was originally a Manitowabi. She married at the age of thirteen, right after residential school, and took on my grandfather's name.

For Geniusz (2009), Biskaabiiyang approaches to research begin with the Anishinaabe researcher, who must look at his or her own life and how he or she has been personally colonized in order to conduct research from the standpoint of *Anishinaabe-inaadiziwin*

How the author approached her research

What are the protocols Non-Native Americans have to follow when researching Native American information?

(Anishinaabe "psychology" or "way of being"). Rather than assuming an unbiased stance toward research, a researcher using Biskaabiiyang approaches to research submerges herself or himself within Anishinaabe-inaadiziwin and *Anishinaabe-izhitwaawin* (Anishinaabe "culture, teachings, customs, history"), the very things that she or he is researching. From this position, the Anishinaabe researcher must acknowledge the personal connection to the research because the protocols of Anishinaabe-izhitwaawin require that one always explains his or her personal and intellectual background whenever sharing *aadizookaan* ("traditional legends") or *dibaajimowin* ("teachings, ordinary stories"). To do otherwise takes credibility away from the information presented and insults those who gave that Anishinaabe the teachings.

Therefore, in honour of all the Elders, advisers, and research participants who worked with me on FourDirectionsTeachings.com, and on the subsequent research on the impact of Indigenous Knowledge online, I will continue introducing and locating myself within a Biskaabiiyang approach, as described above. I will also do so as an acknowledgement of spirit and to honour the gifts that each of us is born with because, as Anderson so passionately spells out,

> our failure to ignite and share our spirits is barbarism. Set apart from one another, it becomes easier to succumb to self-interest, indiscriminately accelerated material progress, and the acquisition of *things*. In such a world, our shared purpose, our deeper selves, and love itself, are dimmed. But together we survive. Given a chance, our inner fire can be shared sincerely, which brings light to others. (Anderson, Chiarotto, & Comay, 2017, 64)

I was given a spirit name much later in life. I am still learning what the name means, so I am not totally confident using it publicly. I am also not comfortable speaking or writing in Anishinaabemowin (the Ojibwe language) because I still need to develop my skills. However, I was told by late Elder Lillian Pitawanakwat never to say that I don't know my language, because I was raised hearing it, and the imprint is still there and remains strong. I began learning about Anishinaabe traditional culture in my early twenties, when I was employed as a front-line community worker in Toronto for various not-for-profit Aboriginal organizations. They included Native women's and men's drop-in centres, homeless shelters, and cultural centres.

Based upon my experience as an adult literacy instructor, I formed some initial impressions that led me to believe that the Internet could lead to greater empowerment for members of Indigenous communities. For example, I believed that the personal and flexible ways in which people can explore the Internet are well suited to adult learners who want to gain knowledge at their own pace. I also intuitively felt that such a project might help members of Indigenous communities who are dealing with many significant learning issues related to literacy, perceptions of learning, and learning styles (George, 2002; Hill, 2010). I hoped that it might also help Indigenous Peoples to reconnect with their cultures, especially those who, like me, might have experienced disenfranchisement from their cultural teachings and the idea of Indigenous Knowledge.

With respect to locating myself, my personal experience of colonization is a continued presence that I resist daily. I grew up in a family that struggled with poverty, addictions, lack of education, abuse, institutional violence, and a plethora of health issues. Consequently, at the age of twelve, I was placed in the Catholic Children's Aid Society and remained in group homes and institutions, and, briefly, foster care, until the age of eighteen. I did not graduate with a high school diploma and have generally reached life's milestones much later than others because of post-traumatic stress disorder.

As a researcher, I do not assume or pretend to have an "objective" stance. I am connected to the work that I do because I believe that it can help people who, like me, did not grow up with their cultural teachings and have to find them on their own. I believe that cultural teachings are necessary to overcome the internal pain of colonization because they offer a connection to healing and an alternative to self-abuse. I also believe that the research work presented here needs to be discussed by our respective Indigenous communities since we are in a time of great flux in which, according to our timekeepers, we are entering a new era that will carry us for the next several hundred years.

Since 2010, Indigenous timekeepers from the Mayan, Otomi, Kogi, and Hopi communities have been meeting to discuss the coming of the new dawn, marked by the end in 2013 of a long cycle in the Mayan calendar. For these timekeepers, the end of this period in the Mayan calendar marks the beginning of a new cycle, a new dawn of truth, recovery, reconciliation, and investment in Indigenous ways of being and knowing. In 2015, this group invited me to New Mexico to meet with them to discuss how to share their collective knowledge, through new technologies, for the benefit and health of Mother Earth. I have begun working with them on the Indigenous Timekeepers Project, which will share the interconnections among the Earth, moon, stars, and human consciousness to reveal how we are all part of the Sacred Cycle of Life. For these Indigenous timekeepers, a return to ourselves and to our ways is paramount for our survival.

About FourDirectionsTeachings.com

The online project FourDirectionsTeachings.com was conceived to give expression to Indigenous worldviews through the teachings of Elders and Traditional Teachers from five distinct Indigenous Nations. In the mid-1990s, I was trained as an adult literacy instructor by Priscilla George, founder and former executive director of the National Indigenous Literacy Association, now defunct. George brought together Elders and Traditional Teachers to convey the value of holistic knowledge derived from First Nations teachings. Impressed with how important Indigenous Knowledge was for our adult literacy classes, I began conversations with stakeholders such as George and Nancy Cooper (an adult education worker and academic in the field of adult literacy) on the value of having First Nations teachings made accessible in a respectful manner on the World Wide Web.

no longer existing

FIGURE 1: Main navigation page for FourDirectionsTeachings.com. The circles are representative of holistic approaches to Indigenous Knowledge and intuitively express and reinforce this concept through the user interface design.

The idea was that these teachings would be immediately accessible to front-line workers, who often struggle to find appropriate resources on Indigenous Knowledge. Furthermore, the teachings would be inspirational because the Elders themselves would share their knowledge. An interactive website would provide individual adult Indigenous learners with a sense of empowerment, allowing them to explore the teachings on their own, building their computer literacy skills while engaging with relevant content important and significant to them. These discussions were undertaken in the spirit of front-line community work, and we were able to envision an exciting potential resource that could be accessed by Indigenous learners in the computer rooms of the many drop-in organizations and friendship centres where we held our literacy classes. Several years later FourDirectionsTeachings.com became a reality (see Figure 1).

Four Directions Teachings celebrates Indigenous Oral Traditions by honouring the process of listening with intent as each Elder or Traditional Teacher shares a teaching from his or her perspective on the richness and value of cultural traditions from his or her nation (see Figures 2–5).

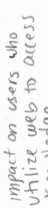

[handwritten margin notes: "impact on users who utilize web to access knowledge"; "what the website is about + Oral traditions"; "Jeff gives his perspective of cultural values"]

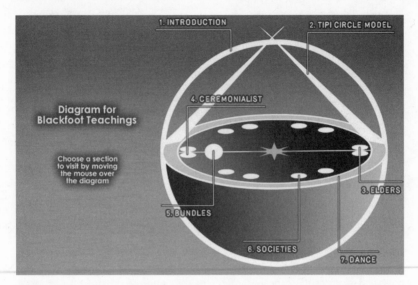

FIGURE 2: Diagram for Blackfoot teachings, Elder Reg Crowshoe and Elder Geoff Crow Eagle.

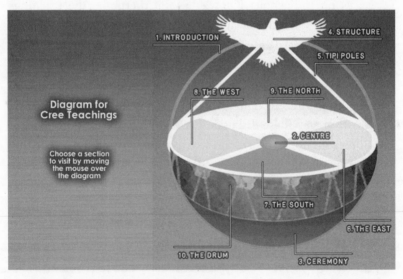

FIGURE 3: Diagram for Cree teachings, Elder Mary Lee.

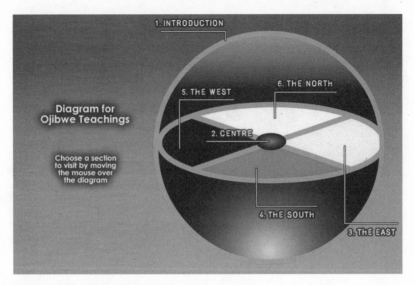

FIGURE 4: Diagram for Ojibwe teachings, Elder Lillian Pitawanakwat.

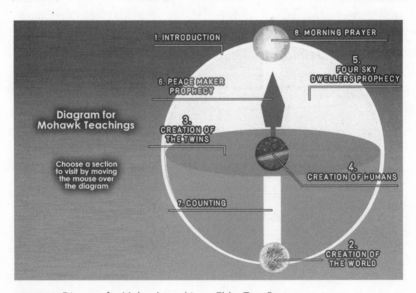

FIGURE 5: Diagram for Mohawk teachings, Elder Tom Porter.

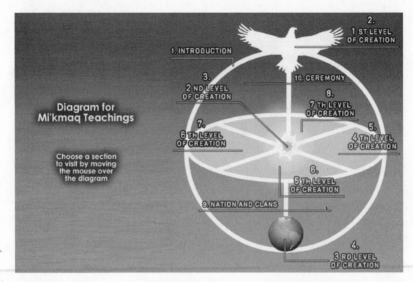

FIGURE 6: Diagram for Mi'kmaq teachings, Elder Stephen Augustine.

In honour of the timelessness of Indigenous Oral Traditions, audio narration is provided throughout the site, complemented by beautifully animated visuals. In addition, the site provides free curriculum packages for Grades 1 to 12 to further explore the vast richness of knowledge and cultural philosophy introduced in each teaching. The curriculum is provided in downloadable PDF and can be read online through the Teacher's Resources link.

Observing Cultural Protocols in the Production
of FourDirectionsTeachings.com

The first person whom I went to see for the production of FourDirectionsTeachings.com was late Ojibwe Elder Lillian Pitawanakwat in 2005 on Manitoulin Island, Ontario. I gave her a traditional offering of tobacco and asked her if she would share a teaching for the website project. Lillian consulted her pipe because she had been asked to do this kind of thing many times before and had refused. But this time, she said, her pipe told her that this project would be done properly and that she could trust it. She therefore agreed to share a medicine wheel teaching with us. But Lillian did more than that. She spent three days with the content producer and me teaching, praying, and

[handwritten in margin: audio & animated visuals is used throughout the site]

taking us through a Sweat Lodge ceremony. I did not request this. Lillian said that the ceremony, song, and prayer were being done so that the project could be undertaken in a good way and that we would have the help and guidance needed from the Creator. At the time, I thought that this was very kind and generous, and I would later come to realize how significant it was. The project received its first teaching after we spent several days meditating on Dreamer's Rock, receiving teachings, and preparing for and undertaking Sweat Lodge, giveaway, and feasting ceremonies.

Several weeks later in 2005 I was in Blackfoot country meeting with Dr. Reg Crowshoe, a Piikani Blackfoot Elder and Traditional Teacher. After I presented him with tobacco, he asked me, "Under what cultural authority are you presenting the project?" I did not know how to answer him. He asked me again. I did not know how to respond. He smiled patiently and began to explain Blackfoot cultural processes and how they involve ceremony and how ceremony represents cultural authority. He articulated Blackfoot processes as a way of demonstrating how cultural and political authority are traditionally recognized and legitimated in Blackfoot societies. He referred to these processes by the acronym VALS, which stands for venue, action, language, and song.

According to Crowshoe, these processes are present in all legitimate Blackfoot cultural transactions, and they are at the foundation of Blackfoot cultural authority. He also stated that these processes are not limited to Blackfoot culture but shared across Indigenous communities and only need to be drawn out and demonstrated. Amazed, I finally realized that Lillian, by conducting ceremonies for the project, had been implementing a process through cultural protocols that gave it spiritual, social, and cultural legitimacy. Excited by the realization, I was finally able to answer Crowshoe's question. I explained that the project had been initiated with a Sweat Lodge ceremony, that we had held a feast and prayed in Anishinaabemowin, and that Lillian had brought out her drum and sung and conducted a Pipe Ceremony. I explained that all of this had been done on sacred ground, at the base of Dreamer's Rock. Crowshoe smiled and said that the process had been a good one and that Lillian had known what needed to be done.

FourDirectionsTeachings.com, uploaded to the World Wide Web in 2006, has been maintained by my company, Invert Media. Access to the site is free. I pay the annual hosting costs for the website since currently there is no funding body specifically committed to online Indigenous Knowledge projects. That said, I have been fundraising to upgrade the site from its original flash HTML to HTML 5, a mobile responsive technology. In its current state, the website is accessible to less than 50 percent of potential Internet users.

It took five years of pitching FourDirectionsTeachings.com before it got approved for funding. The problem was that many community-based arts councils and government agencies did not want to take a chance on infringing on the cultural rights of communal Indigenous Knowledge. Armed with this feedback, I established an advisory committee for the purpose of producing the project consisting of the following people.

DR. MARIE BATTISTE (Mi'kmaq), director of the Aboriginal Education Research Centre, College of Education, University of Saskatchewan; co-author of *Protecting Indigenous Knowledge: A Global Challenge* (2000); and former co-chair of the UN Workshop on Indigenous Heritage in Geneva.

JAMES (SAKEJ) YOUNGBLOOD HENDERSON (Chickasaw/ Cheyenne), professor and research director of the Native Law Centre of Canada, University of Saskatchewan; noted international human rights lawyer and authority on protecting Indigenous Knowledge, heritage, and culture; member of the Sectoral Commission on Culture, Communication, and Information of the Canadian Commission for UNESCO and of the Experts Advisory Group on International Cultural Diversity.

DR. REG CROWSHOE (Piikani Blackfoot), well-known Elder; executive director of the Oldman River Cultural Centre in Alberta; pioneered and initiated cross-cultural programs for institutions across western Canada; honorary doctorate of law, University of Calgary.

DIANE HILL (Katsitsawaks), Mohawk Nation, Bear Clan, Six Nations of the Grand River Territory; consulted for the past twenty years on various Aboriginal educational initiatives internationally and worked to promote culturally based educational strategies in the field of social work and the area of prior learning assessment with the First Nations Technical Institute; completing her PhD in adult education with a focus on Aboriginal approaches at the University of Toronto.

SYLVIA MARACLE (Mohawk), Tyendinaga Mohawk Territory, Wolf Clan; involved in Aboriginal friendship centres for over thirty years, serving as executive director for the Ontario Federation of Indigenous Friendship Centres for much of that time; served as vice-president of the National Association of Friendship Centres, president of the Native Women's Resource Centre, and co-chair of the City of Toronto Task Force on Access and Equity.

[handwritten margin note: It is important to have a committee or advisory counsel; can't do it all alone. Requires collaboration.]

The accomplishments and work of these Indigenous intellectuals and activists speak directly to issues concerning the protection and promotion of Indigenous Knowledge. Their connections to various Indigenous communities also opened doors for me as a producer so that I could meet Indigenous Knowledge Keepers Tom Porter, Mary Lee, Stephen Augustine, Lillian Pitawanakwat, Reg Crowshoe, and Geoff Crow Eagle. Ultimately, the expertise of the advisory committee became crucial to FourDirectionsTeachings.com, which charted new territory in Indigenous education by being on the Internet and raised questions about wider community access to Indigenous Knowledge as well as rights related to its protection and promotion.

Any attempt to represent Indigenous Knowledge on the Internet involves many different risks and raises significant concerns for Indigenous Peoples. Judy Iseke-Barnes and Deborah Danard (2007), in their article "Indigenous Knowledges and Worldview: Representations and the Internet," fear that cultural knowledge online will be usurped and turned into a commodity by Western audiences and that prevailing discourses on Indigenous Knowledge will be in danger of being defined by these audiences. Such a trend removes the Indigenous contexts and Knowledge Keepers from the equation, effectively removing the original Indigenous Knowledge itself. In discussing this issue, Iseke-Barnes and Danard point to commodification of the dream catcher. Now made and marketed online from China, the original teachings or knowledge associated with this cultural item are nowhere to be found in that context. Arguing that "this removal from history and community ensures continued silencing of Indigenous voices," they believe that, consequently, "cyberspace and information technology are limitless in their potential as the modes of transmission for the dominant society to continue colonization practices. Information accessed through the Internet has no context in which to position it and is distanced from the Indigenous peoples that it purports to represent" (28, 33). Iseke-Barnes and Danard argue that the silencing and removal of Indigenous Peoples create opportunities for more stereotyping and commodification of their knowledge and cultures, supporting continued Western colonization. Their article is just one expression of a much wider range of concern about and controversy over putting Indigenous Knowledge on the Internet. Cultural commodification and appropriation by non-Indigenous people are real and have done great damage. Indeed, in a discussion on cultural intellectual property, Miranda Belarde-Lewis (2011) notes that the history of non-Aboriginal people taking and recording cultural property is long and well documented and in fact is chronicled in the collections of museums around the world.

[handwritten: Suggests that museums have denigrated and stolen knowledge]

This history leads many to worry that Indigenous Knowledge will continue to be denigrated or stolen. Winona LaDuke stated in "The Indigenous Women's Network: Our Future, Our Responsibility," that "the intellectual knowledge systems today often negate or deny the existence and inherent property rights of Indigenous people to our cultural and intellectual knowledge by supplanting our knowledge systems. Industrial knowledge systems call us 'primitive' while our medical knowledge, plants, and even genetic material are stolen (as in the Human Genome Project) by transnational corporations and international agencies" (1995, 7). Suffice it to say here that issues of cultural appropriation and the fear of usurpation take many forms *[handwritten: Taking someone's power or property by force.]* when thinking about Indigenous Knowledge on the Internet. Indeed, some scholars argue that Indigenous Peoples should not share their knowledge at all, as in the politics of refusal (Tuck & Yang, 2012). Andrea Smith, a scholar of Native American and Indigenous studies, takes the position in her article "Spiritual Appropriation as Sexual Violence" that "knowledge about someone also gives one power over that person. Withholding knowledge, then, is an act of resistance against those who desire to know you in order to better control you" (2005, 97).

"Withholding knowledge" also protects the sacredness of that knowledge. The need to protect sacred knowledge is reflected in the backlash against depicting the Sundance Ceremony online, which I discuss in Chapter 8 with examples of online postings from members of various Indigenous communities reflecting on this issue. *[handwritten: How do I avoid this in my project.]* Providing knowledge about Indigenous ceremonies online opens many opportunities for misinterpretation, poorly understood appropriation, and various other forms of abuse. Many Indigenous Peoples regard keeping ceremonial knowledge out of public media as a way of protecting that knowledge and of protecting the right of Indigenous Peoples to be Indigenous in meaningful ways: that is, to prevent their knowledge from being denigrated, usurped, or appropriated by settler society. These arguments represent the opposition to putting Indigenous Knowledge online and are fodder for ensuring great caution, hesitation, and care when thinking about the potential for Indigenous Knowledge on the Internet.

Not surprisingly, the advisory group gave me the confidence to proceed with the production of FourDirectionsTeachings.com because I thought not only that I was working for the community but also that the community was involved in the project. Indeed, the advisers were able to open doors to Elders and Traditional Teachers across the country so that I could discuss the project with them and gauge their interest. Furthermore, the presence of an advisory committee and the referrals that came from it assured Elders and Traditional Teachers that a community-based process was being undertaken and that a sense of accountability was in place. Upon hearing that Sylvia Maracle had referred me to him, one Traditional Teacher, Mohawk Elder Tom Porter, quipped, "Well, if you are working with her, then you are moving in some good circles."

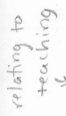

Originally conceived as a national Aboriginal educational initiative, FourDirectionsTeaching.com was developed so that Indigenous communities across the country, both on and off reserve, could benefit from its content. The idea was to provide a culturally sensitive pedagogical aid that could be accessed easily by Indigenous educators, front-line workers in literacy and community wellness programs, and non-Indigenous people working with Indigenous students or teaching Indigenous-themed curricula to all kinds of learners. Today the website has reached far beyond the original target audience and is seen and utilized by Indigenous and non-Indigenous people in many different contexts as a valuable resource for introducing Indigenous Knowledge.

Oral and Visual Storytelling

I am not alone in thinking that the Internet is well suited to introducing concepts of Indigenous Knowledge and value systems. In *The New Media Nation: Indigenous Peoples and Global Communication*, Valerie Alia (2010, xii) cites Paul DeMain, an Oneida-Ojibway journalist, who states that "for the first time Native people are on the breaking edge of information technology in terms of computer systems and the internet,

[handwritten: Support why Internet is good]

which means that we're going back to an old tradition, the oral visual presentation and the storyteller's credibility." DeMain is expressing the idea that the Internet is an effective medium for conveying oral teachings because it can present information in both audio and visual formats, similar to how oral teachings are presented by Elders and Traditional Teachers, who often use visual aids when they are speaking. For example, I have attended many teachings at which the Elder refers to an object such as a pipe when speaking or sketches the four quadrants of a medicine wheel to describe the integral relationships among them. In contrast, written descriptions of oral teachings miss the flow of the teachings, especially with respect to explaining spatial relationships or representing the layers and connections that can be made, for example, among different medicine wheels.

[handwritten margin note: Justification of why oral teaching better then written]

Like DeMain, I see the Internet as a medium that, in some ways, has finally caught up to aspects of Indigenous notions of oral storytelling. According to Alia (2010, 17), others, such as Jim Bell, editor of *Nunatsiaq News*, believe that "the Internet offers a way of *fighting back*—a chance to *send the information the other way*—and therefore can be an antidote to the cultural demolition that has occurred in some other media," notably the racist portrayals of "Indians" in film and television (Kilpatrick, 1999). In thinking about the hypertext functionality and the meaning that arises from the relationships between texts and images, Martin Nakata (2002, 287) notes in his work *Indigenous Knowledge and the Cultural Interface: Underlying Issues at the Intersection of Knowledge and Information Systems* that "the online environment has reconstituted the balance between visual, oral, and textual modes of presenting information in a way that supports cultural perspectives."

In 2009, FourDirectionsTeachings.com was part of a retrospective exhibition on Aboriginal new media called *Codetalkers of the Digital Divide (or Why We Didn't Become "Roadkill on the Information Superhighway")*. The exhibition, a collaboration between A Space Gallery and imagineNative, marked the tenth anniversary of the imagineNATIVE Film + Media Arts Festival. Curated by Cheryl L'Hirondelle, a celebrated Metis multidisciplinary artist and musician, the exhibition was a timely contextualization of what Aboriginal new media practices were pre-Internet in relation to what they have become in the current Web 2.0 paradigm.[5] In her curatorial statement, L'Hirondelle (2009) quotes the late Ahasiw Maskegon Iskwew: "To govern ourselves means to govern our stories and our ways of telling stories. It means that the rhythm of the drumbeat, the language of smoke signals and our moccasin telegraph can be transformed to the airwaves and modems of our times. We can determine our use of the new technologies to support, strengthen and enrich our cultural communities." She then says that

> Aboriginal people have been, since time immemorial, "making things our own" and certainly since the 1960s, finding our own "Indigenous aesthetic in digital story-telling." . . . Yet as we move as fast as bytes of information, catapulted through time and space and by the imperative of our continued survival, it's important to hit the pause button, reflect on our history and pay homage to the agency and ingenuity of our pathfinders.
>
> . . . Like our ancestors before us, we have always been keen to identify new tools to accomplish a necessary survival task. The multi-disciplinary artists honored in this exhibit are renowned masters of this; their example embodies and manifests the imperative of being skillfully adept with a variety of disciplines and media.

This curatorial statement politicizes the act of Indigenous story-telling by making it clear that our stories are part of our survival. This is significant because it introduces the notion of accountability and responsibility, not only to one's personal vision of the story, but also to the broader Indigenous community and its vision of the story. I was honoured that FourDirectionsTeachings.com was part of this retrospective in Indigenous new media, and I was thrilled that the community embraced the site as "painstakingly researched" and "a gift—a map back to our source" (L'Hirondelle, 2009).

The Internet: A New Public Sphere?

In writing about difference, Mark Poster (1995, 13) suggests that "Internet communities function as places of difference from and resistance to modern society. In a sense, they serve the function of a Habermasian public sphere without intentionally being one." For Jürgen Habermas, the "bourgeois public sphere" (Habermas, Lennox, & Lennox, 1964) consisted of places such as coffee houses and taverns where citizens could meet and have informal discussions. For Poster, the Habermasian concept of the public sphere does not really apply to the Internet because the subjects are disembodied and scattered (8). Yet he uses the concept because it is imbued with a sense of democracy in its liberal politics: "The question that needs to be asked about the relation of the Internet to democracy is this: are there new kinds of relations occurring within it which suggest new forms of power configurations between communicating individuals? In other words, is there a new politics on the Internet?" (5).

More than twenty years later we can say unequivocally that there is indeed a new politics. This is evident in the groundbreaking work *Alternative and Activist New Media* by Leah A. Lievrouw (2011). Drawing on the work of Chris Atton, Lievrouw notes how he describes the alternative Internet as "a range of media projects, interventions and networks that work against, or seek to develop different forms of, the dominant, expected (and broadly accepted) ways of doing media" (quoted on 19). Lievrouw then revamps the general definition of new media so as to

> propose that **alternative/activist new media employ or modify the communication artifacts, practices, and social arrangements of new information and communication technologies to challenge or alter dominant, expected, or accepted ways of doing society, culture, and politics.** Their creators take advantage of the recombinant, networked nature of new media infrastructure, and the ubiquity and interactivity that they offer users, to create innovative projects in which people extend their social networks and

interpersonal contacts, produce and share their own "DIY" information, and resist, "talk back" to, or otherwise critique and intervene in prevailing social, cultural, economic, and political conditions. (19)

For Lievrouw, the four main features that make new media new are recombination, networked architecture, ubiquity, and interactivity. Recombinant technologies are designed and shaped by users who, for example, combine existing older systems such as video with new software innovations such as YouTube. Networked architecture, according to Lievrouw, refers to the social consequences, impacts, and circulation activity of a work. Ubiquity is the idea that new media are present everywhere. Interactivity is a necessary condition for social, political, and cultural participation. Lievrouw deduces that this type of interactivity is found in Web 2.0 technology.

The term "Web 2.0" generally refers to user interactivity and was coined in 2004 at a conference dedicated to discussing Internet users who interact and collaborate with each other in social media and who dialogue as creators of user-generated content in a virtual community—in contrast to websites where people are limited to the passive viewing of content. Such interaction was seen as revolutionary because it was immediate and, therefore, occurred in *real time*. Perhaps more importantly, though, it was seen to provide a truer Habermasian space for users to engage and hence be political and social. Websites that did not have a Web 2.0 feature were seen as passé and not interactive. As Lievrouw writes, "we might think of interactivity as a feature of media infrastructure (articulating artifacts, practices, and social arrangements) and participation as a particular form of action supported by that infrastructure; but one depends on the other. 'Interactive' new media offer more opportunities for communicative action, and interaction, than do most traditional mass media formats, and thus more opportunities for participation" (2011, 15).

I have always thought of FourDirectionsTeachings.com as an interactive web project because it articulates a particular form of teachings, which have been combined and designed to impart their significance, as holistic knowledge, through their spatial relationships. The Internet user engages those spatial relationships by interacting with each teaching. In this book, I show through the research participants' interviews that FourDirectionsTeachings.com articulates and embodies a specific "Indigenous artifact," to use the academic term (though it carries some baggage for "overarchaeologized" Indigenous Peoples). The design of the site supports the participation of the user in particular ways, allowing for interactive rather than passive viewing because of how it engages the user to intuitively experience and interact with a representation of holistic knowledge.

After the launch of FourDirectionsTeachings.com in 2006, members of the new media community in Toronto and Banff dismissed it as not being cutting edge because it did not use the latest Web 2.0 technology. Therefore, it was not regarded as "interactive." Their definition and my definition of interactive differ greatly: I do not limit interactivity to the content contributing to and altering activity of Web 2.0. For me, interactivity is embodied in how users can engage with the spatial design of FourDirectionsTeachings.com and thereby learn a great deal about the holistic nature of Indigenous Knowledge through their actual engagement.

Furthermore, some in the new media community (e.g., the Canadian New Media Awards) were unable to appreciate the significance of the project's novelty in making Indigenous Knowledge available online, for they had no reference point for what constitutes such knowledge. In contrast, this book reflects the insight and participation of Indigenous Internet users able to make specific distinctions regarding what constitutes Indigenous Knowledge and who can therefore speak with experience and authority about its impact online. Consequently, there has always been a tension between how FourDirectionsTeaching.com is perceived and defined by settler society and how it is received and taken up by Indigenous communities. I will examine this tension further in Chapter 2 with respect to the choices that I made regarding research design and approach.

Working within an Indigenous Context

My research has verified that significant, respectful, and accurate Indigenous Knowledge can be presented online in ways that can help users to access and become inspired by such knowledge. However, it is important to recognize that *no mere tool, no matter how well designed or used, can ever replace—or even come close to—oral, person-to-person transmission of traditional cultural knowledge.* Consequently, any discussion of Indigenous Knowledge online presented in this book should be digested with these two important principles in mind. As a producer and researcher, I believe that certain aspects of Indigenous Knowledge can be expressed through new technologies and can therefore contribute to the needs of Indigenous communities. I am not advocating the transmission of deep Indigenous Knowledge, or what might be called Indigenous Ceremonial Knowledge, since that is not the topic of my research.

Rather, my interests are in researching the need and potential for culturally sensitive resources that speak to diverse forms of Indigenous cultural heritage and in understanding the connections that can be made between new technologies and Indigenous epistemologies. This research requires us to *look differently,* and it picks up on the work *Native on the Net: Indigenous and Diasporic Peoples in the Virtual Age,* edited by Kyra Landzelius, which inquires about the meanings of "interoperability, connectivity, universality, fluidity, transparency":

> Such are the buzzwords of our digital age. But what do they mean to, and for, peoples outside the mainstream? What do they deliver for Indigenous people on the fringes of power; for subaltern minority populations in diaspora? Can the info-superhighway be a fast track to greater empowerment for the historically disenfranchised? Or do they risk becoming "roadkill": casualties of hyper-media and the drive to electronically map everything? (2006, 1)

There is a general feeling that, if Indigenous Peoples do not stake out a claim on the Internet, they will become colonized in that space too because of their absence. The notion of unjust occupation is ingrained in the hearts and minds of Indigenous Peoples in Canada. It is both physical and emotional, and it applies to the web, as evident in Indigenous discussions of new media, in which—to echo L'Hirondelle (2014)—we hear again the sentiment of not wanting to be "roadkill on the information superhighway."

Indigenous Peoples already know what it is like to be invisible. Being present on the Internet is an act of resistance to further colonization, asserting the visibility and viability of First Nations, Metis, and Inuit and therefore subverting notions of colonialism that would have people believe that First Nations, Metis, and Inuit do not exist.

As a research academic, I work from and with scholarship that has focused on Indigenous Knowledge (represented by scholars such as Atleo, 2005; Battiste, 2000; Geniusz, 2009; Grande, 2004; McGregor, 2005; Restoule et al., 2010; and Simpson, 2011) and has put Indigenous research and methods at the centre of inquiry (Geniusz, 2009; Grande, 2004; Restoule et al., 2010; Simpson, 2011; Smith, 1999; Wilson, 2008). I choose this position because I want my research and cultural work to be proactive and to contribute to dialogue between and across Indigenous circles in academia, leadership, Knowledge Keepers, and grassroots movements. To accomplish this goal, I take my lead from Deborah McGregor, who states that "Indigenous people must move beyond a focus on decolonization (which puts the colonizer at the centre of discussion), to one in which 'Indigenous theorizing' is both recognized and achieved" (2005, 75). Linda Tuhiwai Smith's work *Decolonizing Methodologies: Research and Indigenous Peoples* has greatly informed my practice and thinking, and it speaks to the work that I am doing in this study. Smith states that sharing knowledge is a long-term commitment, which she differentiates from sharing information:

> To me the responsibility of researchers and academics is not simply to share surface information (pamphlet knowledge)

but to share the theories and analyses which inform the way knowledge and information are constructed and represented. By taking this approach seriously it is possible to introduce communities and people who may have had little formal schooling to a wider world, a world which includes people who think just like them, who share in their struggles and dreams and who voice their concerns in similar sorts of ways. To assume in advance that people will not be interested in, or will not understand, the deeper issues is arrogant. The challenge always is to demystify, to decolonize. (1999, 16)

It is important for me as an Indigenous person and an academic to honour the people who participated in this research by making the work accessible to Indigenous communities everywhere. The voices of the research participants, all Indigenous except for one, deserve to be heard. Indeed, their voices fill a void in audience reception/ Internet studies; the concerns and interactions of Indigenous Peoples online are not sought-after topics of research (Nakamura, 2007; Warschauer, 2004). However, though it is important to address that void, doing so is not my primary motivation. My motivation comes from the Indigenous principles of reciprocity and relationship, which consider the needs of the audience to be an integral component of presenting research (Wilson, 2008, 126). In this way, I hope to honour the research participants who generously shared their time and insights with me, and I hope to honour our communities by speaking to them in a way that invites them into a dialogue, because without them it is difficult to move forward.

Like Smith, Leanne Simpson, in her work *Dancing on Our Turtle's Back: Stories of Nishnaabeg Re-Creation, Resurgence, and a New Emergence*, calls for Indigenous Peoples to "delve into their own culture's stories, philosophies, theories and concepts to align themselves with the processes and forces of regeneration, revitalization, remembering, and visioning" (2011, 148). As a producer of an online Indigenous Knowledge project, I have done that work.

FourDirectionsTeachings.com delves into teachings from Elders/ Knowledge Keepers from five distinct First Nations, sharing Indigenous Knowledge from a variety of cultures. For those who have visited the site and used it in their work, FourDirectionsTeachings. com represents a work of "regeneration, revitalization, remembering, and visioning." I will discuss in detail how the site accomplishes these processes with reference to the research participants' interviews. To get there, I will use four tenets that Simpson develops in her work.

Before discussing her framework, I want to note that Simpson is from my territory—Anishinaabe territory—and works closely with Edna Manitowabi, an Elder from my community, Wikwemikong First Nation. I have known Edna all my life, and in fact she was the first Elder to bring me into a Sweat Lodge ceremony. Furthermore, my grandmother's father was Sam Manitowabi. Sam was Johnny Manitowabi's brother, and Johnny was Edna's father, making Edna and I cousins. I state this because I feel comfortable with her teachings and trust Edna as an Elder and Traditional Teacher. So, though I have never met Simpson and know her only through her work and her relationship with Edna, I feel a close connection to what she says because she uses teachings from and the language of my community and territory. Her work resonates with me on a deep level that can only be described as heart based because it is rooted in relationships with the land, the people, the knowledge, and the spirit of what I would call my community. I will discuss these principles and relationships further in this book.

Simpson introduces the following Indigenous concepts: *Biskaabiiyang* ("to look back"), *Naakgonige* ("to plan"), *Aanjigone* ("non-interference"), and *Debwewin* ("the sound of the heart"). These terms are from the language of the *Anishinaabek*; the language is *Anishinaabemowin*. She writes that "I believe we need intellectuals who can think within the conceptual meanings of the language, who are intrinsically connected to place and territory, who exist in the world as an embodiment of contemporary expressions of our ancient stories and traditions, and that illuminate mino bimaadiziwin in all aspects of their lives" (2011, 31). *Mino bimaadiziwin* is living "life in a good way" or "the good life." I agree with Simpson and Smith, and I believe that we need to work from Indigenous contexts and that this means incorporating Indigenous concepts and thinking. So, though Simpson does not purport to offer an Indigenous framework for academics, I respectfully use her four tenets of Biskaabiiyang, Naakgonige, Aanjigone, and Debwewin to explore and draw out the themes presented in my research.

I also use Smith's "twenty-five projects" as a method of exploring and analyzing the interview content from the research participants (1999, 142). These projects are mixed methodologies and practices that put Indigenous goals and interests at the centre of research. By incorporating these Indigenous works into my analyses and theoretical approach, I hope to make transparent how knowledge and information are constructed and represented in this work so that members of Indigenous communities who are reading can be invited into the discussion and appreciate the diverse insights shared by the research participants.

I wholeheartedly believe that our communities need to work together to ensure our survival in a good way. As Smith writes,

> what is more important than what alternatives indigenous peoples offer the world is what alternatives indigenous peoples offer each other. The strategies that work for one community may well work for another. The gains made in one context may well be applied usefully in another. The sharing of resources and information may assist groups and communities to collaborate with each other and to protect each other. (1999, 105)

Having a dialogue across First Nation communities about Indigenous Knowledge online is crucial to the development of policies and protocols that can protect and sustain this knowledge in the present and into the future. Consequently, I will demonstrate in this book how Indigenous Knowledge online is a new cultural form propelling new social relations offline and inspiring new "knowledge production"—and thereby actively contributing to a radical Indigenous resurgence.

For Simpson, resurgence creates life. It propels and nurtures life. For Smith, themes of resurgence are evident in the way that she envisions communities working together:

> The survival of one community can be celebrated by another. The spiritual, creative and political resources that indigenous peoples can draw on from each other provide alternatives for each other. Sharing is a good thing to do, it is a very human quality. To be able to share, to have something worth sharing gives dignity to the giver.... To create something new through that process of sharing is to re-create the old, to reconnect relationships and to recreate our humanness. (1999, 105)

Sharing this research is an act of resurgence because it embraces Indigenous theories and methods and because it facilitates the voices of diverse Indigenous Peoples who want to share Indigenous Knowledge online in respectful and responsible ways. The research participants in this project shared their insights with me because they believe that FourDirectionsTeachings.com is a valuable resource that can inspire other Indigenous communities to invest in Indigenous Knowledge projects online as an important part of regenerating the spiritual, creative, and political aspirations of their nations. This work, then, is a concrete example of Indigenous Peoples engaging in a project that allows us to draw insights from each other and to invite others to join us so that we can find new ways of doing things in a good way.

I will now speak to a finding that has emerged from this research project: how FourDirectionsTeachings.com embodies a new cultural form—what cultural studies might call a new "cultural artifact" (see Hall, 1996)—that I will refer to as "a digital bundle."

[handwritten margin note: Why this project is an act of resurgence]

CHAPTER 1

Are my objects considered Bundle? Do they hold power or used in ceremony

A Digital Bundle

Based upon discussions and input from the people who participated in and contributed to this research, I humbly propose that Indigenous Knowledge projects online such as FourDirectionsTeachings.com should be considered digital bundles. Naming them as such elevates the protocols and responsibilities that come with such a designation and speaks profoundly to how Indigenous communities regard the processes to which such works contribute from and within an Indigenous epistemological paradigm. In Chapters 5 to 8, which focus on the interview data gathered, I will discuss how FourDirectionsTeachings.com has come to be perceived and articulated in this way.

Simply speaking, a general definition of a bundle, from a community-based Indigenous perspective, refers to a collection of things regarded as sacred and held by a person with care and ceremony. A bundle could be a skin or fur bag or wrapping holding an eagle wing or feather, rattle, pipe, or other items used in ceremony, along with medicines such as tobacco or dried plants for smudging. These are just some examples, and there could be a much wider range of more particular things, such as items used in specific ceremonies. More importantly, these sacred items are highly valued and protected, and some are transferred for the benefit, growth, and sustainability of a community

Some bundles can be handed down through a family. Others are community bundles and hold a great deal of power, as do very old pipe bundles, some of which might even go back to the beginning of a specific revealed ceremony or tradition that supports the whole community. In this case, the person holding the bundle must undergo a thorough process of learning about the meaning of the tradition or ceremony and how that particular bundle gets transferred to members of the community. Other bundles can be personal, such as those held by youth who are encouraged to pick up their cultures and make bundles with items that they can use in maintaining their paths. These items can be as humble as a little smudge bowl and some sage or a personal pipe or feather used with little or no public exposure. These personal bundles are protected and cared for, and they are regarded as being imbued with spirit. A bundle is a lifelong commitment (or a commitment that has to be responsibly passed on or otherwise released, never simply neglected or discarded in a disrespectful way).

Beyond these definitions, there is a more "metaphorical" and non-physical use for bundles. For example, Indigenous Peoples working in community governance or development in various ways might sometimes refer more loosely to bundles as collections of knowledge or practice that get passed on. I have also heard Elders talk about how we all carry a bundle in the sense of gifts that we are given by the Creator when we arrive. These kinds of uses seem to be colloquialisms that many accept and understand within Indigenous communities. A bundle can be defined somewhat differently, then, depending on the context in which it is used.

Among different Indigenous Peoples, there are specific cultural definitions and particular attributes of bundles. Because *bundle* is an English word, there is of course no "official" or "traditional" Indigenous definition or "policing" of the word, though there could be concern among various traditional people if it were thrown about carelessly— for example, if "New Agers" decided to announce, without any connection to or understanding of any specific Indigenous community or tradition, that they held "a sacred bundle" and used it to hold "ceremonies" that they made up or improvised from a book or mimicked based upon attending a few real or fake ceremonies.

Therefore, in thinking about a bundle and what it means, we have to be mindful of the care and passing on of bundles (whether physical bundles, special bundles of knowledge, or the gifts that we receive at birth), that they are sacred things, and that there is—or at least could be—a ceremony to go along with that process. For example, when a child is born, there are specific ceremonies for what is done with the placenta, or, when youth take on certain responsibilities for governance through a youth council and are trained by Elders, some ceremony accompanies that process to recognize and demonstrate the sacredness of that new responsibility, whether it is through a metaphorical bundle of knowledge or a physical bundle of items that will help them in their work. Ultimately, all of this implies that a bundle is most often associated with the manifestation of a very important and sacred thing that is spiritual, and not just physical, in nature.

In some ways, FourDirectionsTeachings.com can be considered as a digital bundle because it is a collection of teachings by respected Elders and Traditional Teachers who have shared Indigenous Knowledge that is highly regarded and valued by diverse Indigenous communities. These communities see FourDirectionsTeachings.com as a representation of Indigenous Knowledge ultimately derived from sacred sources—knowledge that must be respected, cared for, and passed down for future generations and hence has the attributes of a community bundle. In this sense, FourDirectionsTeachings.com represents a new cultural form, a new cultural artifact, because it is the first Indigenous Knowledge project online to be considered and referenced by users in a way that implies it can be seen as a digital bundle. Through the research participants' feedback and contribution, and through the producer's reflection on creating the website, I will explore how it has achieved this consideration or recognition.

Internet Activism and Cross-Cultural Knowledge Exchange

In her work, Lievrouw introduces what she calls "five basic genres of contemporary alternative and activist new media projects: *culture jamming, alternative computing, participatory journalism, mediated mobilization,* and *commons knowledge*" (2011, 19). I came upon this work while searching for ways to frame my analysis of Indigenous Knowledge online. Each of the five genres presented by Lievrouw is distinct and delivered in a particular way that can be inspiring and engaging. Indeed, her work inspired me to recognize that Indigenous Knowledge online is itself a contemporary alternative and activist new media project. Yet it is very different from the genres that she outlines. Here I will offer brief descriptions of the genres in order to show how they accomplish tasks very different from those addressed through Indigenous Knowledge online.

According to Lievrouw (2011), the goal of culture jamming is to borrow, subvert, and comment on popular culture. Alternative computing involves highly specialized programmers who develop open software or hack into existing software to modify it for public purposes. Participatory journalism is reporting from the margins that aims to subvert mainstream media broadcasts of the news. "Mediated mobilization extends and activates the power of 'live,' local social relations and organizing—such as kinship and social support networks, professional affiliations or expert advice networks" (20). Finally, commons knowledge projects "challenge or reframe the established, expert knowledge classifications of mainstream cultural institutions and disciplines" (20).

For Lievrouw, these projects "do not only reflect or critique mainstream media and culture, they constitute and intervene in them" (2011, 19). Desperate to find where and how FourDirectionsTeachings. com might fit into this array of alternative new media, I reviewed each genre carefully. However, I concluded that none really fits how FourDirectionsTeachings.com was conceived or how it works. Although aspects of mediated mobilization and commons knowledge projects could be used to describe the work of FourDirectionsTeachings.com, that would be like trying to fit a square block into a round hole.

For example, according to Lievrouw, mediated mobilization "relates to the domain of political/cultural organizing and social movements." She further explains that it "takes advantage of web-based social software tools like social network sites, personal blogs, flash mobs, and email listservs, as well as DIY digital media, to cultivate interpersonal networks online and to mobilize those networks to engage in live and mediated collective action" (2011, 25).

The Idle No More movement[6]—an ongoing Indigenous protest movement—might be described in these terms since it uses Facebook, personal blogs, websites, and listservs to mobilize community flash round dances in public spaces and therefore engages in live and mediated collective action. FourDirectionsTeachings.com does not facilitate the same kind of public presence in the streets.

It has enabled users to act in the sense that many have requested more materials, both for online and for offline use. For example, communities that do not have strong Internet access have requested offline copies of FourDirectionsTeachings.com content or promotional material to hand out in their communities. More importantly, the project has also facilitated connections to Elders presented on FourDirectionsTeachings.com for communities seeking their expertise. Access has been granted to several educational institutions to utilize the site and the curriculum pieces in their classes. However, though FourDirectionsTeachings.com has contributed somewhat to aspects of "mediated mobilization," this term does not really describe its design or approach.

With respect to commons knowledge projects, Lievrouw (2011) writes that they "reorganize and categorize information in ways that can challenge or reframe the established, expert knowledge classifications of mainstream cultural institutions and disciplines" (20). This genre, she expounds, "relates to content of culture itself—the nature of knowledge and expertise, how information is organized and evaluated and who decides" (26). Commons knowledge projects are framed in direct response to established Western knowledge constructs and therefore are seen as radical and subversive of dominant power relations. For Indigenous communities that have never seen their knowledge appreciated or presented in public spaces, Indigenous Knowledge projects online such as FourDirectionsTeachings.com are radical and antithetical to the colonial education and textbooks used throughout North America. It could be argued that FourDirectionsTeachings.com in some ways is a commons knowledge project because of the subversive and alternative position that it occupies. Yet I would posit that this genre is too limiting because it cannot fully acknowledge the depth of the work and the impact of Indigenous Knowledge online. To acknowledge this impact, I argue in this book, we need to think of Indigenous Knowledge projects online as a unique genre.

Although I appreciate Lievrouw's discussion of the five basic genres of contemporary alternative and activist new media projects, none is an ideal fit for Indigenous Knowledge online. However, I am inspired by her thinking about genres and how Lievrouw applies it to activism on the Internet. Indeed, it was her writing on the notion of genre that helped me to envision the concept of FourDirectionsTeachings.com as a digital bundle. She defines genre as

> a type of expression or communication that is useful and/ or meaningful among the members of a given community or within a particular situation. Genres have both *form* and *purpose*: that is, they have typical material features or follow certain format conventions, and they allow people to express themselves appropriately, and to achieve their various purposes or intentions, in a given situation. (2011, 20)

As discussed, FourDirectionsTeachings.com can be considered a digital bundle because it is a collection of teachings by respected Elders and Traditional Teachers who have shared Indigenous Knowledge in culturally specific ways. Hence, the site is a type of expression and communication that is meaningful to Indigenous communities.

Lievrouw (2011, 21) also points out that genres have many other significant facets that make them "relevant for alternative and activist new media projects." "First," she writes, "they help 'mediate' or facilitate communication among members of communities." Quoting the work of Kevin Crowston and Marie Williams, Lievrouw includes their "note that 'Genres are useful because they make communications more easily recognizable and understandable by recipients.'" "Thus," she continues, "genres are the means for creating and maintaining community and social context, and the cultural products of those communities and contexts." Moreover, she argues, genres "can also be so specific to a certain group's worldview or situation that outsiders may not understand them—so genres can also act as boundaries or markers that exclude outsiders and reinforce the power of insiders." Citing Crowston and Williams once more, Lievrouw concludes that "'recognition of a particular genre is one sign of membership in a particular community.'"

In thinking about Indigenous Knowledge online as a particular genre, such as a digital bundle, it is possible to see how such projects can mediate and facilitate communication among members of Indigenous communities. Furthermore, a genre such as the digital bundle only comes to life as a cultural product for the people who recognize and understand it as such, and therefore it speaks to the notion of a certain group's worldview—one that outsiders might not understand. For example, outsiders or non-Indigenous people might not understand the impact of FourDirectionsTeachings.com because they have little or no reference point for Indigenous Knowledge and consequently tend to ignore (and deny funding for) such sites.

For some Indigenous Peoples, a site such as FourDirectionsTeachings.com is regarded as a sacred collection of Indigenous Knowledge that must be respected, cared for, and passed down for future generations—in many ways embodying the attributes of a community bundle. Thus, the meaning of genre and its implications for insider community membership, as described above, are applicable and will become evident in Chapters 3 to 8, in which the research participants share their feedback and insights on the potential for Indigenous Knowledge online. That said, the time has come to elevate the work that Indigenous Knowledge is doing online by naming it and providing it with its own genre. I suggest that digital bundle is an apt name for this genre since it signals how such projects can act as boundaries or markers that reinforce the power of insiders—Indigenous communities for which the respectful protection and promotion of Indigenous Knowledge online is of paramount significance.

Finding the language to discuss Indigenous Knowledge online has been challenging. The difficulty of the task is not surprising. Upon reading *Subversion, Conversion, Development: Cross-Cultural Knowledge Exchange and the Politics of Design*, edited by James Leach and Lee Wilson, I couldn't help but notice how the editors summarized the book by stating that "this volume has demonstrated the different ways in which modes of life, trajectories of practice, ways of knowing, imaginaries, and particular values feed into and shape alternative uses and reuses of technologies in ways that have the potential to challenge this appropriative knowledge form, the epistemological assumptions, and the social values that guide most ICT production today" (2014, 242). Yet the editors coordinated a collection of empirical cases and theoretical examinations "that focus on alternative cultural encounters with and around information technologies (alternative, that is, to the dominant notions of media consumption among Western audiences)" (1). To change the appropriative knowledge form and the epistemological assumptions and social values that guide ICT production today, we need to stop positioning *difference* as *alternative*. To truly change is to adopt positions and discourses grounded in cultural knowledge that stand alone and apart from the dominant notions of media and consumption preferences of Western audiences. Much of the Indigenous content in Leach and Wilson's collection, published in 2014, focuses on postcolonial databasing: that is, the preservation and digitizing of Indigenous cultural artifacts or Indigenous Knowledge in various forms. In the context of Indigenous Knowledge online, methods for assembling knowledge from Indigenous academics to create new knowledge was coined as an "Indigenous Knowledge commons."

Although these types of projects are important, I would argue that they merely pick up Western alternative and activist Internet projects and insert Indigenous content. Indeed, Leach and Wilson recognize that the discourse surrounding ICT production and analysis is limiting and exclusionary of Indigenous concepts and worldviews. In fact, they note an absence of Indigenous ICT accounts: "For one thing, rather surprisingly, while global transformations wrought by ICT's are widely trumpeted, we have remarkably few accounts of ICT initiatives that have meaningfully privileged local knowledge and understanding. The reciprocal effects on the development of these technologies and accompanying social forms in different contexts remain underrepresented" (2014, 231). Reading this work made me realize that my frustrations with Internet studies and the discourse surrounding the web and activism in ICTs are grounded in the contested nature of this space, where settler or Western knowledge and perspectives and Indigenous Knowledge and perspectives are not always equally well represented, to say the least. As a result, my efforts to retool and refashion ICT for the purposes of Indigenous Knowledge through FourDirectionsTeachings.com entail retooling and refashioning the discourse surrounding the web and activism in order to speak adequately to the different contexts that Indigenous Knowledge online has for Indigenous communities.

To truly understand the work that FourDirectionsTeachings.com is doing online, and to adequately represent and frame this research, I needed to draw from the fields of Indigenous Knowledge, resurgence, and activism in Internet studies. I could then describe the concepts and introduce the language that I need as a producer and academic to discuss Indigenous Knowledge online. I hope that my work can contribute to the ongoing dialogue that Leach and Wilson refer to in their conclusion: "We consider an emphasis on ongoing and reflexive dialogue, through making and use, with people in all sorts of places and with different histories and imaginaries can only enhance the positive subversion, conversion, and ultimately development of future technologies" (2014, 242). Like bundles carried by Elders and Traditional Teachers, FourDirectionsTeachings.com is transportable and can be accessed when needed and activated at particular times and places when alone or with a group. Also, like a physical bundle that is carried, the digital bundle stores knowledge and teachings and takes care of them through the process of adhering to protocols. Ultimately, a digital bundle represents a positive subversion on the Internet by offering an Indigenous history and imaginary that dares to challenge colonial ideologies by asserting the power and presence of Indigenous Knowledge.

Ten years ago I wrote that "the Internet has the potential to reinforce and reinvigorate (without 'reinventing' or replacing) traditional forms of thought and ways of interpreting the world around us that are grounded in authoritative and once communally held sources and symbols" (Wemigwans, 2008, 35). Projects such as FourDirectionsTeachings.com show how Indigenous Peoples are expressing Indigenous Knowledge online in ways that contribute to the reflection of Indigenous ontology and values on the World Wide Web.

CHAPTER 2

DECOLONIZING THE DIGITAL

The notion of a digital bundle demonstrates that online spaces can be defined and validated through cultural protocols. Distinct from digital storytelling through its grounding in cultural protocols, Indigenous Knowledge online is a new kind of tool or resource—and hence a new opportunity to support the ways in which Indigenous communities are decolonizing the digital.

I begin from the premise that FourDirectionsTeachings.com is a novel cultural form on the Internet that challenges existing dominant social configurations of power. The site does so by contributing to social and political transformation from the periphery of mainstream society through helping to revive the cultural foundations of Indigenous communities. To discuss the impact of this project, I employ social theory, cultural analysis, political critique, as well as Indigenous methodologies and theories that pull from the work of Taiaiake Alfred (2009), Wendy Makoons Geniusz (2009), Leanne Simpson (2011), and Linda Tuhiwai Smith (1999).

As I noted in Chapter 1, Indigenous Knowledge online is an emergent phenomenon. A culturally appropriate methodological theory is required to analyze and comprehend the multifaceted features, circulation, and effects of Indigenous Knowledge online. To this end, I discuss my research strategy and design and introduce Simpson's (2011) four tenets of Biskaabiiyang, Naakgonige, Aanjigone, and Debwewin. In the next section, I discuss the relationship that I see between these four tenets and Alfred's (2009) five mantras. I then briefly introduce Smith's (1999) twenty-five projects as a framework for thinking about Indigenous Knowledge on the Internet. I conclude the chapter with an in-depth look at what it means to be Indigenous on the Internet.

Positive Inversion

When I produced FourDirectionsTeachings.com, I envisioned an online project that embraced Elders and celebrated Indigenous Knowledge for Indigenous Peoples. I did not create the project to teach non-Indigenous people, yet many use the site. I was pleased to hear that the site was being used to train teacher candidates at the Ontario Institute for Studies in Education at the University of Toronto. However, I have also received feedback that is less pleasing. For example, a non-Indigenous distributor in England who markets teepees for a living wrote to get permission to reference Mary Lee's teaching on the construction of the teepee in his teepee camps. I recommended that he refer his clients to FourDirectionsTeachings.com, where they could experience the teaching for themselves. Refusing to give him permission to take any part of the teaching out of its original context is firmly to reject the reduction of the teaching to superficial sound bites, which turns the teaching into a marketing ploy and thus appropriates the Indigenous Knowledge of that teaching. Cultural appropriation by non-Indigenous people is the root cause of centuries of degradation of Indigenous Knowledge. It is my hope that this man will respect my wishes, but notions of Indigenous copyright are very different from those of Western copyright. Belarde-Lewis frames cultural intellectual property from an Indigenous perspective:

> Communal sensibilities regarding tribal, clan or family
> ownership versus individual ownership, as well as

stewardship, or a caretaking type of relationship, prevents many Native and Indigenous communities from being able to place monetary value on these belongings. . . . The investment in their creation includes the entirety of whole Indigenous systems of knowledge: the process of learning the associated prayers, learning where in the community the materials are gathered, knowing how to make the physical pieces, and internalizing their function within the community. (2011, 18)

My experience both as a producer and as an academic has informed me that there is a far deeper level of commitment that includes personal responsibility and accountability. Indeed, the participants who contributed to this research project questioned me about my role as a cultural custodian and how I plan to transfer the responsibility for FourDirectionsTeachings.com when I am no longer able to care for it. This question about the role of the cultural custodian frames responsibility and accountability to the wider Indigenous community regarding care and maintenance of the site, but it also acknowledges the deep commitment to interrelationships and relationality and how these relationships come into being through the process of ceremony. The cultural transference of the site, then, becomes a very important responsibility that must be considered and attended to in the future because, as a bundle of knowledge, it must be transferred lovingly and with great care, according to cultural protocols.

When I reflect on what people are doing with FourDirections-Teachings.com, I think of Mary Lee, who told me that only teachings transferred through cultural protocols become real teachings. Anything else is speculative or, at best, imaginative, for it is processed through a single individual outside the community and outside cultural protocols. In some ways, this brings me peace. Furthermore, having gone through this intensive process of research, I see the project differently because of the people who spoke with me about their experiences, hopes, and dreams. I understand now that introducing non-Indigenous people to Indigenous Knowledge and worldviews begins a much-needed dialogue in relation to all facets of community life. The implications of the teachings for everything from political economy to social organization and the environment are of value to both Indigenous Peoples and non-Indigenous people. More importantly, I see the necessity of having Indigenous communities and non-Indigenous people understand the ethics of Indigenous Knowledge and how it is acknowledged and accessed within Indigenous community protocols, even when found on the Internet.

It is vital for me as an Indigenous researcher to speak politically and personally to Indigenous communities so that we can begin a conversation on these important issues. So, in the spirit of delving into Indigenous philosophy and epistemology, I have constructed my research to reflect the four Indigenous tenets that Simpson (2011) introduces in her work: Biskaabiiyang, Naakgonige, Aanjigone, and Debwewin. I employ these tenets as theoretical principles to discuss Indigenous Knowledge online and how it produces and contributes to Indigenous resurgence through particular processes that Alfred identifies in "Being Indigenous: Resurgences against Contemporary Colonialism" (Alfred & Corntassel, 2005). He describes these processes as "mantras of a resurgent Indigenous movement," and they include Land Is Life, Language Is Power, Freedom Is the Other Side of Fear, Decolonize Your Diet, and Change Happens One Warrior at a Time (613). In discussing these processes and tenets, I also bring in Smith's (1999) work on the twenty-five projects/methodologies to frame the research data that I gathered for this study.

Through these lenses, each giving a unique view from three diverse and widely acknowledged Indigenous scholars, I explore the questions under consideration in this book in a way that connects and juxtaposes interrelated principles and perspectives. The idea is not to achieve coherence or meaning through a linear or literary methodology. However, moving through the ideas in this way, and exploring some of the many possible ways in which they relate to and shed light on the issues being explored, might help us to affirm meaning in relation to the questions being considered *in a way that ensures a relatively rigorous Indigenous perspective.*

The Four Tenets

Biskaabiiyang

Leanne Simpson (2011, 51) explains that Biskaabiiyang means "to look back" in order to recreate "the cultural and political flourishment of the past" and to reclaim "the fluidity around our traditions," thereby "encouraging the self-determination of individuals within our national and community-based contexts" and "re-creating an artistic and intellectual renaissance within a larger political and cultural resurgence." I recognized that Biskaabiiyang is embodied in the project of FourDirectionsTeachings.com because the project celebrates cultural survival through Indigenous Knowledge grounded in the Oral Traditions of our ancestors. By sharing this work digitally, we are reclaiming the fluidity of our traditions by choosing and adapting how to represent, restore, and reframe teachings, so that even an introductory presentation on Indigenous Knowledge can reach out to communities nationally and inspire individuals to remember and reclaim. In this way, I understand that Biskaabiiyang is a process of decolonization because it means that we pick up the things that have been left behind. I have heard cultural teachers refer to this as "picking up those bundles," such as our songs, dances, teachings, and knowledge.

In thinking about Biskaabiiyang, I think about vision and how our vision needs to include all that we know to the extent that we can. I also think about what Simpson says regarding "being ethical about our responsibilities for resurgence within a Nishnaabeg ontology" (2011, 147). As a producer and researcher, I can see how FourDirectionsTeachings.com is part of Biskaabiiyang, which Simpson calls "a process by which we can figure out how to live as Nishnaabeg in the contemporary world and use our gaa-izhi-zhawendaagoziyang ['that which was given to use in a loving way'] to build a Nishnaabeg renaissance" (50–51).

Furthermore, I have come to understand that as the producer of FourDirectionsTeachings.com, and as an academic writing about Indigenous Knowledge online, I have a tremendous responsibility to respectfully acknowledge and to accurately reflect what the research participants have shared with me. FourDirectionsTeachings.com is more than just a website on Indigenous Knowledge; it is a gift of teachings that carries responsibility for the next seven generations and indeed resembles important aspects of what Traditional Teachers might call a bundle. Acknowledgement of the work in this way implies a huge cultural responsibility. Biskaabiiyang is integral to thinking about the project and the roles and responsibilities of a producer, academic, and Anishinaabekwe.

Naakgonige

In discussing Naakgonige, Simpson states that planning is an important process in resurgence, "a way of collectivizing, strategizing and making the best decisions possible in any given context" (2011, 147). This principle was central to my discussions with research participants, all of whom expressed warnings about how to proceed with having Indigenous Knowledge online. Indeed, many participants reflected on Indigenous culture in contemporary contexts and stressed the importance of respect and responsibility, echoing what I read from Simpson, who states that Naakgonige means "to carefully deliberate and decide when faced with any kind of change or decision. It warns against changing for the sake of change, and reminds Nishnaabeg that our Elders and our Ancestors did things a certain way for a reason" (56).

As a producer, I had to allay people's fears about having Indigenous Knowledge online when I first proposed the project. I did not feel comfortable making decisions on my own because I understood intuitively that those decisions were not mine alone to make. I sought community advisers, seen as people who take the protection and promotion of Indigenous Knowledge seriously, to help me develop the project. Now, at this stage in my work, I am seeking community members once again to engage in a dialogue about the next steps based upon my research findings.

I therefore appreciate how Simpson positions Naakgonige as that which "encourages one to deliberate and consider the impacts of decisions on all aspects of life and our relationships—the land, the clans, children, and the future"—and requires "individuals, clans and communities to carefully deliberate, not just in an intellectual sense, but using their emotional, physical and spiritual beings as well" (2011, 57). I believe that we are in a place and time in which we need to make decisions together as communities regarding how we are going to strengthen our cultural foundations and regenerate our intent to be Indigenous (Alfred & Corntassel, 2005, 614). FourDirectionsTeachings.com is part of this process because it contributes to the strengthening of cultural foundations by providing Indigenous Knowledge and worldviews online. In doing this work, FourDirectionsTeachings.com helps to regenerate our intent to be Indigenous.

Aanjigone

In considering the meaning of respect from an Indigenous perspective, Simpson writes that we are to deeply cherish each other—to truly see one another and cherish what we see. She states that "this teaching flows into Aanjigone ['non-interference'] in that we are to be very slow to judge one another, very careful with our words and actions to not bring those negative attributes back onto ourselves and our families" (2011, 125). I understand this to mean that we are to extend patience and kindness and that Aanjigone is a part of claiming and testifying and negotiating. With respect to change, Simpson states that "Aanjigone ensures that if change or transformation occurs, it promotes Nishnaabeg ways of being and prevents Zhaaganashiiyaadizi ['assimilation']. It also ensures that the interrogation or critique of decisions—or the consideration of all the possible consequences of a particular decision—is focused on the concept or decision rather than an individual" (54). The principle of Aanjigone is vital for thinking about Indigenous Knowledge online because it means that we have to set our fears aside and think beyond and outside ourselves about the next seven generations to come. For Simpson, Aanjigone "means to focus within" and "to think carefully and strategically about our responses rather than blindly reacting [to colonizing forces] out of anger" (56). I see this process as a meditative space in which healing and restoration occur through deep feeling and reasoning. Rather than force change out of preconceived agendas, we try to hear and see deeply what lies behind things so that we can more truly affect them from our common sacred bond.

FourDirectionsTeachings.com emulates this principle by being a space in which visitors can experience the teachings at their own pace. The teachings are not interpreted for them; rather, they must come to their own conclusions through active listening. In this way, FourDirectionsTeachings.com is a space in which visitors can experience Indigenous Knowledge without judgment and within the Indigenous principle of non-interference.

Debwewin

Simpson translates Debwewin as "the sound my heart makes," meaning "truth" (2011, 17). I have also heard that Debwewin means "heart based" or what one knows intuitively: that is, one's inwardly derived truth. In writing about Debwewin, Simpson draws from Anishinaabe ethnologist and storyteller Basil Johnston and Anishinaabe law scholar John Borrows to get at the notions of diversity and individuality in the meaning of truth. Simpson quotes Johnston:

> Our word for truth or correctness or any of its synonyms is *w'dae'b'wae*, meaning "he or she is telling the truth, is right, is correct, is accurate." From its composition—the prefix *dae*, which means "as far as, inasmuch as, according to," and the root *wae*, a contraction of *wae-wae*, referring to sound— emerges the second meaning, which gives the sense of a person casting his or her knowledge as far as he or she can. By implication, the person whom is said to be *dae'b'wae* is acknowledged to be telling what he or she knows only insofar as he or she perceived what he or she is reporting, and only according to his or her command of the language. In other words, the speaker is exercising the highest degree of accuracy possible given what he or she knows. In the third sense, the term conveys the philosophic notion that there is no such thing as absolute truth. (59)

Simpson then goes on to state that "these explanations are consistent with John Borrows' explanation of diversity in terms of Nishnaabeg thought. Borrows explains that difference exists within Nishnaabeg thought. Rather than positioning this difference as 'tension' or in an oppositional framing, diversity and difference are seen as necessary parts of the larger whole" (59). So, though we might recognize a diversity of truths, as captured in the statement "all Creation stories are true," we must still strive to reach those insights from a place of Debwewin—truth. The principle of Debwewin is integral to how we write, read, envision, discover, and share as Indigenous communities, and hence it is critical to mobilization. Without it, we would lack a sense of faith and trust in what we know.

Regenerating Indigeneity

In the interviews that I conducted, themes of Indigenous resurgence, survival, cultural revitalization, and transformation were consistently discussed and debated by the participants. Many were not willing to make hard and fast statements; rather, they took care in ways that I believe are related to some of the principles listed above. What became clear to me through each interview was the work that individual research participants were undertaking to regenerate what Taiaiake Alfred refers to as "being Indigenous." For him, this means "thinking, speaking, and acting with the conscious intent of regenerating one's indigeneity" (Alfred & Corntassel, 2005, 614).

For Alfred, there are particular pathways that lead to Indigenous resurgence movements. I will now define and discuss these pathways. Although some are more applicable than others with respect to Indigenous Knowledge online, or to how the participants in this research discussed the issues important to them, all mantras/pathways are worth noting.

LAND IS LIFE

Our people must reconnect with the terrain and geography of their Indigenous heritage if they are to comprehend the teachings and values of the ancestors, and if they are to draw strength and sustenance that is independent of colonial power, and which is regenerative of an authentic, autonomous, Indigenous existence.

LANGUAGE IS POWER

Our people must recover ways of knowing and relating from outside the mental and ideational framework of colonialism by regenerating themselves in a conceptual universe formed through Indigenous languages.

FREEDOM IS THE OTHER SIDE OF FEAR

Our people must transcend the controlling power of the many and varied fears that colonial powers use to dominate and manipulate us into complacency and cooperation with its authorities. The way to do this is to confront our fears head-on through spiritually grounded action; contention and direct movement at the source of our fears is the only way to break the chains that bind us to our colonial existences.

DECOLONIZE YOUR DIET

Our people must regain the self-sufficient capacity to provide our own food, clothing, shelter and medicines. Ultimately important to the struggle for freedom is the reconstitution of our own sick and weakened physical bodies and community relationships accomplished through a return to the natural sources of food and the active, hard-working, physical lives lived by our ancestors.

CHANGE HAPPENS ONE WARRIOR AT A TIME

Our people must reconstitute the mentoring and learning-teaching relationships that foster real and meaningful
human development and community solidarity. The
movement toward decolonization and regeneration will
emanate from transformations achieved by direct-guided
experience in small, personal, groups and one-on-one mentoring towards a new path. (Alfred & Corntassel, 2005, 613)

What strikes me about these pathways is how some of them connect
and ally with Simpson's (2011) tenets discussed above. For example,
Biskaabiiyang fits with the pathways of Land Is Life, Language Is
Power, and Decolonize Your Diet. Land Is Life is about reconnecting.
To reconnect, we need to look back and claim, name, and reframe the
meanings of those territories that are rightfully ours. With respect
to Language Is Power, looking back and picking up the language
means making a commitment to language revitalization, restoration
of Indigenous worldviews, and creation of ways to learn—which ultimately means being responsible for resurgence within an Indigenous
ontology. This resurgence also relates to the principle of Naakgonige,
with Indigenous ontology as the basis for planning. Decolonize Your
Diet is also about looking back to find those medicines and ways of
eating and being that nourish us in the best ways possible.

In thinking about the notion that Freedom Is the Other Side of
Fear, I can see how this pathway resembles the principle of Aanjigone
as a way of coping with and addressing our fears of colonial domination. To even consider Naakgonige is to entertain the idea of transformation or change, yet Aanjigone reminds us that we cannot force
this change, that we need to allow the space and time to heal, because
that is how we become spiritually grounded. Transformation and
change can be planned but not actualized until we are grounded
spiritually through our own healing and insight. Perhaps knowing
that transformation is possible is what drives the individual to want
to heal and be free from fear.

Finally, the pathway Change Happens One Warrior at a Time relates directly to all of the research participants in this project who work to foster meaningful relationships in their communities. These warriors seek Debwewin, and they are committed to sharing what they find and what they create through the process of mentoring and learning from one another.

In articulating the relationships that I see between Simpson's four tenets and Alfred's five pathways, I am making connections to Indigenous principles and methodologies as a way of applying an Indigenous research design for my work. In keeping with this goal, I will now turn to the work of one more Indigenous scholar, Smith (1999), on the twenty-five projects/Indigenous methodologies. This work provides a frame for the research data that I have gathered for this study.

Twenty-Five Projects/Indigenous Methodologies

Linda Tuhiwai Smith devotes a chapter of *Decolonizing Methodologies* to listing twenty-five projects that are not a definitive list of activities but an attempt to bolster Indigenous communities, researchers, and activists with the information that there are processes and methodologies that can work for them (1999, 161). The projects listed are still relevant today and resonate as powerful methodologies that can provide an Indigenous framework for thinking about how Indigenous Knowledge online contributes to Indigenous resurgence.

Just as I have drawn attention to the relationship between Alfred's five mantras and Simpson's four tenets, so too I can make connections between Smith's twenty-five projects and Simpson's four tenets. I list these tenets below as categories into which I place Smith's twenty-five projects, demonstrating the connections that I see between them. I have purposely left the numerical order of each project as it is presented in Smith's book to demonstrate my reordering of them to reflect the relationships and connections that I perceive. These categories are not immutable and merely represent guides that I believe work for my study.

BISKAABIIYANG

3. Storytelling
4. Celebrating survival
6. Indigenizing
8. Revitalizing
12. Representing
15. Reframing
16. Restoring
18. Democratizing
20. Naming
22. Creating

NAAKGONIGE

5. Remembering
7. Intervening
9. Connecting
13. Gendering

AANJIGONE

1. Claiming
2. Testimonies
17. Returning
19. Networking
21. Protecting
23. Negotiating

DEBWEWIN

10. Reading
11. Writing
14. Envisioning
24. Discovering
25. Sharing

Smith's twenty-five projects represent methodologies concerned with the broader politics and strategic goals of Indigenous research (1999, 143). As Smith explains, methods frame and shape the analyses and help to qualify the kinds of questions asked. So, though these twenty-five projects are presented within the context of Maori scholarship, as an Anishinaabe scholar I respectfully utilize them in an Indigenous framework to connect to the Anishinaabe tenets outlined by Simpson and then to think broadly about activation and agency through Mohawk scholar Alfred's work on pathways. I combined these various Indigenous scholars' works so that I can apply an Indigenous methodological, theoretical, and analytical framework to my research. I wanted to immerse myself, and this research work, in an Indigenous paradigm of analysis, and therefore I had to be creative in doing that ethically, respectfully, and conscientiously. I hope that it inspires other Indigenous scholars to search for Indigenous methodologies and theories that might be applicable to their work and that it provides proof to settler educators that using Indigenous theories and analyses is possible and indeed productive.

Placing the twenty-five projects into the four categories has helped me to develop a framework into which I can put the research data. Of course, I want to stress again that these categories are not fixed; rather, they help me to organize my analysis using Indigenous contexts and paradigms specific to this research project.

Being Indigenous on the Internet

Given the ubiquity of the Internet, cyberspace—like any popular medium before it—produces cultural narratives that contribute to our misunderstanding of race (Nakamura, 2007). Valerie Alia (2010), a media scholar, writes that the Internet is fast becoming a vital medium for Indigenous Peoples. Others note, however, that "far less is known about the uses and experiences of ICT's by groups decentered from the dominant institutions and idioms. This is especially true for Indigenous peoples, who have long been delegitimized by ruling cultural norms and isolated (economically, politically, geographically) from centers of influence" (Landzelius, 2006, 1). Lisa Nakamura (2006) also argues that popular Internet studies are not interested in the experiences or analyses of people of colour on the net. This is evident in her article "Cultural Difference, Theory, and Cyberculture Studies: A Case of Mutual Repulsion." So, not only is far less known about the uses and experiences of people of colour on the Internet, but also the theorizing and analyzing of such experiences are marginalized. This book addresses this gap in the literature by introducing how Indigenous research participants think about and use the Internet and thereby privileges and explores the notion of "being Native on the net."

Furthermore, by combining Indigenous methodological and theoretical applications for this work, I am privileging Indigenous analyses and methods in the study of the Internet and thereby challenging the predominantly Western Internet field to consider Indigenous theoretical understandings. This approach keeps company with scholars such as Megan Bang. In "Repatriating Indigenous Technologies in an Urban Indian Community," she and her co-authors discuss the important shift away from the use of technologies only for representation and communication and "toward the new innovations of technologies as authoring tools" (2013, 708). They quote Juan Francisco Salazar, encouraging us to "consider indigenous media as a socio-technical system of relations where technology becomes a cultural construction appropriated according to relevant cultural codes and social relations" (709). Putting forward the notion of a digital bundle for identifying Indigenous Knowledge projects online speaks directly to this strategy and offers a new genre to Western Internet theory.

A digital bundle is inclusive of—and indeed executed according to—local Indigenous cultural protocols and therefore speaks directly to Bang and co-authors' notion of Indigenous technology, "where our knowledge keepers, our Elders and our cultural producers are the architects and engineers of that construction process" (2013, 709). Taking on the roles of architect and engineer in our own techno-logical processes will replace what George Sefa Dei (2012, 102) calls our "cultural estrangement" with our "cultural engagement." For Dei, this shift is key, for it "affirms the centrality of local cultural ways of knowing and local voices in the dialogue on education. . . . Learning must liberate all knowledges" (104). Having Indigenous Knowledge projects online validated by the community creates rich learning environments that are intercultural, deeply respectful of local knowl-edge, and ultimately transformative in that they root "knowledges and practices into their appropriate soils, cultural contexts, histories and heritages" (105). This approach to Indigenous Knowledge in turn provides alternative learning sites for educators and learners that can transform educational institutions from locations of mere sur-vival(ism) to sites of contestation over knowledge, power, and social transformation.

For Dei, we cannot achieve academic and social excellence in our communities by mimicking colonial standards of what counts as intellectual. Decolonization is about producing our own knowledge projects and not continually challenging and subverting epistemological imperialism. Dei states that "community is shared space, thought and body. It is a collective more powerful than a sea of individuals. The power of community (however defined) prevails over the fragmentation of individuals, each locked in her/his own subjectivity and discursive agency" (2012, 108). For Dei, to privilege community is to develop a radical critical consciousness of knowledge and knowledge production. Doug Anderson writes that "our combined light is the real meaning of civilization." He elaborates that "the great Nehiyaw (Plains Cree) Chief Payepot exhorted his people to remember this truth on his deathbed in 1908": "My people, love one another. I want you to keep together. You don't know what the future holds. There will come a day when carts will no longer need horses. The white man may even be foolish enough to try to fly. Mark my words. Stay together. Love one another" (Anderson, Chiarotto, & Comay, 2017, 64). This conception of community built upon the foundation of love is radically different from the definitions of communities lauded today as network or platform societies.

In fact, Martin Nakata writes that "knowledge recovery led by Indigenous communities would not look the same as that led by scientists, developmental technologists, and conservationists (even when participatory) . . . selecting and privileging some Indigenous knowledge whilst discarding and excluding others" (2002, 283). Nakata notes that, if what Indigenous communities choose to document is of no apparent value to others, then the cost of documentation can be an obstacle. This is evident in the preferences of non-Indigenous government funding bodies that select which knowledges get recovered. For example, in Canada and the United States, huge amounts of funding are available for online digital collections of Indigenous artifacts, yet Indigenous Knowledge projects and language projects online continually struggle to find funding.

FourDirectionsTeachings.com was rejected twice by the Canadian Heritage Partnerships Fund because it was thought that the project was completed even though there were numerous calls from many other First Nations communities that wanted to have their teachings represented on the site. And there are many more First Nations, Metis, and Inuit who would love to have their teachings and knowledge featured on the site. The Inukshuk fund also rejected any proposal to expand the site to include an Indigenous language component. These rejections demonstrate significant obstacles to expanding the site and indicate that community demand was not enough to compel these Canadian government funders. This disregard for what Indigenous communities want is not only a symptom of colonization but also represents a worldview unable to conceive of notions of community, language, and knowledge outside its own limited perceptions and understandings.

In fact, the field of Indigenous education also has to resist imperialist understandings of knowledge and culture. Nakata makes the important point that,

> even though we don't find many references to Indigenous knowledge until quite recently, for the last three decades the field of Indigenous education refers instead to cultural appropriateness, cultural content, cultural learning styles, culturally responsive pedagogy, Indigenous perspectives— issues but not knowledge. This reflects the influence of anthropology in the human sciences as a way of understanding Indigenous peoples and communities. (2002, 285)

For Dei, "cultural decolonization is critical to address cultural colonization through developing critical consciousness, a radical and mobilizing new awareness to knowledge and knowledge production" (2012, 110). Hence, we need to make research transparent and accessible to Indigenous communities. Nakata (2002) offers the concept of the cultural interface as a way of thinking about knowledge on the intersecting nature of discourses and systems of thought.

Nakata's notion of the cultural interface accepts that all knowledge systems are culturally embedded, dynamic, responsive to changing circumstances, and constantly evolving. It is not about competition or usurpation; rather,

> it is about maintaining the continuity of one when having
> to harness another and working the interaction in ways that
> serve Indigenous interests, in ways that can uphold distinc-
> tiveness and special status as First Peoples. Indigenous
> interests will include the recovery and maintenance of
> knowledge but not without understanding, for example,
> what happens to that knowledge if documented and stored
> according to disciplines and technologies that have evolved
> in another Knowledge system. (2002, 286)

The cultural interface is about meta knowledge: that is, knowledge about knowledge. Nakata states that "Indigenous peoples need meta knowledge . . . as the basis for their interactions with the multitudes of intersecting, often conflicting or competing discourses emerging from different systems of Knowledge" (286–87). It is precisely for this reason that I have explained and elaborated Indigenous paradigms of knowledge—so that we can better understand the work that Elders and Knowledge Keepers perform in our communities versus the personal knowledge acquired by Indigenous educators, politicians, business and legal professionals, and so on. In making these important distinctions, and in having a community understanding and consensus (or at least a shared conversation) regarding these distinctions, we can then begin to distinguish the work of various Indigenous Knowledge projects online.

Nakata, like so many others, stresses that the web is an unbounded and chaotic discursive space: "It contains endless possibilities. Indigenous peoples must be involved at a deeper level than merely providing Indigenous 'content' or 'voice' if we are to use it for our own interests" (2002, 288). So, while we are no longer bounded by the gatekeepers of broadcast media—film, television, radio, books— we still need to be mindful of how we make our contributions online, because our choices will affect the next seven generations. Nakata cautions that this may involve change but change in our own long-term interests, rather than that imposed by bigger interests that may seek to coerce us unfairly. Change that incorporates into our own knowledge all the ongoing developments brought about by the convergence of other systems of understanding, so that our own corpus of knowledge, derived within our own historical trajectory and sets of interests, keeps expanding and responding to that which impacts on daily life and practice. (286)

Margaret Noori echoes the impact of daily life and practice in her work on Indigenous language online: "We must use the same methods and resources used by instructors of the dominant competitor. If our children type, text, process their English words, and place them in a wireless web environment, then we must do the same with Anishinaabemowin" (2011, 6).

Yet we must also avoid being co-opted by knowledge systems not sensitive to, or unable to perceive, our worldviews. Kim Christen experienced this all-consuming knowledge tsunami when her project, Mukurtu Wumpurrarni-Kari Archive 2007 (which she created with the Warumungu Aboriginal community in the central Australian town of Tennant Creek), became embroiled in the Information Wants to Be Free meme. Christen writes that over the course of a few weeks the Mukurtu archive became framed by Internet journalists in relation to one of the most controversial contemporary legal, social, and economic debates: digital rights management (DRM). This is a hot button issue because of high-profile corporations that use digital "locks" to regulate consumer use instead of copyright or other legal tools (2012, 2872). Christen emphatically states that DRM was never central to the archive itself; rather, Aboriginal cultural protocols were at the core of the project.

These protocols restrict access to content on the site based upon Clan affinity, gender, community role, cultural rite tied to life stage, et cetera. Basically, the site incorporates, as Christen notes, a wider range of ethical and cultural concerns into its digital tools and thereby subverts the narrow notion of information freedom that character-izes discussion of the cultural commons. Specifically,

> memes like "information wants to be free" and general calls for "open access" undo the social bearings of information circulation and deny human agency. Shifting the focus away from information bits and bytes or commodified content, indigenous cultural protocols and structures for informa-tion circulation remind us that information neither wants to be free nor wants to be open; human beings must decide how we want to imagine the world of knowledge-sharing and information management in ways that are at once eth-ical and cognizant of the deep histories of engagement and exclusion that animate this terrain. (2012, 2889)

So, like Nakata (2002), Christen emphasizes that human agency is paramount to how Indigenous communities produce and disseminate knowledge. Even within the new technologies, we must—as Nakata implores—incorporate our own knowledge into the convergence of other systems of understanding so that our own corpus of knowledge, derived from our own historical trajectories and sets of interests, keeps expanding and responding. The concept of a digital bundle is a response to this need for emerging Indigenous technology strategies because it makes the distinction between Indigenous Knowledge sites invested with the sacred teachings of Elders and Knowledge Keepers versus sites such as Deepening Knowledge, which helps educators to access Indigenous educational resources. The former is imbued with the local cultural protocols for each community represented by the Elder or Knowledge Keeper, whereas the latter is informed by sound educational practices that reflect the personal/acquired knowledge of educators committed to Indigenous education.

In thinking about social media as a possible repository for Traditional Knowledge, Joanne Waitoa acknowledges that "it can be difficult to navigate the online world with respect to indigenous values. The concept of best practice and literacy around social media is something that would benefit all users, minimizing the scope for harm" (Waitoa, Scheyvens, & Warren, 2015, 53). She also outlines some of the difficulties, such as the risk to Indigenous Knowledge, which can be easily replicated and disseminated through social media and thereby infringed because Indigenous intellectual property is bypassed or derailed when customary law, social relations, and responsibilities are ignored (49). This represents a tremendous loss for community. However, in reflecting on a research participant's feedback, Waitoa shares that

> if people have a kawa (protocol) that governs how they treat people socially then there's no reason why that kawa shouldn't carry through to the Internet and their relationships online or their engagement online, that kawa should still follow through. . . . It's a good illustration of how we in this day and age . . . as Maori communities should be able to maintain kawa while having these different interfaces that we have to engage with. (53)

I totally agree! It is possible to apply cultural protocols to the Internet. One way that FourDirectionsTeachings.com has achieved this is by creating a biography section for each Elder/Knowledge Keeper. The biography locates the Elder in his or her community and illustrates why and how that Elder is recognized as such by the community. Furthermore, the teaching/knowledge is grounded and authenticated by acknowledging the Elders and the cultural protocols that they possess: that is, their cultural authority to share teachings and knowledge as they see fit. As a producer of FourDirectionsTeachings.com, I understood that you can never dictate to Elders what you want; rather, they share which teaching/knowledge is appropriate for the particular time and place. I explained to each Elder approached for FourDirectionsTeachings.com that the teaching would be broadcast across the world once on the Internet. Each Elder decided what to share on the basis of this knowledge. So kawa was enacted during the development and production of FourDirectionsTeachings.com. This enactment of kawa was perhaps best exemplified by the initiation of the project through ceremonial protocols with Lillian Pitawanakwat that were later, during the development process, validated by Reg Crowshoe as having the appropriate cultural authority.

Perhaps for this reason the participants in this research so passionately discussed their feelings of authenticity and trust regarding the site, often stating that they believed it was done in a good way and that the culture and spirit of the teachings translated through the interface of the computer screen. One participant even thought that the project should have a note about tobacco and that, after visiting the site, a user should offer some tobacco. The offering of tobacco is an Indigenous protocol, which in this case would acknowledge and thank the Elders for their teachings and express gratitude for the knowledge that the person received. In this way, Indigenous cultural protocols are followed by those able to perceive the gift of the digital bundle and, according to protocol or kawa, humble themselves by placing down their tobacco.

Waitoa found in her study of Facebook use within the Maori community that political empowerment is possible, especially for young Maori, but that *kaumatua* ("Elders") were excluded because typically they do not use social media. So, while Facebook according to Waitoa increases awareness of political issues and alternative perspectives by aligning with Maori *tikanga* ("values/customs") through *tino rangatiratanga* ("self-determination") and *whanaungatanga* ("relationships/networks"), other aspects such as cultural misappropriation conflict with Maori values (Waitoa, Scheyvens, and Warren, 2015, 45). Waitoa also concludes that, because Facebook is a corporate entity, "it is becoming increasingly difficult for non-profit organizations to disseminate ideas when Facebook is controlling how many people see posts unless organizations opt for paid promotion. Furthermore, there is no guarantee of privacy with concerns of government and corporate surveillance" (54). Ultimately, one message that comes from being part of a social platform society and being "networked in" is that we are also part of a corporate platform society in which users are corralled like cattle into specific networks for the benefit of big business.

The Culture of Connectivity: A Critical History of Social Media by Jose Van Dijck discusses how we have moved from a culture of connectivity to a platform society. He constructs his argument by looking at the historical evolution of the Internet from Web 1.0—the ability to author and disseminate work and communicate freely on the Internet by offering everyone the ability to be his or her own broadcaster—to Web 2.0, which, "virtually overnight, replaced dot.communism by dot.commercialism" (2013, 10). The technology of Web 2.0 enabled users to contribute content to the web through various existing platforms such as Facebook, My Space, Flickr, YouTube, Wikipedia, et cetera. They became known as social media and "connoted the Web's potential to nurture connections, build communities, and advance democracy" (4). For Van Dijck, these social media sites are intentionally masked corporate sites that advertise a free participatory culture online so that they can benefit from the agency of users who create and share content for free. Their presence in the millions on these various platforms creates a cash cow for the corporate owners of these platforms who exploit user information and presence for other corporations and business interests seeking to connect with potential buyers and better understand their potential respective markets.

For Christian Fuchs, these platform sites are even more insidious. In writing about Edward Snowden, Fuchs explains that "the National Security Agency (NSA), through the Prism programme, obtained direct access to user data from eight online/information and communication technology (ICT) companies: AOL, Apple, Facebook, Google, Microsoft, Paltalk, Skype and Yahoo" (2017, 5). In this way, these so-called democratic platform sites become the tools of surveillance by the government and the neoliberal corporate tools of the rich.

Yet among Indigenous users these sites are tremendously popular. Acushla Dee O'Carroll, like Joanne Waitoa, writes about how Maori identity is formed using social networking sites (SNS). In *Maori Identity Construction in SNS*, O'Carroll demonstrates that the construction of Maori identity is being found in non-traditional spaces:

This raises some important questions [on] . . . how information and knowledge of Maori identity [are] transferred and
disseminated. Despite some participants commenting that
they continue to engage in their marae [a cultural gathering
place for Maori, where formal greetings and discussions
take place], there remains a growing concern amongst communities . . . that some Maori whanau [extended family or
family group] are leaving their tribal lands and not necessarily returning. Further queries are raised around the practical impacts on our marae if Maori are accessing intrinsic
tribal knowledge from sources other than the marae and
what is lost when that knowledge is accessed through means
other than oral transmission. (2013, 12)

These are crucial questions and speak to the urgency of communities that engage in dialogues on the notion of a digital bundle,
which identifies and defines sacred teachings and incorporates Elders
and Knowledge Keepers into the process while honouring cultural
protocols throughout all stages of production and delivery. Perhaps
most importantly, the notion of a digital bundle acknowledges—by
virtue of its deferral to respected Knowledge Keepers—that sharing
and disseminating aspects of Indigenous Knowledge online, though
important for various reasons, can never fully reflect, let alone replace,
the oral transmission of traditions on the basis of real spiritual connection. As Nakata (2002) states, it is imperative that Indigenous communities understand the meta knowledge of Indigenous Knowledge.
This understanding is especially important with regard to Indigenous
Knowledge online. It is also prescient with respect to social media
and the infrastructure of the Internet itself.

The Internet—Idle No More!

In reflecting on the Internet and how that technology contributes
to the degradation of the environment, Cheryl L'Hirondelle (2014)

urgently stated that "I am also concerned for the environment in cyberspace because the question still remains: how do we not become roadkill on the information superhighway?" She and I had attended the day-long Euphoria and Dystopia symposium at which we had been privy to the words of Sheelagh Carpendale from the University of Calgary, who had spoken about data barons and data serfs. L'Hirondelle elaborated on what Carpendale had said: "Her point was that there was a time where an application would cost $399.00, but now we're down to nano-dollars where an application only costs $3.99. At $3.99, making sales in the millions is possible, whereas before only a thousand would sell at $399. So our economy has changed significantly because of usage." She was referring directly to the Internet economy, in which millions of dollars are made by brokers such as iTunes that can sell a song for one dollar a million times over. L'Hirondelle elaborated: "And that was Sheelagh's point about data barons and data serfs; telecommunications companies are making huge amounts of money because they are the brokers of packets and parcels, bits and bytes. Ultimately, they're also the ones who are able to make money off of information because they control the networks." Controlling networks is about ownership, and that is what marks the difference between data barons and data serfs. The former are the landlords, whereas the latter are the renters and hitch-hikers of the Internet. For that reason, L'Hirondelle noted that

> what I would like to see is our people actually create our own networks so that we can be part of that economy and have greater control. I would like to see us have our own telecommunications company where we are selling bandwidth. It's important, because we know that the Idle No More movement, at one point, was hijacked. So there are ways that people can infiltrate networks and shut people out. I think for the future, as Native people continue to assert their rights, it will be necessary for us to have control over our own networks. It's the only way we won't be shut out or shut down and run over on the information superhighway.

Rob McMahon's PhD dissertation, "Digital Self-Determination: Aboriginal Peoples and the Network Society in Canada," offers some important insights regarding the links between networked digital infrastructure development and the autonomy and agency of Indigenous Peoples (2013, iv). His work presents a coherent argument on how Indigenous Peoples can shape and use networked digital infrastructure to support their self-determination. Like L'Hirondelle, McMahon sees the power imbalance of data barons and data serfs as being embodied in colonial structures and relationships surfacing through the development of broadband infrastructure, which all too often bypasses Indigenous territories. McMahon's and L'Hirondelle's advocacy for ownership of broadband networks by Indigenous communities is prescient and worth investigating—especially now as telecommunication giants bully new and independent service providers.

Ownership of the network hardware that connects us is worth exploring, but so are the applications that Indigenous communities currently use. L'Hirondelle alluded to this when she noted how the Idle No More movement was "hijacked" online. For the purposes of connecting, Indigenous communities have gravitated to social media sites, on which they have participated in what Lievrouw (2011) calls "mediated mobilization" through movements such as Idle No More. However, as noted by L'Hirondelle, these sites are not secure. Indeed, McMahon cautions that

> a vibrant Indigenous social media presence suggests that many Indigenous peoples may be bypassing "Web 1.0" platforms to move directly to easier to use—but less customizable—"Web 2.0" platforms that are owned and operated by third-party commercial entities. I suggested this lack of control and ownership over such information appliances threatens to constrain the future potential of Indigenous peoples to use these platforms to assert self-determination. (2013, 286)

McMahon warns against these corporate social media sites as he quotes Evgeny Morozov, who identifies that "third-party social media platforms are also used for state surveillance as well as activism. . . . For these reasons, [McMahon] focused on examples of social media platforms that Indigenous people have shaped into community-based platforms of engagement" (286).

The Idle No More movement certainly demonstrated the propensity of Indigenous communities to use popular social media sites, but it also demonstrated the ability of state surveillance to infiltrate such sites and co-opt opportunities for Indigenous social activism. Ownership, then, applies not only to the broadband infrastructure that connects us but also to the ownership, design, creation, and maintenance of online Indigenous projects, whether they are digital bundles, language websites, educational portals, or social hubs. Indigenous communities must take control to own and operate broadband infrastructure and to disseminate Indigenous Knowledge in ways that suit their interests, needs, and cultural principles.

CHAPTER 3

APPLYING INDIGENOUS METHODOLOGIES AND THEORIES

The Recruitment Process

As a researcher, I seek to understand Indigenous and other users' responses to Indigenous Knowledge projects online. After launching FourDirectionsTeachings.com in 2006, I received over 100 unsolicited emails regarding the project, and I kept a log of potential research participants. I selected individuals who self-identified their professions or roles in their communities and described why they were interested in FourDirectionsTeachings.com.

A range of people contacted me, among them teachers from elementary, secondary, and postsecondary programs and adult education programs. These educational institutions included public schools, colleges, and universities. I also received emails from various children's aid societies and penal institutions from across the country interested in using the site to train social workers, foster parents, and parole officers. I also received requests from many program managers and workers seeking culturally relevant aids for their community-based educational programs. Generally, these people worked in health services, family and social services, penal institutions for

Indigenous adults, and youth correctional facilities. There were also many Indigenous community programs operating in drop-in centres and friendship centres that offered adult literacy, youth mentoring, parenting classes, life skills, and professional training. I also received many emails from both Indigenous and non-Indigenous individuals who just wanted to express their gratitude for having access to an Indigenous Knowledge site—especially from artists and people who work in the arts who felt inspired and energized by the teachings.

It was an honour to hear from all of these people. As the years passed, many of the people with whom I originally had contact moved from their jobs, but fortunately a good number of people were still in reach. In general, the highest turnover rate was among adult educators. Some of the adult literacy/education programs that connected with me originally included the Native Women's Resource Centre, the Seven Generations Education Institute, the Circle of Nations Learning Centre (which I quoted in an article that I wrote in 2008), the Seniors Education Centre for Continuing Education at the University of Regina, and the Institute of American Indian Arts distance learning program. In the end, I contacted approximately twenty people, and initially twelve people accepted the invitation to participate. Unfortunately, I was unable to secure any adult educators and might consider this demographic for a future research project. I also contacted potential participants based upon strong referrals from people aware of my work as a producer of FourDirectionsTeachings.com.

I used FourDirectionsTeachings.com as a way of recruiting people and initiating conversations with potential research participants. I reassured the participants that the purpose of the interview was to examine and discuss how Indigenous online projects are perceived and used and to reflect on Indigenous Knowledge representation and how communities are affected (or not) by having this knowledge online. My goal during recruitment and throughout the interview process was to mitigate any power differential that I held as the producer of FourDirectionsTeachings.com by stressing my academic research focus on examining the phenomenon of using online technology to explore Indigenous Knowledge.

The Interview as a Reciprocal Exchange

As a researcher, I have always valued Indigenous approaches to research that emphasize the importance of and need for reciprocity. One of the main tenets of Indigenous research is how it will serve Indigenous communities and demonstrate reciprocity for those who participate in it (Wilson & Restoule, 2010). As the producer of FourDirectionsTeachings.com, I have offered the project freely on the Internet, where diverse Indigenous communities and groups have engaged with it. In this way, a gift has already been presented to Indigenous and non-Indigenous communities alike, putting me in a unique position as a researcher, because research participants are using a project that I helped to provide.

I found that using FourDirectionsTeachings.com as an introductory platform for discussion really helped to launch each of the interviews into a wider discussion on Indigenous Knowledge, the Internet, and the implications of the two in the field of education. From the start of the interviews, I found that having a common referent gave participants comfort and helped to guide the interviews. I also found that most participants were happy to be involved, seeing their participation as a way of giving back to a work that they personally valued and appreciated.

I am honoured that all of the participants agreed to be identified in this book. However, initially, one research participant chose not to be identified in order to protect her work in the community. All are respected professionals in their fields, and the work that they are doing is vital to reinstating what it means to be Indigenous and what it means to articulate Indigeneity and Indigenous worldviews to all Canadians. They are passionate about their work and eager to contribute to the dialogue on Indigenous Knowledge and the Internet. Revealing the participants also honours their roles as agents of change in their unique contexts—examples of change that happens one warrior at a time (Alfred & Corntassel, 2005).

The Research Participants

I have organized the research participants into three groups: educators, cultural arts workers, and system workers (those who work in organizations/institutions such as child welfare systems and penitentiaries). My rationale for this categorization is that, throughout the recruitment process, I noticed that the people who expressed the most interest in FourDirectionsTeachings.com worked in the field of education, were engaged as cultural arts workers, or were employed in organizations and institutions that provided services to or worked directly with Indigenous communities. Generally, the organizations represented are health, the penal system, and social services. For ease of description, I refer to this last group as system workers since we often hear people in the community refer to them colloquially as being "in the system."

Ten individuals took part in this research project. I will begin by introducing the educators (four) followed by the cultural arts workers (three) and then the system workers (three). I began with twelve participants but lost one person (grouped with the cultural arts workers) who left their organization and did not leave forwarding contact information and another individual working in the system.

I begin with an overview of each research participant and how each was recruited for this study. I then introduce what the participants do and why their particular work was of interest to me as a researcher looking at Indigenous Knowledge online. These introductions go in order of each participant's location, beginning in the east of Canada, where the sun rises, and ending in the west, where the sun sets. I then discuss "being Native on the net" as a way of introducing how each participant uses the Internet to facilitate his or her own work.

Educators

DR. LARRY CHARTRAND

Larry Chartrand teaches in the Faculty of Law at the University of Ottawa. He is Metis, and his Metis roots originate in the prairie region going back seven generations. His paternal family was displaced from the Red River area. When I asked him if being Metis informed his interest in Indigenous law, he said, "Yes, I would say so ... not only for personal reasons but academic reasons too; when I started law school, [I began] looking at Aboriginal Rights, and I have pursued that ever since" (2013).

I first became aware of Chartrand's connection to FourDirections-Teachings.com when Natalia Crowe, one of his law students, emailed me to say that she had just gone through the course syllabus for Aboriginal Legal Mechanisms and saw the website listed there. I quickly emailed her back and asked for more specific information. She sent me a direct quotation from the syllabus, which read "please review each Indigenous Nation's Tradition (on FourDirectionsTeachings. com) as it corresponds to the Indigenous national law descriptions in the Borrows textbook" (Crowe, email to the author, February 5, 2012). On reading this, I knew that I wanted to interview Chartrand to discuss the field of Indigenous law and to find out how an online project such as FourDirectionsTeachings.com became required reading in a law course.

Before contacting him, I researched Chartrand online and found his research interests posted on the University of Ottawa website, where it states that he takes

> an interdisciplinary approach to Indigenous peoples' issues including work involving Aboriginal rights and Treaty rights as understood from the perspective of Canadian law, International law and Indigenous legal traditions. Main areas of focus currently include Indigenous Identity and citizenship, Métis issues, Treaty interpretation and modern Treaties, Indigenous self-determination and sovereignty, critical Indigenous theory, decolonization, Indigenous justice reform, and Indigenous legal traditions.[7]

On reading this statement, I was immediately impressed by and interested in his work and wanted to know how Chartrand incorporates Indigenous Knowledge into the study of law.

DR. ANGELA NARDOZI

Angela Nardozi is project manager of the Deepening Knowledge Project facilitated by the Ontario Institute for Studies in Education (OISE) at the University of Toronto. The project reaches out to teacher candidates to help inform them about Indigenous education. I became aware of this project when Nardozi contacted me to speak about FourDirectionsTeachings.com at a teacher conference at OISE. I was amazed at the number of teachers familiar with the project and actively using it.

When I asked Nardozi to introduce herself, she began by telling me that she grew up in Markham, Ontario, and attended Catholic schools. She has a strong background in teacher education, receiving her Bachelor of Education degree at OISE in 2008 and then working in an Aboriginal summer literacy camp in a Treaty Three First Nations community near Kenora, Ontario, for two months. Nardozi does not identify herself as Indigenous or having any Indigenous lineage. She told me that her time in that First Nations community "completely changed my life. . . . It changed my whole academic direction." She elaborated that "I'd already been enrolled to do a master's in something completely different, then [decided], no, I want to go back to the community as much as possible" (2014).

Her desire to "go back" resonated with what Nardozi (2014) called "a tugging interest in Indigenous issues." However, up to her time in that First Nations community, she had never really had a connection to any Indigenous community. Now that she did, she knew that her parents would not approve. "My parents, being very Italian and strict, I knew they would be nervous about it, because they had a lot of stereotypes. So doing the master's . . . was my way to justify going back to visit the community a lot."

Nardozi (2014) succeeded in doing her master's degree with the permission of that First Nations community, where she studied "youth in the community and why or why not they were pursuing postsecondary education." For a non-Native researcher such as Nardozi to gain the support of an Indigenous community is a tremendous validation of trust and acceptance. It demonstrates an insider status that non-Indigenous researchers are rarely granted.

Since then, Nardozi has acquired her PhD from OISE and is teaching and working as an ally. Her community experience and the fact that she had been a teacher candidate helped her to acquire the role of project manager for the Deepening Knowledge Project. Each year Nardozi, along with her team (mostly Indigenous academics), do presentations, conduct outreach, and curate the Deepening Knowledge website. The site states that

> the Deepening Knowledge Project seeks to infuse Aboriginal peoples' histories, knowledges and pedagogies into all levels of education in Canada. The project is a part of the Ontario Institute for Studies in Education, University of Toronto, which is located on the territories of Anishinaabe and Onkwehonwe peoples.
>
> On this site you'll find information about the history and traditions of First Nations, Métis, Inuit and Native American cultures, information about the challenges facing Aboriginal communities today, and curricula for incorporating this information into your teaching practice.[8]

Since its inception, the Deepening Knowledge Project has used FourDirectionsTeachings.com in its presentations to teacher candidates and as a resource for teachers seeking Indigenous curriculum resources. On the current version of the Deepening Knowledge website, FourDirectionsTeachings.com is listed prominently under the "Student Resources" section: "These resources offer students the opportunity to explore Aboriginal topics at a level that is engaging and age-appropriate. Accompanying each resource is a suggested grade level, indicated in brackets. These ratings are only a guide, and it is up to the individual teacher to determine what is appropriate for her or his classroom."[9] This section of the Deepening Knowledge website helps teachers find resources suitable for elementary and secondary school students. Throughout our interview, Nardozi informed me how the Deepening Knowledge website and FourDirectionsTeachings.com help to educate teachers and teacher candidates on Indigenous worldviews and reassure them that there are resources out there for them to access.

DR. RAINEY GAYWISH

At the time of our interview, Rainey Gaywish was the program director for Access/Aboriginal Focus Programs at the University of Manitoba. She did her PhD dissertation on the work of Edward Benton Banai, Grand Chief of the Three Fires Midewiwin Lodge, focused on the revitalization of the Midewiwin spiritual tradition through the Three Fires Society. Thus, it was not surprising when Gaywish (2014) introduced herself to me as a member of the lodge. She began our interview by saying,

> I'll start formally. *Boozhoo.* My Anishinaabe name is Zhooniyah Waubizee Iquay, Silver Swan Woman. I am a Cree Anishinaabe woman. I grew up in the Interlake region of Manitoba. I am recently Treaty, through Bill C-3. Growing up, I identified as a "halfbreed." In my childhood, that wasn't a derogatory term. My family was very proud of our Aboriginal ancestry. And, while I don't speak the Cree language, I am trying to learn Anishinaabemowin, the language of the Ojibwe. I am a member of the Midewiwin Three Fires Lodge, and I am Third-Degree Midewiwin.

I became aware of Gaywish in 2012 when the Copyright Office of the University of Manitoba contacted me requesting permission to photocopy and distribute the transcripts from the Ojibwe and Cree sections of the FourDirectionsTeachings.com site. I was intrigued to see a university course titled "Aboriginal Spirituality" and that it was specifically and formally using FourDirectionsTeachings.com. I was also excited to note that the University of Manitoba wanted ongoing permission so that it could store the information on the university's server for future use. I happily granted permission but was curious to learn more about the course and how and why Gaywish was using FourDirectionsTeachings.com in her work.

Her work as a program director is to develop and offer programs that meet the needs of First Nations communities. Gaywish (2014) states that the "mandate is accessible, relevant, accredited postsecondary programs." To that end, she has developed and implemented a number of culturally relevant and culturally respectful certificate and diploma programs, such as the First Nations Community Wellness diploma. The University of Manitoba website describes the courses in the program in the following way: "Each of the courses incorporates knowledge of 'western' concepts and traditional philosophies and knowledge systems of Aboriginal people as they relate to mental health and wellness."[10] Here an epistemological binary is clearly articulated between Western concepts and traditional philosophies and/or knowledge systems of Aboriginal Peoples. In my research interview with Gaywish, we explored in depth the meanings of these concepts and their impacts on education.

DR. JOHN BORROWS

John Borrows (2013) introduced himself by stating, "I am Anishinaabe from Cape Croker/Neyaashiingmiing. My family all lived there. I continue to keep those associations strong because of that and because of my work. I am a law professor." I became aware of Borrows through my contact with Chartrand, who coupled FourDirectionsTeachings. com with *Canada's Indigenous Constitution* (Borrows, 2010). From my research interview with Chartrand, I also learned more about Borrows and discovered that he cited FourDirectionsTeachings.com in one of his books on Indigenous law. Borrows has been teaching law for almost thirty years. Here is how he was described on the website of the University of Minnesota Law School on his appointment to the Robina Chair in Law and Society[11] in 2008:

> Borrows was appointed professor and Law Foundation Chair of Aboriginal Justice and Governance at the University of Victoria in 2001. Previously, he taught law at the University of Toronto (1998–01); the University of British Columbia, Vancouver (1992–98), where he was

director of the First Nations Law Program; and Osgoode
Hall Law School of York University, Toronto (1994–96).
At Osgoode Hall, Borrows was the founder and director
of the Lands, Resources, and Indigenous Governance
Program. He has also been a visiting professor at Brigham
Young University, Dalhousie Law School, the University
of Waikato Law School in New Zealand, the University
of New South Wales in Australia, and Arizona State
University. . . . He writes and speaks prodigiously on such
issues as Indigenous legal rights and traditions, treaties
and land claims, and religion and the law. His research
interests include Aboriginal, constitutional, and environmental law. . . . In 2007, he received Canada's highest academic honor: fellowship in the Canadian Society of Arts,
Humanities, and Sciences. He also has been honored with
a Trudeau fellowship for research achievements, creativity,
and social commitment and with an achievement award
from the National Aboriginal Achievement Foundation for
outstanding accomplishment in the field of law and justice.[12]

Borrows (2013) continues to teach at the University of Victoria. In my
interview with him, he made it clear that he looks "for sources that
pull on Elders' understanding of what our laws, our values, our stories,
our traditions are." Consequently, he utilizes and references FourDi-
rectionsTeachings.com in several of his courses. I asked him specifically how online Indigenous projects affect the field of Indigenous law
and in which ways these connections are made.

Cultural Arts Workers

ÉMILIE MONNET

I was introduced to Émilie Monnet when she contacted me via email
to request permission to link to and quote teachings from FourDi-
rectionsTeachings.com for her performance piece *Bird Messengers*, a
project that premiered in Montreal in May 2011. I found a description

of *Bird Messengers* on her website: "A captivating interdisciplinary performance by Émilie Monnet and Moe Clark, where theatre, visual projections and music transport audiences from the symbolic realm of ancestry to a contemporary, living mythology. Created during a residency at the MAI in Montreal, this performance is inspired by Aboriginal storytelling and ancestral teachings."[3] Monnet was particularly inspired by Mary Lee's teepee pole teachings and how the seven values in them represent an Indigenous worldview related to community and well-being.

When I asked Monnet (2013) to introduce herself, she began by telling me about her family: "My mom is an Anishinaabe member of the Kitigan Zibi Algonquin community in Quebec, and my dad is French from France. I grew up in France until I was five. After that my dad would send me and my sister to France every summer, so I am really connected to that side too." As an artist and activist, Monnet explained, she does not want to box herself in because she explores art from a contemporary Aboriginal experience that celebrates her Aboriginal and French European identity. She is interested in collaborations between artists of different cultures and disciplines. Monnet has travelled extensively and worked with Indigenous communities all over Latin America and Canada.

Her website in 2013 stated that her work "experiments and creates from a place where languages, imagination and memory intersect; telling stories with theatre and media art forms that weave the symbolic realms of dreams and mythology—both personal and collective." Her goal is to use art as a tool "to create more consciousness in people and empower youth and sensitize people to the richness, diversity and resilience of Indigenous cultures and worldviews."[4] Impressed with her mandate, I wanted to learn more about how Indigenous Knowledge informs her work, where and how Monnet has accessed such knowledge, and what it means to her process as a contemporary Aboriginal artist.

MONIQUE MOJICA

I have known Monique Mojica for many years and actually hired her for the audio scripting of the female Elder voices on FourDirections Teachings.com. She narrated the words of both the late Ojibwe Elder Lillian Pitawanakwat and Cree Elder Mary Lee. When I sat down with Mojica (2014) and asked her to introduce herself, she went beyond the normal introductions, given our familiarity with each other, and elaborated on the evolution of her identity as an artist:

> I'm working on embracing "artist scholar" as a title, and I have written and published several essays on Indigenous performance theory. I've been a performer all of my life; I come from a theatre family, a performing family. I am third generation of four generations of performers, and my mother started me training when I was three years old. I am going to be sixty years old in a week. So I've been doing this for fifty-seven years; that's more than half a century.

Her artistic trajectory spans a lifetime of work in which Mojica has gone from victim to victor: "I cease to identify with my own victimization and no longer recognize my reflection as 'the victim'" (2008, 164). Instead, Mojica (2014) has become passionate about "finding ways to put Indigenous Knowledge in the centre of my creative practice." She remains committed to telling stories and exploring work from the experience of Indigenous women, which she states is very different from the perspective of Indigenous men and often is not heard. However, her approach to her work has evolved by delving into the heart of Indigenous Knowledge paradigms, where Mojica seeks to understand the social, ceremonial, and architectural structures and the cultural aesthetics that inform particular Indigenous Knowledges in order to comprehend how they are encoded and how that particular knowledge can be applied to art being created now. She writes that "I spent a long time digging around in massacre imagery and now I must call out to other spirits because transformation *is* a continuum and I must conjure myself into another place on my map" (2008, 166).

Intrigued with the trajectory of her artistic vision and her original contribution to the FourDirectionsTeachings.com site, I invited Mojica to be a research participant to get her thoughts on the site after all of these years. I wanted to know how she finds and works with Indigenous Knowledge and to get her thoughts on whether it should exist online. As an Indigenous artist with over half a century of experience, she shared more insight and expertise with me than I could have imagined.

CHERYL L'HIRONDELLE

I first met Cheryl L'Hirondelle at the Banff New Media Centre's Interactive Project Laboratory during the Banff Boot Camp in 2003. She was one of the first Indigenous new media artists whom I had the privilege of meeting in person, and I was excited to hear about her work. Over the years, we have kept in touch. Currently, L'Hirondelle is a PhD candidate at University College Dublin/SMARTlab. She is also a curator and musician.

When I asked L'Hirondelle (2014) to introduce herself, she began in the Cree language. She then translated for me that she is "a Cree woman and a boat person, which in Cree is the old way of saying a European." She also identified herself as Metis and part of the Pekanoe Metis colony, where Edmonton now sits. She said that this part of the country is referred to in Cree as Beaver Hills, and therefore she introduced herself in Cree as a Beaver Hills woman.

It was evident that L'Hirondelle has a great affinity with and connection to her home. This is why I have chosen to identify her place of being as Alberta rather than Ontario; although she is currently living and working in Toronto, it is clear that her home, the place that she is connected to, is the Beaver Hills.

Like Mojica, L'Hirondelle has had a long artistic career. It was a challenge for me to decide on a bio to best describe her work, for there are many available on the Internet. After much deliberation, I finally decided to select the bio from the Banff New Media Centre, the place where we first met:

> Cheryl L'Hirondelle is an Alberta-born interdisciplinary artist of mixed ancestry (Cree / Métis / German / Polish). Since the early 1980s, she has created, performed, and presented work in a variety of disciplines (music, storytelling, performance art, theatre, video, and net.art). She has also worked as an arts programmer, cultural strategist/activist, arts consultant, producer, and director—independently and with various artist-run centres, tribal councils, and government agencies.[15]

What I like about this bio is that it reflects her many talents and abilities but also lists her community-based work as an arts programmer/curator and activist and her work in artist-run centres and tribal councils. Working in communities with Elders is where her work began, and it is clear that after many years abroad in the arts L'Hirondelle is circling back to community and the importance and vitality of Indigenous Knowledge. This return is evident in how she describes her current arts projects and her work in graduate school.

It was clear from our discussion that she has been doing some deep thinking about the relationship between new media and Indigenous communities, and I am grateful to have engaged in a research conversation with her. She introduced me to insights and ideas about custodianship of Indigenous Knowledge on the Internet and the impact of and potential for that type of work for generations to come. I owe L'Hirondelle a great deal of thanks for her thoughtful and novel insights.

System Workers

DONNA BOURQUE AND PRISCILLA LEPINE

I was introduced to Donna Bourque in November 2007 when she contacted me via email to request more material and resources that would help with a new program that she was developing for inmates focused on healing and cultural awareness for the 98 percent of inmates who identify as Aboriginal. I remember being touched by her email and saddened by the high percentage of Aboriginal men in jail. I spoke to

Bourque again more recently when she accepted my invitation to be a research participant, bringing with her Priscilla Lepine, a new hire and the first coordinator for offender programming in the Northwest Territories. I was happy to include Lepine in the research interview.

Since 2007, Bourque has moved from being program coordinator to being case manager at the Fort Smith Complex, where she oversees the male inmate population. Her work includes overseeing program referrals and release plans for each inmate. She has been working with corrections for thirty years.

Lepine has worked for the government of the Northwest Territories for approximately twenty-eight years. She began in the field of social work for six years and then moved into teaching for nineteen years at a local college where she taught social work and then Native studies courses on the processes of colonization, their impacts, and the mechanisms for decolonization, with an emphasis on reflection and healing. With regard to her current position, Lepine (2014) said that it is new: "They call it the coordinator for offender programming, and there is no position like it in the Northwest Territories in any of the other jails. I work with both the female and male inmate population. My job is to provide professional development for staff and to develop Aboriginal healing programs for inmates."

Both women clarified their Indigenous identities. Bourque (2014) stated, "I'm northern Cree. My dad is Metis, and my mom is Cree, Chipewyan, and French. I have some Ojibwe in there too." Lepine (2014) said,

> I'm Metis. My family is from Fort Smith; we've been here since time immemorial. I have a great-grandfather several generations back who was one of the voyageurs that came up to this area and married my Chipewyan great-grandmother, so became a part of the Chipewyan community, and so I grew up in a Chipewyan community and identify with the Chipewyan people. I also have Cree and Mohawk heritage; however, I did not grow up in those cultures so don't have the same connection to them. My dad was from Poland, but

he was the only relative I had from there, and since he lives so far away from his homeland our family did not have any connection to that culture. Despite all of these affiliations to different cultures, I am identified as Metis in this community, partly because of how the federal government establishes Indian identity. As you can see, identity and affiliation can be very complex for a person of mixed ancestry.

Bourque and Lepine are passionate about their work and believe that coming from Indigenous backgrounds affects how they relate to imprisoned men. Bourque (2014) elaborated:

> All our guys are majority Aboriginal, so what I find is, because they know I'm Aboriginal, they feel more comfortable talking to me; they're more open; they know that I've probably experienced racism and the impact of the residential school system. They'll say to me, "Well, you know what I mean—you're Native. You know how it is." So it helps in that way.

Lepine (2014) added that

> we're really from a small community, and we're fairly isolated. We're a community of about 2,500 people. When I was growing up, there were about 1,000 people here. Our nearest community is 265 kilometres away, and there's nothing in between but wild land, no gas stations. There are a couple of pit stops, some cabins off the road, that sort of thing. So, growing up in a small isolated community, everybody knows everyone else. And growing up in the North is small too. I went to Akaitcho Hall, a residential school named after a chief from the Yellowknife Dene. I got to know a lot of people; plus teaching at the college I got to know a lot of people from the North. So you get lots of connections. When I meet one of the inmates, I ask them

where they are from. They'll tell me, and I'll say, "You know so and so," because I usually know people in most of the communities. This helps establish a connection between them and me. It is an age-old Aboriginal method of establishing a relationship. The North is small, and we know a lot of each other.

It is evident from their descriptions that Bourque and Lepine come from a tightly knit community that shares a collective experience of oppression. During our interview, they discussed the importance of creating culturally focused programming for the inmates as a way of dealing with low self-esteem and oppression. Both Bourque and Lepine have studied and researched Indigenous Knowledge for several years and are committed to using it in their programs. I wanted to learn more about their process and why they think that it is important and relevant to bring Indigenous Knowledge into the prison system in the North.

JANETTA SOUP

Janetta Soup sent me an email on February 14, 2012, to request permission to link to FourDirectionsTeachings.com and to use some of the animated pieces in a health project. She explained that it was for "First Nations Cancer Care, one of the professional development training courses that we offer to health care providers working within or for First Nation communities" (email to the author, February 14, 2012).[16] Soup said, "as you are aware, design and development of on-line materials can be very taxing ... which is why we want to know if we can reference the work your organization has already created." I was happy to comply.

In our interview, and in her initial email to me, Soup identified herself as a proud Blackfoot woman. She grew up in the small town of Cardston, Alberta. She lived on the reserve side, the largest reserve in all of Canada and home to the Blood tribe. Her current work with the Saint Elizabeth First Nation, Inuit, and Metis Program involves "helping health-care providers that are working within and/or for

First Nations, Inuit, and Metis communities and providing them with resources to deliver services to those communities" (2014). In relation to this objective, her organization works in partnership with different areas within health care. As Soup noted, "I actually worked on a project that was taking the Canadian physical activity guidelines and making them more culturally relevant."

In 2015, Soup and her team worked on a project with the Alberta Health Services Aboriginal Health Program. The project involved developing an online course in the realm of Aboriginal awareness and sensitivity learning. This course was made available to all of Alberta Health Services, which has over 95,000 staff, according to Soup. The vision of the Saint Elizabeth First Nation, Inuit, and Metis Program is to honour the human face of health care. Consequently, the organization has developed First Nations courses on cancer, diabetes, chronic obstructive pulmonary disease, elder care, and, most recently, trauma. This body of work is committed to enhancing the capacity of health-care providers in various First Nations, Inuit, and Metis communities. Soup shared that her team works in partnership with various communities and other organizations.

At the time, Soup was one of five engagement liaison workers. The other four were located in Winnipeg, Mississauga, Red Lake, and Montreal. Soup (2014) described to me how they are organized virtually and noted that the manager and program assistant are based in Winnipeg: "We're a virtual program; all our work is done online." Intrigued by the setup of the organization and the amount of work that it is producing and delivering, I wanted to know how much of it relies on access to Indigenous Knowledge online and why this is important for the field of health care.

BRENDA DUBOIS

The last participant originally chose to remain anonymous (an option provided to each potential participant). At the time of our interview, Brenda Dubois was working in the child services sector. In respecting her choice, I will not identify the province, city, or centre in which she worked at the time of our interview. Currently, Dubois is a highly respected and much-valued Knowledge Keeper at the Aboriginal Student Centre at the University of Regina. Prior to this position, she worked for almost twenty years in child and youth services, providing programming and services to families with children under the age of eighteen. In addition to working with families, Dubois explained in our interview, she has been advocating for thirty years for families to get their children back and supports the Aboriginal Family Defence League and efforts dedicated to murdered and missing women and Indigenous People. After sharing this initial information, Dubois (2014) spoke about family origins:

> To honour my mother, I'm part Metis; to honour my father, I'm part Cree/Saulteaux. I consider myself an urban refugee because I had to move to the city because of lack of employment in my community. I was taken as a small child to some of the ceremonies. At that time, they were still being held in hiding. Thirty years later, in the city, when trying to initiate a Pipe Ceremony or a feast, people from the community would say no because they said it was witchcraft. So we realized we needed to learn more and proceed carefully.

Dubois has initiated many programs rooted in Traditional Knowledge. One of them provides Talking Circle training to forensic psychology interns and to families in the communities. She explained that Talking Circles are a great way for families to do problem solving and really hear each other. Sweat Lodges and Coming-of-Age Ceremonies are also important for Indigenous families. She also noted that many of the people working in the social services field are not Indigenous and require cultural awareness training, which she has also provided.

Over the years, Dubois has had many debates and battles with agency managers over creating diverse Aboriginal programming because they continuously challenge her on whether such programming is effective. Her reply to this challenge was that "all of our ceremonies would not have survived this many years without being best practice[s]. You may not believe in them, but we do. Ceremony is the foundation of our belief system" (2014). I was moved by her struggles and insights and was curious to learn more about how Indigenous Knowledge informs her work in social services. In particular, I wanted to know about the impact or value of Indigenous Knowledge online for Aboriginal families who access social services.

Indigenous Knowledge in the Classroom

All of the educators who spoke with me use the Internet as a resource in their classrooms, and many of them specifically use websites to introduce and present Indigenous Knowledge. Indeed, Larry Chartrand (2013), who began teaching Indigenous law in 1993, noted that "at that time there were no Internet resources at all. Now it's the first place students go in the pursuit of knowledge. Books are secondary." For Angela Nardozi (2014), the only non-Indigenous participant in this study, the Internet is a pillar of strength for training teacher candidates. She acknowledged that "the Deepening Knowledge website became a central focus to our work, as it has alleviated teacher fears about not having access to trusted resources." She emphasized that, "in our presentations, we actually introduce our website first as a way to reassure them that we understand and empathize with their fears— that they think there's nothing out there. We let them know that Dr. Restoule has approved everything on the website and that it can function as their 'one-stop shop' to research and access for Indigenous resources online." These fears also apply to Indigenous educators such as Rainey Gaywish (2014) who are concerned about the representation of Indigenous Knowledge online:

> When it comes to preparing higher education that expresses our own Indigenous worldview, our own perspectives, our own teachings, and the knowledge of our Elders, we are at a disadvantage because so much research on our communities has been done by non-Aboriginal people. It is these

scholars who present our worldview, our teachings, our history, our everything! Finding anything that's been developed by our own people and that talks about our worldview is like finding a diamond. I highly value those resources.

Both Indigenous and non-Indigenous educators struggle to address the imbalance of scholarship from an Indigenous perspective and the lack of quality Indigenous educational resources; these are common struggles in the field of education. Gaywish (2014), who teaches the "Native Studies" and "Aboriginal Spirituality and Native Medicine and Health" courses for the First Nations Community Wellness diploma, said that she uses FourDirectionsTeachings.com in both courses "because the content on that site is very relevant to what students should be learning."

Nardozi (2014) indicated that few websites are highlighted in the Deepening Knowledge Project, but FourDirectionsTeachings.com is one mentioned in every presentation:

> We like to show the navigation screen page where it shows icons representing the five First Nations because we have a really hard time communicating to the teacher candidates how diverse First Nations are. When teacher candidates hear that there are so many different Indigenous Nations across Canada, they get really anxious and ask, "Do I have to teach about all of them?" I tell them, "No, but you can begin by honouring the territory that we're on." I also tell them that the FourDirectionsTeachings website will give you some insight into the Anishinaabe/Ojibwe teachings and Haudenosaunee/Mohawk teachings, whose territories make up the province we live in.

Educators such as Nardozi stressed that there is a lack of good-quality Indigenous Knowledge resources online. This sentiment was echoed by other participants. Chartrand (2013) relayed that, "although Indigenous Knowledge has become more and more present online, it's certainly not a significant aspect of what is available yet. So I have to pull from other sources like language sites, which are helpful, but they are not geared to teaching the fundamental philosophies and teachings; they are geared toward teaching the language." Websites focused on the fundamental philosophies and teachings that make up Indigenous Knowledge are so limited that, when I asked participants to name other websites like FourDirectionsTeachings.com, they could not name any. This was a surprising finding for me as a producer and an academic, and it led me to question whether a distinction should be made between Indigenous *Knowledge* sites and Indigenous *information* sites. When I put this question out to the research participants, most agreed that there were more Indigenous information sites than Indigenous Knowledge sites.

Most of the websites used by educators relate to their specific fields and, for the most part, are text based. For example, John Borrows (2013) relies on legal databases regarding court decisions, and he seeks out blogs such as *Turtle Talk* from Michigan State University with Matt Fletcher. Borrows noted that about six of his colleagues make regular contributions to this blog and that there are good links from that blog to other Indigenous websites. He also uses the Navajo Nation's website frequently because the Navajo have a tribal court, and decisions are listed on the site: "On this website, they talk about how their code of ethics can be practised before those courts, which is great. I also try to find that kind of information for other tribes, like the Sioux, Leech Lake, or Cherokee; many nations in the United States have tribal courts, so they'll have that kind of material." Borrows also visits the Tribal Court Clearing House, a site that deals with tribal law more generally in the United States. More importantly, he noted that "on this site there is also discussion of traditional law. There's nothing graphic like yours or the Nature's Laws website, but it is a great—I guess text-heavy—website because it gives you access to what people are writing about and what their constitutions look like, et cetera."

For Gaywish (2014), sites such as the National Aboriginal Health Organization (NAHO) site are great for cultural resources: "They did excellent research and have published many articles. In their archives, you can find quite a lot of information on midwifery and Traditional Knowledge." Gaywish used the past tense because, as she imparted, this organization was axed by the Conservative government of Stephen Harper. She also noted that

> FourDirectionsTeachings.com is different from other sites that I use, like NAHO, because of the audiovisual design. Most sites I access for Indigenous Knowledge are text based and do not offer this rich audiovisual experience. I like the fact that you can still print off the transcripts and have students refer to them, but the real value is the access to the teachings. It is the next best thing . . . to having an Elder in the classroom with you.

This notion of "having an Elder in the classroom" was brought up many times by the educators, who highlighted a profound desire to have that kind of cultural knowledge and presence in the classroom. Having an audiovisual representation of an Elder's exact words supports the work of the educators and demonstrates to the students that this knowledge is alive and well, existing among Elders and Traditional Teachers living and working in their respective communities. Indeed, all of the educators said that they would like to see more Indigenous Knowledge projects online that they could access for their classrooms. Chartrand (2013), for example, said that "I would like to see more nation-specific teachings regarding social order. Or perhaps even a framework for looking at Indigenous worldviews as opposed to Western worldview perspectives. It would be great to see how the teachings from various First Nations communities are relevant today, but that's wishful thinking." Sadly, to have this type of work online right now is "wishful thinking" not because it is not possible—it is totally doable from intellectual and technological standpoints—but because very few funding agencies or organizations are currently committed to getting this type of work done. This is a great disservice to the movement of Indigenous resurgence and to the field of education in Canada.

Indigenous Knowledge in Art and Activism

The Internet is useful for the Indigenous artists and activists whom I interviewed. Émilie Monnet (2013) noted that "the Internet is a big resource for me when researching Indigenous Knowledge and cultural teachings. The last piece I worked on focused on cultural prophecies. I am also very interested in Creation stories, so I search for that online as well." As Monique Mojica (2014) mentioned, "I am always searching for good photos of clothing from a certain era, or depictions of Indigenous tattoos, and those kinds of things that inform my art practice and interests. I also use the Internet to research photographs, books, archives, and maps. I certainly used it to find where all the mound sites are, for my current project." In reference to the Idle No More movement, Cheryl L'Hirondelle (2014) stated that "the Internet is definitely the way that we find out about things that are happening now." In fact, she researched the meaning behind the movement online because she was curious about its name, wondering where it originated and why:

> I immediately found footage online of a teaching that happened in Alberta with Sylvia McAdam. She was speaking in Cree and mentioned the term *Meechquasquo*, and the *Ogichetaw*, the male version. . . . I was very excited to hear her talking about the Ogichetaw because roughly translated it means "warrior society" or "dog soldiers" or "providers"; there are so many different attempts to try and translate it. Usually, this word is used in reference to the men, so I was surprised to hear it being used with respect to the women. I contacted Joseph, now my adopted brother and formerly my ex, and said, "I'm sending you a link. You got to check this out." It turns out he knew the woman who was speaking, and we were able to discuss it further. It was the first time I've heard about a protest that is based in our history and our worldview and is being conveyed in our language. Being able to learn about Idle No More on

the Internet in this way has to be one of the most profound things that the Internet has given me.

The Internet informs the artistic and activist practice of the participants whom I interviewed and expands what they know about Indigenous Knowledge. This expansion in their thinking has impacts on their work in their respective fields.

The Internet is also an important point of access and connection. For Monnet (2013), access to language and community is found in a popular social media site that she resisted for many years but eventually joined because it addressed her need for access to Indigenous language support:

> I found a language dictionary online and quite a few language groups on Facebook. It's a nice way to share information. I found a link to Basil Johnston doing an interview on the radio because people will also post events and links to other resources. I've been on Facebook for two years. I really resisted at the beginning because I was concerned about privacy issues and corporations, but I eventually logged on because it is really practical for sharing information and being in touch, and there are a lot of Indians on Facebook!

Mojica (2014) also uses Facebook to access a number of websites, though she noted that "I forget the names of those sites because I am following links." The ability to access radio stations such as Native America Calling and Indian Country Today online means that she can hear the latest news, such as when Carter Camp died and then Charley Hill right after him. It also means that she can keep up with what is happening elsewhere, such as when she was in London, England, and could get accurate updates from people in Elsipogtog First Nation (New Brunswick). As Mojica said, "I could then talk about this story in Europe because I knew I could trust the information that I was receiving. So it's about trusting who is doing the reporting and who are the people being discussed."

Like Monnet, Mojica (2014) is also a Facebook user:

> Facebook is a way for me to connect with family and friends that live very far away and that I have not seen for a very long time. I love that I can share Idle No More flash mobs with my family in Panama and that they can connect with me and say, "Hi, Auntie, what's going on? What's happening with Ngobe Bugle?"—which is another nation in Panama.
>
> Demonstrators there were blockading a road and getting killed and being assassinated for protesting Canadian mining. I could see what collaborators and artists were doing in Panama City, so to support their actions and get the word out I connected them with supporters of Mining Watch Canada. This connection helped them to connect with people that are on the ground in Ngobe Bugle so that the international community, including Canadians, could be informed. As an activist, I find it's really important to have this access online, especially because I have community [members] spread out over several continents.

For Mojica, Facebook provides a connection to family members across distances, while the Internet helps her to make connections as an artist and activist. Monnet accesses language groups on Facebook, which provide her with a sense of extended community. Having access via the Internet means that artists have a sense of connection and access to Indigenous communities both locally and internationally.

For L'Hirondelle (2014), a keen observer and scholar of the Internet, access is revealed by the ways in which Elders and Traditional Teachers interface with the Internet:

> A phenomenon I've seen online recently is that there are now Elders on Facebook that are putting up daily or weekly postings. I know one of these guys personally, and he's by

no means a plastic shaman. I am happy to see that he's alive. He's an old man who's decided that Facebook is the place where he needs to post every day or every week. So I think it's really beautiful. I might have had problems with that a year or two ago, but now I'm like, "Wow, that's so great."

Access to the Internet for cultural workers is a *route*—a way to connect to community, whether through Facebook language groups, Indigenous news outlets, or even Elders who post messages on Facebook. People are finding ways to reach out and support their collective interests as Indigenous Peoples through the Internet. For this reason, I think, L'Hirondelle does not have a problem with an Elder posting on Facebook. As her comment suggests, what we think about Indigenous Knowledge online and the contributions of Elders and Traditional Teachers is changing.

However, there is still great caution and concern about what gets posted online, how, and by whom. As Monnet (2013) said,

I have found that the information online speaks more to my interests than mainstream media, but you always have to be careful. So I always check the sources to see whether the information is accurate and how knowledgeable the person is who is doing the posting. Where are they getting their information? Are they contributing to cultural appropriation? All these things are important to me when searching for information and resources online.

Monnet echoed the concerns of L'Hirondelle, who clarified that the Elder whom she was referring to was "by no means a plastic shaman." So, though these cultural workers find great value in accessing Indigenous Knowledge and cultural information online, they also express great caution and concern about how to read those resources.

Indigenous Knowledge in the Community

Indigenous People who work in the health-care, social service, and penal systems suggest that finding Indigenous resources online that can support their work in their communities is essential to delivering first-rate programming for their clients. I was deeply moved by the passion and empathy of the system workers whom I interviewed and how hard they must work within their institutions to implement culturally sensitive programming appropriate to addressing their clients' needs. For example, Donna Bourque (2014), who works with Priscilla Lepine, has been collecting and saving research information for years on her "favourites list."[17] She noted that

> I have healing programs and organizations, information on the residential schools, the Truth and Reconciliation Commission, and information on Native counselling services. Most of the sites I look at deal with healing because that's been my goal, to have a healing program in the correctional facility here. I've been pushing for this for years. Before Priscilla came, it was just a few staff who would get together and do different programs with the inmates. We would collect resources, and when we weren't sure we would go and check the Internet.

Likewise, Lepine (2014), the first person to work in the newly created position of coordinator for offender programming in the Fort Smith Complex, Northwest Territories, has created multiple folders:

> I have folders that have sites for Aboriginal corrections, Aboriginal cultures, Aboriginal education, Aboriginal healing, and Aboriginal crafts (because I like to use hands-on cultural activities to help foster a healing dialogue for the inmates while they craft). I also have folders on federal Indian legislation, because we've all been impacted equally by federal legislation, which is also our common

thread today. So under each of those folders I have tons of sites that I go to. I like the Aboriginal Healing Foundation site and go there often for information and links to other Aboriginal organizations.

Access to this kind of information helps Bourque and Lepine to do their jobs. With an almost 100 percent Indigenous incarceration rate, it is justifiable that these resources would be offered through the penal institutions themselves, but that is not the case; people who work in penal institutions with Indigenous populations must find these resources on their own and bring them in to work. For this reason, Lepine (2014) stated that, "like Donna, I also keep up online with what is going on down south." Searching online to see what is happening "down south" is important not only for corrections staff but also for organizations that focus on Aboriginal programming. For these women, keeping up with what is happening "down south" is staying on top of what is current. Lepine elaborated:

> The Internet is very useful to us because we are in an isolated community, and while we do have access to a local library and a college library they are only as good as the people that order the books and resources. I know from working at the college if I want to get an interlibrary loan—from, say, the University of Saskatchewan—by the time the book or video gets here it would have to go back in the mail because of the length of travel time. Plus, it's really hard to find good resources on DVD. There's a lot of really old stuff that's out there now and not a lot of new stuff being made. I see this especially when I visit the library. What I like about the Internet is that you can find archives, video clips, and current content.

The Internet helps to facilitate access to materials that Bourque and Lepine would otherwise have difficulty accessing because of their location in the North. Furthermore, as Lepine indicated, the popularity of

DVDs has waned, and not a lot of new content is being offered through that medium, likely because of the expense of production and distribution. The nature of content delivery is changing, and new releases can now be offered via the Internet through downloading and streaming.

Lepine and Bourque acknowledge that, though there is a lot of online content on Aboriginal policy, federal legislation, and Aboriginal cultures, there is not as much on Traditional Knowledge or Metis teachings. In fact, Lepine (2014) said,

> it would be great to have more Traditional Knowledge from Aboriginal perspectives online. Gabriel Dumont Institute has a lot of Metis Traditional Knowledge on their site presented through testimonials and that sort of thing. So I've gone there quite a lot because that's one site that I have found that has teachings about Metis culture. Other than that, there's not a lot on the Internet. There seems to be a lot on the medicine wheel, but there could be more detailed descriptions on it. I make Metis sashes, which I use as a teaching tool to explain the culture. One of the things I was just researching online and emailing my contacts about was the pattern for Louis Riel's sash. I am also interested in Metis women's shawls. So those types of resources are specific things that I look for which are really hard to find on the Internet.

So, though Bourque and Lepine can access some Indigenous resources online, they hinted that this is only the tip of the iceberg. It is clear that they think more could be done. In this they are not alone.

Janetta Soup (2014), who makes online resources for the health-learning field, stated that, though she can generally find First Nations perspectives online, she has a more difficult time locating Metis and Inuit perspectives online. In discussing her work, she said that

> there are multiple ways that I research information in regards to Indigenous Knowledge. When I was researching

elder abuse, I started with a Google search on First Nations elder abuse. I took a look at the organizations and then went deeper by reading various documents that the organizations put out. From there, I looked at the reference guide to see what else is out there. Personally, I find that I can access quite a bit of information from a First Nations perspective, but trying to find information from a Metis or Inuit perspective is far more challenging.

This disparity of information is a concern for Soup because the mandate of the Saint Elizabeth First Nation, Inuit, and Metis Program is national in scope regarding health issues among Indigenous Peoples. As a result, as Soup explained, "it is important for our project work with Alberta Health Services to include these perspectives as well. There is actually a wisdom council and an Aboriginal Health Program, and there are a few council members with Metis and Inuit backgrounds. So we also work with them to access additional information and recommendations."

Access to resources informed by Indigenous perspectives and teachings is key for Indigenous system workers who create and provide programming and training for clients. As a result, it is now common to have Elder councils and traditional councils affiliated with such programming and training to ensure that Indigenous perspectives are respected and reflected appropriately. Indeed, I believe that such councils are required for Indigenous Knowledge resources online.

Brenda Dubois (2014), the Indigenous social worker who provides services for Indigenous families, believes that innovative grassroots programming created by Indigenous communities eventually gets distributed to the larger mainstream society: "Online I found the Aboriginal Mental Health Resource Unit. It was really good because they looked at Aboriginal approaches and explained it so that non–First Nations people could understand it. So the ripples of what we are doing in the community [are] being shown out there as well." As a front-line social worker who works with many non-Indigenous people, Dubois often feels the stigma of having to defend and explain Indigenous Knowledge and approaches in her programming. So, for Dubois, having Indigenous approaches reach mainstream society is necessary for Indigenous front-line workers and community well-being because it promotes cultural understanding and respect.

Dubois (2014) is proactive about accessing Indigenous resources on the Internet and, when possible, distributing them to clients. However, sometimes even good resources are challenged by communities because of their content, even though they "are useful for the community." She discussed one of the sites in particular:

> Sean Mayer has done comic books throughout the years. He's got a web page called HealthyAboriginals.net, and I use it quite a bit. His comics were really cool, and we would distribute them to our community so that kids could take them home. Eventually, families would be talking about the topics of suicide and bullying, or gangs, and stuff like that, so his comic books brought up really important issues. I was sort of upset when he pulled his suicide comics because of people's feedback. It was like our community was saying, "Don't talk about it again," and I was like, no, those comic books provided an opportunity for parents to understand that, potentially, some of their kids may be having suicidal thoughts. Hiding the issue doesn't mean the issue is going to go away.

I am sure that Dubois is not alone in thinking this way, but how do such controversial issues get discussed? It would be unfortunate if Mayer felt bullied by a small group in the community to give up his content on suicide. Obviously, not everyone in the Indigenous community feels the same way, but how we deal with controversy online or how we address what should be discussed publicly is not clear. There are no parameters or protocols for such discussions and conflicts, but perhaps there should be to ensure that everyone in our respective communities is heard and invited to the table. Dubois raised some important concerns regarding what gets profiled publicly online.

Lighting New Fires for Indigenous Knowledge Online

Manuel Castells states that "the new power lies in the codes of information and in the images of representation around which societies organize their institutions, and people build their lives, and decide their behavior. The sites of this power are people's minds" (2004, 425). He elaborates by stating that "voiceless insurgents have a voice" through the new networks of communication appearing on the Internet every day. For Castells, these voices have a chance of seizing power in people's minds by challenging dominant cultural codes with alternative values that flow from the realm of the symbolic. In this way, Indigenous communities have an opportunity to inform the mainstream and to communicate laterally with each other by reclaiming what Makere Stewart-Harawira calls "the invisibilized indigenous histories and the insurrection of subjugated indigenous cosmologies and ontologies [that] are critical aspects of indigenous peoples' resistance to the homogenizing impulse of modernity and its manifestation in current forms of globalization" (2005, 23). In fact, Stewart-Harawira argues that "the teachings handed down by our ancestors, including the interdependence of all existence, [are] key to political and social transformation for indigenous peoples and [are] central to a globally transformative framework" (200).

As I have noted throughout this chapter, the participants in this study use Indigenous Knowledge on the Internet both as a means of education for Indigenous and settler societies and as a means for Indigenous resurgence and resistance. However, such work faces many challenges. Chartrand (2013) captured this well when he said that "it would be great to see how the teachings from various First Nations communities are relevant today, but that's wishful thinking." He is not alone in his desire to see more Indigenous Knowledge online. Educators such as Nardozi also stressed the need for more Indigenous Knowledge sites, as did Lepine, Bourque, and Dubois. Furthermore, Dubois strongly believed that having Indigenous resources online that reach mainstream settler society is necessary to promote community well-being, cultural understanding, and respect.

Why is such work considered unattainable? As I have suggested, one reason is that the political will does not exist currently to push for such work. To bring it about, Indigenous communities need to come together and discuss Indigenous Knowledge online as a necessary and viable educational strategy for Indigenous Peoples. Furthermore, settler/mainstream educators, policy makers, and government bodies need to be educated on Indigenous Knowledge, for generally they remain unaware of it, as do most Canadians. In the next chapter, I consider this ignorance and the subsequent lack of support in a discussion of issues related to reframing and naming.

In *Native on the Net*, we are challenged to think about a range of questions:

> How are Indigenous voices, in turn, electronically reaching new audiences and creating new horizons for speakers as well as listeners? How do marginalized peoples perceive and position themselves in relation to global computer networkings, and how do these sociotechnical apparatuses figure in local lifeworlds? In what ways are interactive media environments changing the subjectivities and practices, both online and offline, of peoples historically de-centered from "the action"? (Landzelius, 2006, 2)

In the following chapters, I address these questions from an Indigenous analytical perspective by employing Nishnaabeg principles of Biskaabiiyang, Naakgonige, Aanjigone, and Debwewin. These four principles help me to articulate how Indigenous Peoples use the Internet currently and how they envision an Internet that will light new fires for Indigenous Knowledge.

CHAPTER 4

BISKAABIIYANG
("TO LOOK BACK")

I n writing about Biskaabiiyang, Leanne Simpson draws from
the work of Wendy Makoons Geniusz (2009), the Anishinaabe
scholar and respected language teacher introduced in Chapter 1.
Geniusz notes that "through Biskaabiiyang methodology, this
research goes back to the principles of anishinaabe-inaadiziwin ['culture, teachings, customs, history'] in order to decolonize or reclaim
anishinaabe-gikendaasowin ['that which was given to us in a loving
way']" (quoted in Simpson, 2011, 50). Here we see how notions of
claiming, restoring, and reframing, and many of the methodologies
that Linda Tuhiwai Smith (1999) describes, are all themes that resonate within the meaning of Biskaabiiyang.

In this chapter, I explore the Indigenous principle of Biskaabiiyang
as a way of providing important cultural insights into how the research
participants encountered and processed FourDirectionsTeachings.
com and other Indigenous Knowledge websites. I connect this
concept with Smith's methodologies, particularly those of storytelling, celebrating survival, Indigenizing, revitalizing, representing,
reframing, restoring, democratizing, naming, and creating. Through
this approach, I hope to demonstrate how Indigenous voices are

reaching new audiences through the Internet and how computer networking and interactive media are affecting the practices and thinking of diverse Indigenous Peoples and non-Indigenous people in Canada. My perspective here also draws from Taiaiake Alfred's (2005) pathway of Land Is Life, which entails reconnecting and looking back in order to claim, name, reframe, and ultimately restore and create ways to learn, thus contributing to Indigenous resurgence from within an Indigenous ontology.

Storytelling

> *Story telling, oral histories, the perspectives of elders and of women have become an integral part of all indigenous research. . . . For many indigenous writers stories are ways of passing down the beliefs and values of a culture in the hope that the new generations will treasure them and pass the story down further.* (Smith, 1999, 144–45)

Smith's notion of storytelling sets a precedent for Indigenous Knowledge. Storytelling can even set a precedent in the legal sense of the term. John Borrows (2013) told me that he uses FourDirectionsTeachings.com in every Indigenous law course that he teaches. He believes that Indigenous teachings and traditions provide opportunities to have conversations and, more importantly, to deliberate on what they tell us. Indigenous teachings and traditions, then, provide the standards for judgment. They are the authorities, the guidelines, and therefore the precedents. Borrows explained that they are the criteria that we can use in making decisions and resolving disputes today.

As a producer and an academic, I had no idea that FourDirections-Teachings.com or Indigenous storytelling more generally was being taken up in these ways. Of course, after engaging with Borrows, the notion of teachings in a legal context made perfect sense in that the values and beliefs inherent in these stories inform cultural mores. As Borrows (2013) elaborated in the interview,

Indigenous and Anishinaabe Knowledge are those authorities, those standards for judgment, as they are the criteria
by which we measure what we are doing and whether or
not it's appropriate. I see these traditions, these stories, as a
precedent, and they therefore require a sense of deference
from us. As we look to the Elders, we look to the teachings,
the traditions, to be able to guide our behaviour today. So
law isn't just something that's said in a legislature or produced in a court judgment, although it can be those things.
It is more broad than that; it is our way of understanding
what we should be doing in the world because of the teachings and knowledge that have been passed on to us by our
ancestors through our Elders.

This definition expands the notion of Indigenous storytelling and its
importance for future generations beyond the realm of being a cultural treasure. For Borrows, Indigenous stories attain the status of
legal precedents that beckon us to consider them seriously as standards or principles for making decisions about how we live as a society
and how we take up our responsibilities as individuals in a community. Consequently, it is important for Borrows that students understand that "as they practise law, they can take these teachings and use
them in how they work to serve community and to see that these stories of growth and reciprocity are a part of the values that they should
be taking on as Anishinaabe or Indigenous lawyers."

The curatorial work of Cheryl L'Hirondelle (2009) likewise suggests how her practice intuitively embraces long-held Indigenous
notions of growth and reciprocity as values that she employs when
thinking about her projects and how she presents them to the community. For her, the highest value of Indigenous work online is giving
back to the community rather than being merely about the individual
artist's self-expression, for example. L'Hirondelle was a participant in
one of the first North American think tanks on Indigenous Peoples
and the Internet, held in January 1994 at the Banff Centre.[18] This gathering was a pivotal moment for her and has stayed with her:

When I had the opportunity to curate for ImagineNative, I wanted my first curatorial project to be an homage to that first think tank at Banff. It was there that I remember hearing from Dr. George Baldwin (an Osage sociologist and a technologist) and Randy Ross (Cherokee) that "we don't want to end up roadkill on the information superhighway." They were the creators of Indian Net BBS and active with Native communities in the United States about getting into technology because they believed that otherwise we will end up roadkill on the side of the information superhighway. So as an homage to that first think tank, and to some of the first websites and examples of technologies that bowled me over and made me realize that technology was an important tool for survival, I curated ten outstanding works. (2014)

L'Hirondelle still has a powerful connection with the ideas that she faced in her first encounters with issues regarding Indigenous digital technology. In her current projects, she sees Indigenous content on the Internet as an important tool for the *survival of Indigenous Peoples*.

Reflecting in her interview on her own work as an artist and producer of new media projects, L'Hirondelle (2014) said that

after I made *Dene Cree Elders Speak* and presented it at an Elders' gathering in northern Saskatchewan, something really interesting happened after the presentation. People began to come up to me and say, "I've got a story to tell you," and they'd just start telling me their story right there, and it took me about a couple of minutes to realize what was going on—and then it came: they wanted to have their stories told on the website. "I want my children to hear this story." It was so amazing. It was like I reached them on another level where they could understand that computers could be more than just "avoidance machines." That phrase comes from a senator from the Saskatchewan Federation of Indians, an ex-chief, who said he used to be able to walk into the band office and have a conversation with people, but now with computers people have their backs to the door, so the computers just become a way for people to avoid talking. My presentation made those Elders feel hopeful that technology could be a good thing and used in a good way that isn't just shutting them out but is actually putting them back in front of their grandchildren.

Indigenous storytelling, then, is a political act of survival because it connects the values and beliefs of the past to those of the present. This realization is growing on Elders and technology dissenters who first saw the Internet as part of the world of "avoidance machines." For Borrows and L'Hirondelle, to be able to look back, to practise Biskaabiiyang by accessing Indigenous storytelling on the Internet, means that they can rekindle culture, teachings, customs, and history for their students and audiences. In doing this work, they actively contribute to Indigenous resurgence by privileging Indigenous storytelling and recognizing its value as a precedent for Indigenous Knowledge.

Celebrating Survival

Celebrating survival accentuates not so much our demise but the degree to which indigenous peoples and communities have successfully retained cultural and spiritual values and authenticity. . . . Events and accounts which focus on the positive are important not just because they speak to our survival, but because they celebrate our resistances at an ordinary human level and . . . affirm our identities as indigenous women and men. Celebrating survival as an approach is also a theme running through the collections of elders' stories. (Smith, 1999, 145)

As a full-time artist, Émilie Monnet (2013) is committed to bridging her two interests of "how art processes can foster transformation and empower the youth, and how art can sensitize people to the cultural richness, diversity of teachings and resilience of Aboriginal world-views." Through her artwork, Monnet celebrates survival in a positive way that embraces the main tenets of Biskaabiiyang. For example, her award-winning work *Bird Messengers* was inspired by "Aboriginal sto-rytelling and ancestral teachings." She also directed *Songs of Mourning and Songs of Life*, "a performance that looked at the imprints of genocide on Aboriginal and Rwandan communities, and the power of the drum to heal and contribute to the process of mourning." In this way, Monnet draws on the cultural and spiritual values of Indigenous communities that she engages with to inform and inspire her artwork.

Monnet (2013) wants to build bridges internationally with Indigenous communities in Colombia. She states that "being able to work with youth and create opportunities for the transmission of knowledge and skills is also very important to me." It is heartening to hear that she is doing this work and that finding and accessing Indigenous Knowledge online contributes to her practice. Since Monnet believes that "our worldviews are a treasure for the whole of humanity," she wants to spend her life contributing to Indigenous resurgence by celebrating survival in her artwork and in working with Indigenous youth.

Indigenizing

The term ["indigenizing"] centres a politics of indigenous iden-tity and indigenous cultural action. (Smith, 1999, 146)

For Larry Chartrand (2013), "the whole field of Aboriginal Rights and Treaty Rights is fundamentally racist and discriminatory because it is based on the doctrine of discovery."[19] As a result, he is committed to teaching his students to think critically about the rights of Aborig-inal Peoples, especially given the historical context and the fact that Canadian history has generally been a one-sided story. Chartrand also teaches Indigenous traditions and principles from a variety of

First Nations. His intention is to inspire students to pick up—to look back—Biskaabiiyang in order to bring forward what has been left behind. In this way, Chartrand centres and privileges a politics of Indigenous identity in order to inspire Indigenous cultural action.

His broader goal is to Indigenize law school and eventually to have an Indigenous law department that will explore how Indigenous law can be reinstated in the mainstream public sphere. Chartrand (2013) stated in his interview that "so much of the teaching that I do is about how we can get Canadian law to recognize the validity of Indigenous law again. What principles and reforms do we need to undertake to achieve that end?" Like John Borrows, Chartrand uses FourDirectionsTeachings.com in his law courses, and he considers Indigenous Knowledge online as a huge benefit to his work and vision, clearly related to Indigenous resurgence from a legal perspective.

Revitalizing

> *Indigenous languages, their arts and their cultural practices are in various states of crisis. . . . The indigenous language is often regarded as being subversive to national interests and national literacy campaigns.* (Smith, 1999, 147–48)

A healthy way of looking back is the recovery of critical aspects of Indigenous cultures found in Indigenous languages. Revitalizing these languages is a key concern for many of the research participants. For example, Monique Mojica (2014) said that she would like to see Indigenous languages on the Internet: "Language is so important because it encodes perception, and, if we're talking about putting Indigenous Knowledge(s) in the centre, you have to know the language. Even simple things in a language tell you a lot about a culture." Cheryl L'Hirondelle (2014) echoed this statement:

> Language resources are critical for future generations because they need to know that our languages are

Earth-based languages. So through our languages you're talking to the Earth; you're talking to the elements; you're talking to the plants, animals, and bugs when you're speaking in one of our Indigenous languages. Language is also inherent in our ceremonies, and our ceremonies are part of the alchemy, that unquantifiable alchemy, that keeps the Earth spinning.

These women understand that Indigenous languages encode Indigenous worldviews. I respect that L'Hirondelle referred to Indigenous languages as Earth-based languages and that she—like Mojica—sees how language encodes our perceptions and understandings. Indeed, L'Hirondelle (2014) explained how the Cree worldview is built upon the metaphor and autonomy of the Cree language:

> That is why it is important that we continue to learn our languages, our ceremonies, and our teachings. Otherwise it's a real conundrum if we don't, because we will no longer be able to recognize the source when it is in plain sight. That is why in Native communities people are recognized and valued when they see someone who had dedicated their life to a particular knowledge. That's how we start to know what we carry in this world.

The ability to recognize the language and understand its meaning is key for accessing Indigenous Knowledge. It is also understood that it takes dedication over a lifetime to be recognized as a Knowledge Keeper.

John Borrows (2013) elaborated this point when he discussed the importance of the Ojibway language and access to respected community Knowledge Keepers:

> Other cultural sources that inform my work include referencing Anishinaabemowin. I find there's lots of information packed in the etymology of words. So going to people

who know the language like Basil Johnston—he is a person that lives in my community and that I talk with—he himself is a source of knowledge, not just for knowing the language but for carrying an understanding of the teachings and history as well, so accessing people from the community is important too.

Like L'Hirondelle, Borrows acknowledged that people from the community who dedicate themselves to particular knowledge must be respected. Learning is not done in isolation or outside the community. It is immersive and entails building relationships. For this reason, people must identify their community, or they lack a foundation from which to speak to and engage with others.

It is not surprising, then, that many of the research participants said that they would like to see more language resources online. Monnet (2013) combines online learning with offline learning in teaching herself the Northern Algonquin language:

> The Golden Lake website has a lot of resources where you can hear how to pronounce words. They also share a lot of materials on how to learn the language and songs. These sites are important to me because they support my learning. More and more, I am incorporating Indigenous languages into my projects. These sites also help me to find words that I can bring to my language teacher so that we can discuss the root of the word and have a discussion about its uses. So having access to language helps to start a dialogue.

Like Monnet, many of the research participants use online language resources to extend their grasp of Indigenous Knowledge. They understand that Indigenous languages inform our ceremonies and that ceremonies are key to discerning Indigenous Knowledge.

Unfortunately, as Alan Corbiere, a respected Anishinaabemowin language teacher and researcher, mentioned in conversation in September 2014, there are very few good beginner Indigenous language websites, and there is a lack of coordination for comprehensive language learning that links beginner, intermediate, and advanced learners. Funding for such projects is scarce. As a producer who has tried to include Indigenous languages in current online projects, I have been turned down numerous times when applying for funding to support such projects. As Smith indicates above, there is a lack of political will to support Indigenous language campaigns.

Nonetheless, the individuals who spoke with me are proactive about seeking Indigenous Knowledge resources both online and offline. Indigenous language resources online would benefit many people and help to address the crisis of losing Indigenous language speakers. However, developing such resources needs to be a coordinated effort, requiring the political will to fund online projects that can connect existing Indigenous language sites and categorize them for learners into beginner, intermediate, and advanced levels. This would aid users so that they don't get lost and frustrated on the World Wide Web.

More importantly, new online resources have to be developed to address language-learning gaps, of which there are many, according to language expert Corbiere. Like Chartrand's suggestion for Indigenous Knowledge sites, Indigenous language sites that accomplish these goals could become a reality with sufficient political will and adequate funding. By providing such projects online, Indigenous communities would be contributing to Indigenous resurgence through Biskaabiiyang by picking up their languages and thus their Indigenous Knowledge.

Representing

Indigenous communities have struggled since colonization to be able to exercise what is viewed as a fundamental right, that is to represent ourselves. The representing project spans both the notion of representation as a political concept and representation as a form of voice and expression. In the political sense colonialism specifically excluded indigenous peoples from any form of decision making. States and governments have long made decisions hostile to the interests of indigenous communities but justified by a paternalistic view that Indigenous peoples were like children who needed others to protect them and decide what was in their best interests. Paternalism is still present in many forms in the way governments, local bodies and non-government agencies decide on issues which have an impact on indigenous communities. Being able as a minimum right to voice the views and opinions of indigenous communities in various decision-making bodies is still being struggled over....

Representation is also a project of indigenous artists, writers, poets, film makers and others who attempt to express an indigenous spirit, experience or world view. Representation of indigenous peoples by indigenous people is about countering the dominant society's image of indigenous peoples, their lifestyles and belief systems. It is also about proposing solutions to the real-life dilemmas that indigenous communities confront and trying to capture the complexities of being indigenous. (Smith, 1999, 150–51)

Importantly, for Smith, the act of representing is inextricable from the need to hear the voices of Indigenous Peoples. Monique Mojica (2014) spoke about how early in the dramatic project that she was working on the dramaturge identified the tension in her work between the invisibility of Indigenous Peoples and the invisibility of effigy mounds: "For example, there's a huge burial mound in Scarborough; over 500 people are buried there. It's in a nice little residential roundabout where people have their suburban homes surrounding it. The mound is enormous; there's even a plaque at the top, and yet it's invisible on the landscape." Mojica noted that these earthworks can be right in front of you—they are everywhere—but you don't see them if you don't know they are there: "So the tension here between duration and invisibility is overwhelming. Much like how our hypervisibility is being displayed in ethnographic congresses and human zoos, which have morphed into Hollywood—and yet the duration of who we are as a people remains invisible, just like the mounds." This tension is exemplified in how colonialism has excluded Indigenous Peoples from representing themselves, and hence their true forms remain invisible, despite their presence and duration, like the earth mounds. Instead, what is made visible through colonialism is the distorted and inhumane caricatures of Indigenous Peoples.

For this reason, Rainey Gaywish (2014) thinks that there is room for a lot more sharing. She believes that having access to tools such as FourDirectionsTeachings.com is helpful for educating Indigenous Peoples and non-Indigenous people alike about what it means to be Indigenous and is, therefore, a way of responding to colonialist stereotypes. As she mentioned, "I always come back to the prophecy of the Seven Fires, which tells us that there will be new people who will emerge and will pick up what's left on the trail." For Gaywish, having Indigenous production teams working carefully and respectfully with Elders and Traditional Teachers to put Indigenous Knowledge on the Internet is an example of new people emerging to pick up what has been left on the trail.

Gaywish (2014) noted that such work is important not only for Indigenous Peoples but also for non-Indigenous people to access:

> We know that we need good allies who understand. We also know you can't address racism if you don't touch people, really reach out and connect with who they are. Teaching tools like FourDirectionsTeachings.com help to accomplish these goals. It helps people to learn that understanding doesn't just exist in your head. You have to feel it. It is personal. It is emotional. It is what we call heart-based learning. Any knowing that has any real staying power is heart based, and that is also how we know it is good.

In the prophecy of the Seven Fires, it is understood that the bundles are knowledge bundles and that, when we pick them up, we are picking up and retrieving our Indigenous Knowledge. This is why

I refer to FourDirectionsTeachings.com as a digital bundle; for the research participants, it embraces and embodies important aspects of Indigenous Knowledge, and, therefore, in many ways it is representative of a knowledge bundle.

In contemplating this notion, I asked the research participants whether or not they distinguished between Indigenous Knowledge and Indigenous information online. Mojica (2014) indicated that Indigenous Knowledge cannot really be found online:

> When I look at a website that is presenting Indigenous Knowledge, I consider that to be ultimately Indigenous information because of the medium through which that knowledge is being filtered. In order to be a recipient of Indigenous Knowledge, that knowledge has to be transmitted through a one-on-one or shared communal experience. Indigenous Knowledge is transmitted through ceremony, and I don't think that Indigenous Knowledge can be transmitted over the Internet.

I also believe that Indigenous Knowledge is transmitted through ceremony and that certain types of it must remain in the ceremonial realm. However, I also think that there are many ways to introduce people to Indigenous Knowledge online so that they can *begin to learn* and have a basis to *find a context* for deep understanding and knowledge transmission. Mojica echoed this sentiment:

> In my opinion, the best way the Internet can function is by being a landmark showing you which way to go and which questions to ask and providing you with the insight to know that, in order to dig deeper, you have to go out and seek the knowledge. You have to participate in ceremony to be a recipient of Indigenous Knowledge. How and where you find these ceremonies [are other questions].

As the producer of an Indigenous Knowledge project online, I would never propose that the Internet become a repository for Indigenous Knowledge. Indeed, I do not believe that it can fulfill that function because I agree with Mojica: people must go into their communities and engage with their Elders and Traditional Teachers and languages and ceremonies to truly grasp Indigenous Knowledge. That is why the introduction to FourDirectionsTeachings.com says that on the site you will find a mere introduction to some of the teachings.

Where I differ from Mojica is in my belief that some aspects of Indigenous Knowledge can be effectively transmitted through the Internet. To digress for a moment, I want to share a touching story from a hospice worker whom my family knows personally. Shortly after FourDirectionsTeachings.com was launched, this hospice worker told us that a young Mohawk man in his care dying of AIDS had been watching Tom Porter's Mohawk teaching over and over again. The teaching seemed to bring the young man so much peace so close to his death that he watched it repeatedly, surfing back and forth and really exploring the concepts. The hospice worker also shared that the young man had experienced a significant degree of alienation from his own culture. I did not know this man, but I believe—based upon the hospice worker's story—that Porter's teaching had touched this young man's heart. We are taught from an Indigenous point of view that learning is not just in our heads but in our hearts too. I often think of this man and wonder what he would have said about being able to receive a teaching through the Internet. Was he a recipient of Indigenous Knowledge? Or was he comforted by something that he might have known, remembered, or just learned? We will never know. All I can know is that the process we used with the Elders and Traditional Teachers to share their knowledge was done in a good way and that it seemed to allow the beauty of the words and ideas to touch the heart of this young man.

Regarding the difference between Indigenous Knowledge and Indigenous information online, eight of the ten research participants affirmed FourDirectionsTeachings.com as an Indigenous Knowledge site, and only two—Mojica and Borrows—saw it differently.

Priscilla Lepine (2014) was one of the eight. She noted that there are few Indigenous Knowledge sites but a plethora of New Age cultural sites that appropriate Indigenous Knowledge:

> There are more Indigenous information sites than Indigenous Knowledge sites. I also think there are too many New Age cultural appropriation sites, which is scary. Who holds the Traditional Knowledge and who has the right to transmit it [are] important to consider. I don't like to use the word *own*, but I guess that's kind of how it's described, so, yeah, for sure one of the things I am always cognizant of when I'm going on the Internet is who is running this site? So I like to find out who created the site and who's running it and where their information is coming from.

Cultural appropriation, Lepine noted, is a complicated topic to talk about because not everyone has the same idea of what it means. Traditional Knowledge is a fairly new topic for many people working in government and education. As Lepine stated,

> I've been to quite a lot of meetings around the territories, when I was working in education, to discuss how to incorporate Traditional Knowledge into the college. At this point in time, the government has been developing policies that say they can't hold Traditional Knowledge or anything to do with Traditional Knowledge because it belongs to the culture and the holders of the knowledge. So it's a very intricate topic to be dealing with on the Internet and in meetings.

Indigenous Knowledge is indeed a complicated topic. It is not something that can be regulated by Western policies and guidelines. It is governed, rather, by the protocols of the community, and because Indigenous communities are distinct, each having its own set of cultural protocols, a blanket policy cannot be applied. Each community must be respected and its cultural protocols adhered to so that Indigenous community values are regarded and deferred to when discussing and presenting Indigenous Knowledge.

Lepine (2014) noted that, though there are more Indigenous information sites, there are not enough in her particular field. When she is online, she searches for sites that can help her to achieve her professional goals: "I am in the helping field. So I'm looking for information that can help people with healing, and with finding themselves, and [with] validating their story—to feel like they have a place on this Earth."

For Lepine (2014), access to more information on Aboriginal healing online can help her with programming for the inmates with whom she works. Currently, seasonal programming brings inmates out onto the land for a fishing camp. For such programs, she invites Knowledge Keepers from the local community to work with the inmates at specific times of the year, and "being out on the land is a big component of our programming and something that we are trying to develop and expand." Lepine also noted that "sometimes funding is an issue because it costs money to bring in Traditional Teachers and Elders. It also costs money if we decide to go out and see them. We have to cover travel costs, per diem, honorarium, et cetera. So being able to access some cultural knowledge on the Internet would be effective because of funding issues." For Lepine, access to Indigenous Knowledge online would help to offset some of these costs while fostering culturally relevant programming. She also pointed out that the era of the residential school curriculum is not behind us:

> Today we talk about residential schools as if it was in the past, but our school system still delivers a curriculum that is no different than what was in the residential schools. In terms of education, we are moving at a glacial pace with respect to including Aboriginal ideology in the curriculum. I think that is also the big thing that's missing on the Internet: that is, access to Aboriginal curriculum nationwide.

With regard to representation, the right of Indigenous Peoples to respectfully contribute to curricula is still being denied by a paternalistic educational system. If the political will existed, then the existing curricula could be overhauled and revitalized in a timely manner. Instead, government will and lack of funding to support such work result in reluctant change that, to use Lepine's phrase, is "moving at a glacial pace." As a producer of Indigenous content online, I agree with Lepine and believe that advances in Indigenous curricula could be achieved nationwide through the Internet.

Donna Bourque (2014) also offers a critique of Indigenous Peoples' representation in the educational system and, like Lepine, sees the Internet as a potential space in which to address the oppression, racism, and ignorance perpetuated by colonialism:

> Canadians are not educated on what has happened to Aboriginal People. We need to have more sites online that teach people about the treaties and about history from an Aboriginal perspective. We need these resources because they are not offered in the schools. These historical truths are not offered anywhere. Even if we had just one site that says "this is what happened, this is why treaties were signed, this is what was understood." It is so very important to have good resources, especially now when Aboriginal people are becoming more vocal with movements like Idle No More.

Indigenous Peoples are desperate to have their say, to represent themselves. Movements such as Idle No More, as Bourque noted, bring Indigenous voices into the public sphere; however, with little context in which to support their voices, their messages get lost in a sea of racism and ignorance in Canada. Bourque explained that,

> sadly, Idle No More has brought racism to the forefront in Canada and has demonstrated that racism is alive and thriving, which is evident when you read posts online in response to Idle No More. I've read "Indians all want

something for nothing. They get everything for nothing." Yet these very people who make these hateful and hurtful comments will turn around and talk about Nelson Mandela and slavery and the Holocaust of the Jews with such compassion—but they won't take the time to learn about what happened to Aboriginal People in their own country. Education is so desperately needed. I am a Treaty Indian. I get five dollars a year. I've never had a free house in my whole life. I pay taxes, and I've worked full time for thirty years.

I agree. Online resources that depict and address historical truths are desperately needed. Furthermore, these resources need to exist in plain sight so that Canadians can stop hiding behind their ignorance. In today's world, it is unacceptable to meet a person with a high school education who doesn't know about Mandela or hasn't heard of the Holocaust (though this can happen). The same needs to be said regarding Indigenous treaties, colonial history, and colonial oppression; it is unacceptable that Canadians should be ignorant of these topics and demonstrates a failure to be a responsible citizen of Canada. To end racism and oppression, and to rebuild our communities, Bourque said, "people [Canadians] need to be educated, and the Internet is the best place to do it!"

Representation of Indigenous history and treaties on the Internet, especially if leveraged into public educational systems, could help to end hostile relations between Indigenous Peoples and Canadian settler society—or at least provide a reference point for dialogue and hopefully intelligent engagement that would go beyond the tiresome reproach that Indigenous Peoples "get everything for nothing." Such online work would challenge these racist statements and engage in the project of decolonization, which would ultimately contribute to Indigenous resurgence. This type of work would present a much-needed corrective history from an Indigenous worldview. How it is done would constitute whether it is Indigenous information or Indigenous Knowledge.

John Borrows (2013) explained that he does not really differentiate between Indigenous information and Indigenous Knowledge when doing research online:

> I can see how it would be separate, and I can understand the arguments that would be made in that way, but I don't really filter the world that way. What I do is look at the people. So it was because of Sakej, and knowing about Reg and Lillian, there's still this sense of being led by people, as opposed to categories of knowledge. So it's somewhat an older way, I guess, of filtering information for me, which is still relational, personal.

Borrows made an important point with respect to filtering knowledge through relations and through personal insights. Indeed, many of the research participants identified the same themes when asked about how they validate Indigenous Knowledge and Indigenous information that they find online. This feedback is discussed in relation to Linda Tuhiwai Smith's methods of claiming/testimony, returning, networking, protecting, and negotiating, outlined in Chapter 7, in which I discuss the principle of Aanjigone. I include their feedback in those sections because it specifically speaks to methods and approaches that they used either consciously or unconsciously when making assessments of knowledge. However, I chose to keep the feedback from Borrows here because he was challenging the representation of Indigenous Knowledge and Indigenous information as a whole. As he explained in his interview,

> I don't really see Indigenous Knowledge as separate from anything in the world. So when I go online I am not filtering what I find there as either Indigenous Knowledge or Indigenous information. [He discussed Indigenous language websites.] . . . Again, looking at these websites, I'm not asking the kind of question that you are or that I'm thinking that you're posing. It's just I'm wanting to

learn about the language, and there could be Indigenous [Peoples] or non-Indigenous peoples producing it with different kinds of perspectives, and if it feels good I take it in.

For Borrows, knowledge is attained through his intuitive ability to relate to the content and to trust himself to choose to accept or reject particular content. Still, he considers his networks and looks at community relationships and contexts as guides for gauging his trust: "Like FourDirectionsTeachings.com, I trust it because of the people who are speaking, and the people who are involved as consultants in the project. Of course I've never met you before now, but I'm getting a sense of the good things you're doing as well."

Issues of representation, then, are critical for how Indigenous Peoples discern voice. That is, who is doing the representing? Why? From the feedback provided by the research participants, it is clear that issues of representation are tied to Biskaabiiyang because that is where we find Indigenous Knowledge, language, and cultural information.

It is this type of content that counters what Smith (1999) calls the dominant society's image of Indigenous Peoples, their lifestyles, and their belief systems. Grounding new images of Indigenous Peoples in their knowledge, languages, and cultural information is at the core of addressing representation by Indigenous Peoples. Representing this content on the Internet requires that we confront the paternalism still present in many forms of government, local bodies, and non-governmental agencies that decide on issues that affect Indigenous communities: "Being able as a minimum right to voice the views and opinions of indigenous communities in various decision-making bodies is still being struggled over" (Smith, 1999, 150).

Reframing

Reframing is about taking much greater control over the ways in which indigenous issues and social problems are discussed

and handled. . . . The framing of an issue is about making deci-
sions about its parameters, about what is in the foreground,
what is in the background, and what shadings or complexities
exist within the frame. The project of reframing is related to
defining the problem or issue and determining how best to solve
that problem. . . .

[There is a] constant need to justify difference experienced by
many other communities whose initiatives are about changing
things on a holistic basis rather than endorsing the individual-
ized programme emphasis of government models. The need to
reframe is about retaining the strengths of a vision and the par-
ticipation of a whole community. (Smith, 1999, 153–54)

The Deepening Knowledge Project at OISE, University of Toronto, is all about reframing how teachers in the mainstream educational system teach students about Indigenous Peoples in Canada. Angela Nardozi (2014), the project manager, explained that teachers do not feel comfortable teaching students about Indigenous Peoples in Canada for many reasons. They think that the curriculum is outdated, and more importantly they do not feel equipped to teach in this area because of a lack of adequate training. They lack confidence and knowledge as well as access to good resources. To better understand why teachers think that current curricula are outdated, one only needs to reflect on Nardozi's experience of mainstream education and how Nardozi was taught about Indigenous Peoples:

I remember growing up in high school. I was a pretty smart kid. I got a lot of A's, and yet I came away from high school thinking that Native People worshipped animals. I only graduated ten years ago, so what does that say about the curriculum in our schools? Now I see teacher candidates who are completely surprised by the fact that there are so many diverse Indigenous Nations in Canada. They have internalized the notion that there is only one kind of Indigenous person, and that is the stereotypical image of the Native with the plains war bonnet and the teepee. So what they are learning is very new for them.

Nardozi elaborated that "my work with teacher candidates has shown me that many people have had similar experiences, learning very little and very inaccurate information about Indigenous Peoples while going through school." The current curriculum on Indigenous Peoples and their histories is in desperate need of an overhaul, and teachers' understanding of history from social and political contexts able to shed light on current issues is desperately required.

The Deepening Knowledge Project provides teachers with resources that they can trust. The project seeks to reframe responsible citizenship in Canada by emphasizing that "we are all treaty people." Nardozi (2014) acknowledged that the training of teachers is new for them:

> We encourage them to think about how they can teach current events and history from a social justice perspective that acknowledges and respects the rights and sovereignty of Indigenous People. So many teacher candidates are really starting from scratch. The level of not knowing is intimidating for them. That is why I'm always encouraging them to first start with the Deepening Knowledge site because we've collected so many resources there, which will help them to think through all of the issues and information they are digesting.
>
> Moreover, we emphasize that in the particular territory where Toronto is located we are all treaty people, so what we are learning about is not just for Indigenous People but for all of us, as active and responsible Canadian citizens. Our work takes a tiny step toward decolonizing a curriculum that is so out of date that even teachers feel alienated by it. So, while our work is a small step, we feel that it is clearly not enough; there is so much more that can be done.

The fact that FourDirectionsTeachings.com and other Indigenous Knowledge sites are contributing to the Deepening Knowledge Project, and the fact that the success of the project is predicated on the Deepening Knowledge website, demonstrate how educators in the community are using Indigenous Knowledge projects online to reframe past wrongs. Here Biskaabiiyang is helping to reframe culture, teachings, and history in a good way and helping teachers to differentiate between a colonial curriculum and approach and a decolonial curriculum and approach. Having allies such as Nardozi committed and sensitive to such issues, and visionaries such as Jean Paul Restoule, who initiated the project, is necessary and of great value to the goals of Indigenous resurgence.

Restoring

> Indigenous peoples across the world have disproportionately high rates of imprisonment, suicide and alcoholism. Some indigenous activists regard these rates as the continuation of a war.... Restorative justice in Canada, for example, applies concepts of the "healing circle" and victim restoration which are based on indigenous processes. These systems have been discussed widely and used to motivate other societies to develop better ways of dealing with offenders and victims. . . . Restoring is a project which is conceived as a holistic approach to problem solving. It is holistic in terms of emotional, spiritual and physical nexus, and also in terms of the individual and the collective, the political and the cultural. Restorative programmes are based on a model of healing rather than of punishing. . . . Health programmes addressing basic health issues have begun to seek ways to connect with indigenous communities through appropriate public health policy and practice models. (Smith, 1999, 154–55)

For Donna Bourque (2014), programming focused on healing is vital in helping inmates to restore themselves from the brokenness that they have experienced. She is aware that many inmates come from the Far North and therefore are Inuit, Innu, and Dene, yet they are more open with her, even though she is Northern Cree, "probably because they understand that I have experienced the same racism and fallout of residential schools as they have." Understanding that they have a shared experience of colonialism and oppression supersedes the lack of Indigenous resources with which to speak to each group's particular cultural background. It would be ideal to have all of those particular Indigenous resources, but bringing in just some Indigenous resources has proven to be an ordeal. As Bourque elaborated,

> we've got a long way to go, and that is why for years I've been advocating for Aboriginal healing programs in the correctional facilities, because we need to target our inmates. We need them to begin to believe in themselves and to be proud of who they are and where they come from, because it is the only way that they are going to be able to build up their self-esteem and move forward in life.

Bourque uses Indigenous Knowledge resources and information online to help her with restorative justice programming. She realizes that not all of the resources can be culturally specific to the inmates, but she noted that inmates appreciate the resources even though they might not be from their particular cultures. Bourque referred to the Ojibway medicine wheel and Cree teepee pole teachings on the FourDirectionsTeachings.com site in her interview:

> We used the medicine wheel as a part of the case plan for the inmates, and the alcohol and drug counsellor used it as part of the release program. She would do a medicine wheel with the inmates. So we would go on the site and check out the medicine wheel. We used that one quite a bit, but we also used the Cree teepee pole teachings. These teachings helped the inmates to visualize their plan in terms of how they would take care of all aspects of their self—emotional,

physical, mental, and spiritual—when back in the community and in daily life. The inmates enjoyed doing it. Toward
the end of their release, we would always have a case conference where program staff, probation officers, and the
offender would meet. Here the inmate would present their
medicine wheel to the probation officer and explain their
plan and commitment for reintegrating into the community.

For many inmates, taking care of all aspects of the self often means
finding ways to address addictions, deal with anger issues, and confront how to begin a healing process that is restorative for them and
their respective communities. The teepee pole and medicine wheel
teachings address all aspects of the self from an Indigenous perspective. According to Bourque, both an Indigenous perspective and an
Indigenous approach are deeply appreciated by the inmates, even
though they might not directly reflect their cultures.

Just as the experience and impact of racism and colonial oppression have united diverse Indigenous groups in the North, so too has
restorative programming, which seeks to apply a holistic approach
to problem solving by working on the emotional, spiritual, mental,
and physical well-being of inmates and in terms of the collective
experience of decolonization from political and cultural oppression.
Bourque (2014) is committed to restorative programs based upon
a model of healing rather than punishing because, as she said, "it's
the only way we are going to build up their self-esteem and see them
move forward in life." To do this restorative work, Bourque acknowledged, Indigenous resources are key.

Democratizing

*Democratizing in indigenous terms is a process of extending
participation outwards through reinstating indigenous principles of collectivity and public debate.* (Smith, 1999, 156)

Both John Borrows and Larry Chartrand believe that it is important that Indigenous lawyers understand what it means to be Indigenous and to serve their communities as lawyers: that is, to fully understand their ethical obligations. Borrows teaches about treaty protocols as a way of reinstating Indigenous principles of collectivity and public debate. His classes on the Two-Row Wampum, the Twenty-Four Nations Belt, and the Bowl with One Spoon discuss how Indigenous Peoples use treaties/wampum as ways of settling disputes among themselves. Borrows (2013) stated that

> these treaty protocols were then applied to the English, French, and Dutch when they came along. Tom Porter's teaching on the peacemaker demonstrates that there are internal mechanisms for peace and order. The story of the Haudenosaunee working through conflict within their community is derived from these teachings on the peace-maker and the wampum belts as treaties. The Anishinaabe People also use these belts. Maybe they got it from the Haudenosaunee. So they became something we also used in trying to work through internal conflict.

By bringing this knowledge into the classrooms of law schools, Borrows is democratizing Indigenous terms—like the treaties/wampum listed above and the teachings on the peacemaker—to extend participation to the students in his classes by engaging them in an Indigenous discourse that explores protocols for dealing with conflict through Indigenous methods.

Likewise, Chartrand (2013) believes that access to more Indigenous Knowledge online would not only increase the viability of such knowledge but also facilitate social order and reinscribe Indigenous values:

> I would like to see perhaps more in-depth sites of relevant legends and stories of particular nations, whether it is the Dene or the Coast Salish, because one of the most important aspects of a viable legal tradition is to ensure its

accessibility to those who are expected to be bound by it. And so the Internet can certainly offer a means of increasing that viability and legitimacy through accessibility. A lot of the worldviews and philosophical principles, our principles, can be thought of as principles for facilitating social order, and that is what law is all about.

Sharing this information on the Internet benefits not only Indigenous but also non-Indigenous communities and therefore extends participation outward by reinstating Indigenous principles of collectivity and encouraging public debate. Democratizing, then, is successfully employed when using the practice of Biskaabiiyang, looking back at our original treaties and reinstating their value and meaning for the world today.

Naming

> This project takes its name from Brazilian educator Paulo Freire whose saying, "name the word, name the world" (which was about literacy programmes), has been applied in the indigenous context to literally rename the landscape. This means renaming the world using the original indigenous names. . . .
> Naming applies to other things as well. It is about retaining as much control over meanings as possible. By "naming the world" people name their realities. For communities there are realities which can only be found in the indigenous language; the concepts which are self-evident in the indigenous language can never be captured by another language. (Smith, 1999, 157–58)

Naming is about power. Historically colonized Indigenous Peoples were not even given the right or dignity to keep their original names simply because colonial bureaucrats could not pronounce or spell them and changed them to suit their needs. Using original Indigenous names is about returning dignity and power to Indigenous Peoples. It is also, as Smith (1999) contends, about retaining as much control over meaning as possible. For Rainey Gaywish (2014), scholarship pertains to these issues because research and authorship are entrenched in the act of naming. Gaywish noted that, "when it comes to preparing higher education that expresses our own Indigenous worldview, our own perspectives, our own teachings, and the knowledge of our Elders, we are at a disadvantage, because so much research on our communities has been done by non-Aboriginal people." Gaywish referred specifically to FourDirectionsTeachings.com and the importance of having Indigenous scholarship in higher education. She emphasized that she highly values resources developed by Indigenous Peoples because they are few and far between and that much more work still needs to be done.

I believe that naming is vital in looking back because we can find that language and apply it today. In doing so, we "name the word [and] name the world," as Paulo Friere says (1970). I also believe that modern English words used in an Indigenous context can have power. For example, the name digital bundle refers to a specific Indigenous context that comes from the acknowledgement and roots of the traditional bundle. The latter has a specific meaning, as described in Chapter 1, and would likely be recognized and acknowledged only by culturally informed Indigenous Peoples. The context of the term "bundle," I believe, would be lost on those not informed by the Indigenous cultural meaning. In this way, as Smith (1999, 157) states, "by 'naming the world' people name their realities," which, perhaps more importantly, allows for the "retaining [of] as much control over meanings as possible."

Naming is also intensely personal, especially for Indigenous Peoples who straddle two worlds, Indigenous and settler. The ability to name and articulate experience is both empowering and healing. Priscilla Lepine (2014) eloquently captured this experience:

I know one of my biggest frustrations going to university years ago was that I didn't know how to articulate the experiences that I had growing up in a cross-cultural world that wasn't very friendly. However, my experience in Native studies was like going through a healing program where I began to understand how to articulate and validate my own story. Learning how to communicate with people that are not from your culture can be very empowering. So I think the teachings on the FourDirectionsTeachings.com site could do the same thing for the inmates. It could help them see that there are other Aboriginal groups that think the same way they do. Other Aboriginal groups might use different words and different symbols, but the ideas are the same. To me, that's a huge self-awareness moment.

Understanding contextually the Indigenous meaning behind the naming is key. For Indigenous Peoples, this can cross over to diverse Indigenous cultures; as Lepine pointed out, "Aboriginal groups may use different words and symbols, but the ideas [or worldviews] are the same." Recognizing the similarities can lead to healing, especially for inmates who do not yet have access to resources that speak specifically to their cultural backgrounds.

Finally, naming is about unlocking context and meaning and about survival. Cheryl L'Hirondelle (2014) explained how she used YouTube for Indigenous music research, which she then compiled into a long document of YouTube clips that she presented to her supervisor:

There is so much encoded in each song, like when all of a sudden a dancer comes up with an eagle whistle or the drummers play another pushup or two of that song. I know what that means because it is imbued with significance. So YouTube is quite a good source for Indigenous music, even though it doesn't explain the relevance and meaning to you. I had to explain to my supervisor the meanings of each song, and the different contexts of each song, and what it means and what type of song it is. So I had to vet the music and explain it; otherwise, my supervisor would never know the significance of what he is seeing.

Indigenous music is also a source of Indigenous Knowledge. L'Hirondelle alluded to this when she spoke about how much information is encoded in a song. I found it insightful that, if she did not name and explain the songs, her supervisor would not know the significance of what he was seeing. This is true for most of us who are not versed in Indigenous music and therefore miss the symbolism, language, timing, et cetera. Naming these features is another source of Indigenous Knowledge that requires us to look back and learn in order to make transparent the relevance and meaning of Indigenous songs.

Creating

The project of creating is about the spirit of creating which indigenous communities have exercised over thousands of years. Imagination enables people to rise above their own circumstances, to dream new visions and to hold on to old ones. It fosters inventions and discoveries, facilitates simple improvements to people's lives and uplifts our spirits. Creating is not the exclusive domain of the rich nor of the technologically superior, but of the imaginative. Creating is about channelling collective creativity in order to produce solutions to indigenous problems....

Indigenous peoples' ideas and beliefs about the origins of the world, their explanations of the environment, often embedded in complicated metaphors and mythic tales, are now being sought as the basis for thinking more laterally about current theories about the environment, the earth and the universe.

Communities are the ones who know the answers to their own problems, although their ideas tend to be dismissed when suggested to various agencies and governments. (Smith, 1999, 158–59)

In writing about resurgence, Leanne Simpson (2011, 147) states that vision alone is not enough: "Vision must be coupled with intent: intent for transformation, intent for re-creation, intent for resurgence." When I first envisioned FourDirectionsTeachings.com, many people whom I love and respect told me that it would be almost impossible to do. I listened to them but felt compelled to push forward with the project even though people close to me were not confident that it would succeed. When the time came to create the website, I followed my instincts and shared in a collective creativity that brought forth a project with staying power. At that time, I understood intuitively that the vision for this project was coupled with the intent to foster a new way of sharing Indigenous Knowledge with communities, but I had no idea what the impact of Indigenous Knowledge online would be.

Today I see the fruits of that creation and the links between Indigenous Knowledge online and Indigenous resurgence, transformation, and recreation through the many endeavours and fields of the research participants. I am excited by working with the concept of a traditional bundle and transforming it to name Indigenous Knowledge projects online as digital bundles. I continue to learn by exploring with Indigenous communities what it means to envision and represent our knowledge online, and how that work will have impacts for generations to come.

Rainey Gaywish (2014) relayed the prophecy of the Seven Fires, which "tells us that a new people shall emerge and that they will pick up what was left on the trail." This prophecy can be interpreted to mean that the new people will use new ways to ensure survival of Indigenous populations and solutions to Indigenous problems. Gaywish elaborated:

> Using the tools that a higher education provides may be a way of helping our people on their journey to pick up what was left on the trail. With that little bit of knowledge, they can then go back and talk to their grandparents and Elders and Traditional Teachers. They can go back to their communities and experience the ceremonies, the feasts, and the sweats

with some confidence, because at least they will have learned a little bit about what to expect when they arrive. Teaching tools like FourDirectionsTeachings.com are very valuable to introduce that basic knowledge, especially for Aboriginal People who feel disenfranchised from their culture. It can help them feel empowered enough to explore more and ask questions. For non-Aboriginal people, access to Indigenous Knowledge shows them that we are not a vanquished people. We've got a strong history, culture, and traditions that are rightfully ours, that we can teach to them in places like the universities—a good way to raise awareness [of] and respect for Aboriginal People and their communities.

Gaywish clearly sees FourDirectionsTeachings.com as an aid in helping disenfranchised Indigenous Peoples to find a sense of connection. Broken communities can find new tools to help them heal and connect, whether through Native programs in higher education or through Indigenous Knowledge projects online.

Finally, it is well understood that communities know the answers to their own problems, as Cheryl L'Hirondelle (2014) suggested. This is why, with respect to discussing Indigenous Knowledge online versus artistic projects online, she thought that

we need to figure out the work-around. We need to figure out how to regroup as fast as we can, because there is still a lot to do. I do sometimes think that, when you have Cultural Knowledge and Traditional Knowledge, really deep knowledge, it's access to that work-around. It's access to that thing that wasn't plain to the human eye; it isn't in plain sight. So it's where your strength becomes your weakness and your weakness becomes your strength. Maybe if *Drum Beats to Drum Bytes* had continued, we would have worked through these issues, but after Ahasiw passed so did the *Drum Beats to Drum Bytes* gatherings. It's heartbreaking when you lose someone who is so pivotal to the community; a hole exists where that person used to be.

Figuring out the work-around and regrouping in Indigenous new media is also an act of creating. It will involve being imaginative and thinking outside mainstream constructs of new media and ICTs. It will involve fostering new discourses that come from Indigenous meanings, contexts, and languages. This work-around will be a collective effort that will welcome everyone and not limit participation to the technologically advanced or profitable projects or the people who have cultural capital as artists. Regrouping will be about channelling collective creativity in order to privilege Indigenous Peoples' cosmology and ontology. To do this new work, we need to look back at the work that we have done and then—as a community—move forward.

Looking Back Is Our Way Forward

Biskaabiiyang is critical to Indigenous learning because looking back to our stories, ceremonies, and languages reveals and emancipates Indigenous Knowledge. For Taiaiake Alfred (2005), Land Is Life is a pathway on which we can reconnect with the terrain of our Indigenous heritage. In so doing, he believes, we can draw strength independent of colonial power and regenerative of an authentic, autonomous, Indigenous existence. I appreciate his thinking in the practical sense that Indigenous Knowledge is rooted in the lands of our ancestors and Knowledge Keepers. To understand all of the projects/methodologies described above, we need to connect with our communities and Knowledge Keepers because they are rooted in those lands.

Practising Biskaabiiyang entails deep reflection and mobilization or help from the spirit world (Simpson 2011, 147). In reflecting on this notion, I thought about Monique Mojica (2014) and her work with the earth mounds. She told me that

> research is ceremony. You've got to put yourself on the land.
> You've got to protect yourself, you've got to do your feasting
> for your purpose, and you've got to know how much to
> open yourself and allow the energies from those sites and
> those guides [spirit and animal] tell you what you need to
> know—and then you've got to trust it.

Here the idea of Land Is Life comes up again along with the idea that the land is tied to our cultural processes and protocols. Indeed, when my project team began work on FourDirectionsTeachings.com, the first Elder whom we visited, Lillian Pitawanakwat, surprised me by guiding the team through a ceremony, putting us out on the land, and bringing us back to Mother Earth (in the Sweat Lodge) so that we could begin the project in a good way; thus, the project was launched within the cultural protocols of our community. Research, ceremony, and land all become intertwined as we practise Biskaabiiyang.

In this chapter, I have examined how the research participants use Indigenous Knowledge and information online to inform and strengthen their work and their communities. I have made connections between Linda Tuhiwai Smith's (2011) decolonization projects and the research participants' work and my own work as a media producer. These connections have been considered in relation to the principle of Biskaabiiyang, through which we can enact and embrace the decolonization projects so eloquently listed by Smith.

Finally, I have discussed how resurgence is related to how the research participants take up Indigenous Knowledge online. My goal was to demonstrate how Indigenous voices are reaching new audiences and how computer networking and interactive media are affecting the practices and thinking of diverse Indigenous Peoples and non-Indigenous people in Canada. I accomplished this task through an Indigenous analytical perspective that privileges the principle of Biskaabiiyang as a way of honouring Indigenous ontology and contributing to Indigenous resurgence in academic theory.

CHAPTER 5

NAAKGONIGE ("TO PLAN")

With respect to Language Is Power, Taiaiake Alfred states that "our people must recover ways of knowing and relating from outside the mental and ideational framework of colonialism by regenerating themselves in a conceptual universe formed through Indigenous languages" (Alfred & Corntassel, 2005, 613). This pathway is closely related to the process of Naakgonige. For Leanne Simpson (2011), Naakgonige requires that we take time to deliberate carefully before making any concrete decision. All aspects of the self must be engaged in such deliberation: the emotional, the physical, the spiritual, and the intellectual. Only in this way can we ensure that we are fully engaged in the decision-making process. Working in this way is a fairly stark contrast to modern, Western, "colonial" planning processes, which have distinctly utilitarian ends and much shorter timelines in relation to artificial pressures and deadlines (versus natural cycles).

In this chapter, I discuss how the principle of Naakgonige was evident when the research participants discussed their work with Indigenous Knowledge online. I use Linda Tuhiwai Smith's (1999) projects on remembering, intervening, connecting, and gendering as a framework for discussing the information shared by research participants. Although these projects are not language based, I see a connection between them and Alfred's pathway of Language Is Power in that these projects encourage us to think and act in ways free from colonialism and to generate a discourse based upon Indigenous worldviews encoded in Indigenous languages. This chapter reveals how the research participants have resisted colonial agendas by deeply contemplating Indigenous Knowledge online and their responses to it.

Remembering

> *Remembering is painful because it involves remembering not just what colonization was about but what being dehumanized meant for our own cultural practices. Both healing and transformation become crucial strategies in any approach which asks a community to remember what they may have decided unconsciously or consciously to forget.* (Smith, 1999, 146)

To remember is to use our emotional, physical, and spiritual selves in addition to our intellectual selves. Remembering is painful because it brings up all aspects of ourselves, and this is required when deliberating because it means that we are present in heart and mind. Remembering the past and articulating it are parts of the healing process. We need to feel the pain of the past with our hearts and minds and then find ways to move forward. In moving forward from the pain, Naakgonige becomes a crucial strategy for healing and transformation because it puts the power to decide back with the people who have been dehumanized.

Priscilla Lepine (2014) stated that "we have lived through a long period of time where we were ashamed of who we are, and many still haven't healed from that period of oppression and hate." Likewise, Brenda Dubois (2014), who works with Indigenous families in distress, relayed that, in the first couple of family sessions, "we talk a lot about healing. I say, we're going to spend some time looking backwards, but we're not going to get stuck there, because too many people are stuck there." To remember, then, is painful, and for many Indigenous Peoples who have suffered and embodied the impacts of dehumanization the risks of immutability and immobilization are real.

Donna Bourque (2014) outlined some of the historical and social factors that have contributed to the continued suffering of so many Indigenous communities in the North:

> The Northwest Territories had the highest amount of residential schools across Canada. For a population of approximately 25,000–30,000 people, we had fourteen residential schools, which means that many of our people have had the residential school experience and have suffered greatly for it.
>
> I am sorry to say this, but in the North we were raised dysfunctional. It began in residential school, and then that dysfunction was brought into our family homes. We have a high rate of alcoholism and a high rate of suicide. We also have a high rate of FASD [fetal alcohol spectrum disorder].
>
> We also have a very high crime rate in the Northwest Territories, and our people are overrepresented in our jails. There are three men's jails and one women's jail, and in each jail the population of inmates is 99.9 percent Aboriginal.

Looking at the statistics on incarceration, suicide, and addiction, it is clear that the Northwest Territories continues to be plagued by the violence of the past. Remembering is extremely painful work there. For Bourque, remembering is frustrating. She claimed that "the North is always a few years behind the South. Especially when you look at Aboriginal communities in southern Alberta. Those communities are very strong in their beliefs, and they're bringing back their culture." Bourque wants to revive Indigenous Knowledge and culture in the North; however, as she noted, "some Aboriginal people claim that the sweats and cultural practices are the devil's work because they were taught that in residential school. Others are very rigid in their Catholic orientation, which is another unfortunate repercussion from residential school."

Lepine (2014) echoed the views of her colleague:

> So, in corrections, we are dealing with low self-esteem, low self-worth, low self-confidence, and issues around having pride in Aboriginal identity. I also dealt with all these things when I worked in the college, because students who graduated from high school still felt misunderstood by people in higher learning and in the mainstream community. It is so important that we work on these things because everyone in this country has a right to feel pride in their culture, especially the First Nations, Metis, and Inuit Peoples.

For Bourque (2014), the facts that "Aboriginal People have lost their way, and in some ways have lost their culture," mean that we need a plan for both healing and education: "So, until we can educate ourselves about our culture, and the treaties, and why residential schools happened, we cannot begin to come to terms with healing. We need resources to do this, like Aboriginal healing methods, cultural knowledge, and history from an Aboriginal perspective. We need to know where we came from in order to move forward." Like Lepine, she believes that access to Indigenous Knowledge online can help to achieve these goals but that more resources are desperately needed.

Brenda Dubois (2014) is also active in education to help non-Aboriginal people and Aboriginal Peoples alike understand the true history of Canada:

> I will do classes sometimes at universities, and the first things I write on the board are "history," and then beside it I write "our story." There's a lot of stuff that was hidden from this society and that was not even covered in the schools. I remember taking a history class as an adult that was really great because the teacher focused a lot on First Nations history, but I was shocked when she pulled out a poster that

was sent to England that said "Land for Free." That sent me into a tizzy. I couldn't believe it. I don't think many people have seen stuff like this. This land wasn't for free!

For Dubois, remembering is about getting the history right. Misinformation about Indigenous Peoples and their history is a common factor in mainstream educational institutions. Having Aboriginal Peoples and non-Aboriginal people acknowledge this fact is key to planning. To move forward, we must forgive, stresses Dubois, who never turns anyone away from parenting classes on Indigenous cultures and beliefs:

> We want to move to the present so that everybody can have a future, and so we talk about forgiveness in many forms. We then move on to teachings. We start with the cycle of life and the conception of Elderhood and grief and loss. We discuss traditional values and teachings like the teepee teachings and the seven grandfathers. When discussing traditional beliefs, we discuss dance, song, kinship, language, ceremonies, laws, and storytelling and humour. I combine these topics because it's a way to show them how they are all interconnected. At the end, I ask them to consider what is meant by "it takes a village to raise a child." By then, they know the answer.

By then, they know the answer from an Indigenous perspective that draws from Indigenous Knowledge like that found in the teepee teachings, the seven grandfathers, and others mentioned above.

Dubois (2014) greatly values resources online that can help with the vision for educating all people in Canada:

> FourDirectionsTeachings.com is part of putting us on the map, but it is also so much more. You are facilitating knowledge, and so you are part of the knowledge transfer, so I think it's important that you have *Mishooms* and *Kookums*

[grandfathers and grandmothers] who are guiding you. I know that to have Elders speak with you and trust you—that is a gift. Back in the 1980s, we tried to talk to our traditional people, but they weren't willing to talk or allow their voices to be taped or their pictures to be taken. So it's nice to see these old people that are sharing their teachings, because their teachings are going to go on forever through some of the writings that have been made into books and some of the videos that have been created online.

I have always believed that the Elders on FourDirectionsTeaching. com are part of a vanguard for Indigenous Knowledge online. But listening to Dubois discuss the 1980s and the Elders' responses back then really drove home how the Elders on FourDirectionsTeachings. com are now in the forefront of a strategic and carefully considered acceptance of the need to reach people through new media. I also deeply appreciated her insight about me as a producer as part of the knowledge transfer because I appreciate how Doug Anderson (content developer/director) and I contributed to the project in shaping the content, but I have never really found the words to express what that contribution·has meant. Fortunately, through the process of researching and writing this book, I have been challenged to think of contribution from an Indigenous perspective, truly a gift provided to me via the research interviews.

Remembering is an approach, a strategy important to planning, not only for the research participants but also for me as a producer. To move forward, we need to understand where we have come from—both the good and the bad. So to remember is to probe what we might have decided unconsciously or consciously to forget as a community, as Smith (1999) says. Communities located in different areas of Canada might be engaged in different kinds of remembering, depending on their social and cultural needs. So remembering means different work for different communities because of their own social and physical contexts. Evident is that remembering is integral to moving forward and is therefore a part of the process of Naakgonige.

In remembering, we can find ways to heal and transform our communities for the better. Access to Indigenous Knowledge online can facilitate this process of remembering and planning and challenge users to think outside oppressive colonial discourse.

Intervening

> *Intervening takes action research to mean literally the process of being proactive and of becoming involved as an interested worker for change. Intervention-based projects are usually designed around making structural and cultural changes. . . . Intervening is directed then at changing institutions which deal with indigenous peoples and not at changing indigenous peoples to fit the structures.* (Smith, 1999, 147)

I consider intervening to be part of the process of Naakgonige because it entails what we take research to mean, as Smith points out, being proactive and becoming involved as interested workers for change— and that involves a great deal of planning and deliberation. Janetta Soup (2014) embodies this role in her work with the Saint Elizabeth First Nation, Inuit, and Metis Program:

> I have been working with the . . . program for three years. The goal of our project work is to help health-care providers that are working within or for First Nations, Inuit, and Metis communities. We help them by providing resources that are specific to the communities that they work in. This work includes trying to break down barriers and address any concerns that they may have with respect to delivering services to First Nations, Metis, and Inuit communities.

Soup seeks to make changes in the delivery of health care in these communities by training health-care providers to be more culturally aware of the communities in which they work. She and the Saint

Elizabeth First Nations, Inuit, and Metis Program are thus actively engaged in research that privileges Indigenous Knowledge and perspectives.

The program is engaged in intervention in the health institutions that deal with Indigenous Peoples. Soup (2014) elaborated on some of the projects of the program:

> A couple of months ago I worked on a project that was taking the Canadian [physical] activity guidelines and making them more culturally relevant. What we did was come up with a very new interactive online resource. We also mailed out the booklet that's available online.
>
> Currently, I am working with Alberta Health Services and their Aboriginal Health Program. The project involves developing an Aboriginal awareness and sensitivity learning strategy. There are a number of key objectives. The first is to develop an online course that will address all of the Alberta Health Services staff—approximately 95,000 people. We began by working with the project management team that they have on their end. Together we identified what their needs are and what resources and tools they have been using. This information helped us to do a learning needs assessment with them.

In assessing learning needs, the organization demonstrates that its intervention-based projects are holistic in scope and approach and that its work seeks to engage organizations but not proselytize people. The intervention projects are also ultimately accountable to Indigenous communities themselves.

For example, Soup (2014) noted that the Aboriginal Health Program affiliated with Alberta Health Services has its own cultural helpers on her team. She said that, when the time came for review, the team went to the cultural helpers provided by the Aboriginal Health Program. "In addition," she noted, we also seek out health-care providers from different regions across the country to provide feedback on our work. It is important for us to ensure that we validate our work. So we'll find external reviewers who will provide feedback on a course. Consequently, we have a pretty comprehensive process when developing health-care courses. Further, the resources that we offer are national in scope, so we have to be aware of the diversity of First Nations, Metis, and Inuit Peoples across the country.

Awareness of the diversity of Indigenous Peoples in Canada is central to the intervention-based projects and vision of the organization:

> There are a number of ways that we develop resources. For example, about two years ago, I started working for the first time on developing our "First Nations Elder Care" course. This course has different modules, which cover the basics of gerontology. The course has three different parts, beginning with the role of an Elder. So we began by identifying who an Elder is and what are some of the roles and responsibilities they have within their community. We used FourDirectionsTeachings.com to explain and present examples on the important relationship that exists between Elders and the youth.

Access to Indigenous Knowledge online is key to the organization's work, especially because its training resources are offered online. As a result, the organization does a lot of research online and posts links whenever possible for its online courses. Finding Indigenous resources online that can help the workers to do their jobs is greatly appreciated. Soup clarified how FourDirectionsTeachings.com assisted them with their "First Nations Elder Care" course:

> The visuals and the information from the beginning to end were ideally suited to the "Elder Care" course. Diversity is

so important and something that we stress to people—that every First Nations culture is unique and has their differences in terms of teachings, practices, protocols, and even worldviews. There are approximately 630 First Nations communities, with every single one being unique. We know that we cannot possibly represent each one, but it is important to provide examples from the different cultures. So we are grateful for FourDirectionsTeachings.com, because it represents the diversity of the First Nations.

Knowing that Indigenous Knowledge projects online are contributing to such important health initiatives on a national scale is truly inspiring. Widely held misconceptions (e.g., that there is only a singular "Aboriginal culture") can aptly be dealt with in one carefully framed online tool. In this case, an intervention is made that brings a carefully deliberated Indigenous perspective and standard into the context of widespread organizational change—in places where careful deliberation in the full sense of Naakgonige is difficult to achieve. Effectively, agencies that have long histories of perceiving people bureaucratically are at least having their bureaucratic notions widened somewhat through the application of Indigenous perspectives.

Another example of an intervention-based national project is the Idle No More campaign. Monique Mojica (2014), who teaches at the postsecondary level, noted that since the explosion of Idle No More in 2012 everyone wants the "cultural low-down." She felt relieved to have FourDirectionsTeachings.com as a resource to refer people to regarding the many queries that she was receiving:

> So, rather than teach "Indian 101," I say there's this website that will introduce you to some Indigenous Knowledge teachings. One gets tired of explaining these things or being asked to comment on things that are not mine to teach.
>
> So it's important to have a place where I can send people who need to do their homework. I think it takes a load of responsibility off of me, and I don't have to be so smart;

> I don't have to know it all. There's a place where some of
> this knowledge has been deposited.

For Mojica, Indigenous Knowledge resources online embody the act
of intervening. In this way, the "ethno-stress" (Hill, 1992) that she
would normally experience from having to be a cultural teacher to
everyone who requests a cultural intervention in his or her institutional context is alleviated. The term "ethno-stress" refers to ethnicity
linked to Aboriginal identity and to stress from the social realities of
that identity (Hill, 1992, 2). More importantly, Mojica indicated that
some Indigenous Knowledge and teachings are not hers to convey:

> For example, I don't have the rights to teach the med-
> icine wheel. So, when students or people that I meet
> want to know these things, I send them to the website. I
> think a lot of people out there are telling stuff they don't
> have the rights to. So it's good to have something like
> FourDirectionsTeachings.com, because it has been vetted.

This distinction is important, for it is in keeping with Indigenous
Knowledge practices that emphasize accountability and responsibility for Indigenous teachings. Indeed, one must have the rights—that
is, understand the cultural protocols—before proceeding to relate a
teaching. So Mojica made a valid point when she stated that she did
not possess the right to relate certain teachings.

In thinking about the act of intervening, I want to end with
Mojica's (2014) statement that "we have to be in control more and
more about what's there and how it's going to be deposited, because
we've never been in control before. There's a lot of stuff written about
us—but from whose point of view?" Intervening is also about the
process of Naakgonige because we need to know how we are going
to move forward with Indigenous Knowledge online. To intervene is
to plan in responsible and accountable ways for the next seven generations. Intervention requires careful deliberation, integral to the
process of Naakgonige.

CHAPTER 5

Connecting

Connectedness positions individuals in sets of relationships with other people and with the environment. Many indigenous creation stories link people through genealogy to the land, to stars and other places in the universe, to birds and fish, animals, insects and plants. To be connected is to be whole. . . . Forced adoption and dehumanizing child welfare practices were carried out in many indigenous contexts. Being reconnected to their families and their culture has been a painful journey for many of these children, now adults. Connecting also involves connecting people to their traditional lands through the restoration of specific rituals and practices. . . . Connecting is related to issues of identity and place, to spiritual relationships and community wellbeing.

There are other challenges in relation to the project of connecting. Researchers, policy makers, educators, and social service providers who work with or whose work impacts on indigenous communities need to have a critical conscience about ensuring that their activities connect in humanizing ways with indigenous communities. It is a very common experience to hear indigenous communities outline the multiple ways in which agencies and individuals treat them with disrespect and disregard. Connecting is about establishing good relations. (Smith, 1999, 148–49)

Relationship building is vital in creating community well-being. In his law classes, Larry Chartrand (2013) noted, he has a range of students: "Some are Indigenous and are well entrenched in their cultural teachings, and other students have never met an Indigenous person before." Chartrand stated that access to Indigenous Knowledge online helps him to reach all of his students. For example, he appreciates how FourDirectionsTeachings.com can provide basic information to his students about some of the First Nations in Canada: "The site really benefits them by giving them an introductory understanding of Indigenous worldviews and perspectives through the lens of the teachings. The teachings become an accessible reference for all of the students so that they can actually have a meaningful discussion within the class. So it's a valuable resource for all of us." Having Indigenous Knowledge resources that he can bring into his law classes helps him to educate his students about the diversity of First Nations and the connections that can be made to identity and place for Indigenous Peoples.

Similarly, John Borrows (2013) believes that sites such as FourDirectionsTeachings.com really help students to open up their minds: "It's one thing to read; it's another thing to hear me tell a story. But then to actually have a visual attached to that story, it really captures their imagination." He noted that

> I've always been impressed with the graphics, for example the opening with the Thunderbird and the world and the lightning. That image and accompanying script is the very kind of thing that I wanted to talk about in the class, that our Elders still have these ways and that they exist across North America and that we can still learn about these ways.

When I asked Borrows what he thought about having Indigenous teachings online, he said that,

> as a teacher, I felt great because that was what I was trying to do with the course. I wanted the class to see that these traditions are living traditions. They are not just once-up-on-a-time things. They can be applied in contemporary settings. So, to the extent that FourDirectionsTeachings.com helps students see these teachings as living and going into tomorrow, it really felt like it helped me to do my job.

In reflecting on the input of Borrows and Chartrand, one could easily discuss their experiences with various projects that Smith (1999) lists, such as representing, creating, celebrating, and reframing. There is so much richness in what they convey. That is why I stressed that the categories I created are merely to assist me in my analysis and do not represent fixed ranks, because there is so much fluidity. That said, I chose to discuss their insights here because, for me, they resonate with the strategy of connecting—through relationships among students and between teacher and students, which I see as establishing good relations.

Such relations are important for education. People need to feel safe to learn. Angela Nardozi (2014), who trains teacher candidates, knows that learning is also about connecting and that connecting promotes community well-being. However, Nardozi, an Italian Canadian, noted that many people do not know how to make that first connection with an Indigenous community, Elder, or person. FourDirectionsTeachings.com, she said, offers non-Indigenous people a stress-free introduction:

> I feel that the lesson plans and the site have been created so that non-Native people can also access the content. I really try to communicate this point to teacher candidates that this site is made for you, because many teacher candidates are really confused about what to teach, especially very early on; they are thinking, "Okay, now I have to teach a culture." We really try to impress upon them that teaching culture is not the expectation or the goal.

Nardozi's insights illustrate how non-Indigenous people can begin to learn about Indigenous Peoples in Canada and how teacher candidates are not responsible for teaching cultural knowledge but can teach about Canada's relationship with Indigenous Peoples through understanding the Indian Act, the treaties, the residential school system, and so on. Again, such educational approaches fit with Smith's projects on democratizing and intervening, but I chose connecting because I believe that Nardozi's underlying message is about the ethno-stress that non-Indigenous teachers experience when they think about their approaches to teaching about Indigenous Peoples and their histories in the classroom. Here building relationships begins with that first connection, learning about and understanding Indigenous communities and worldviews through Indigenous Knowledge online. The appropriate presentation of Indigenous Knowledge online can be a doorway or transition to connection where none existed before.

Learning helps people to know how and what to ask and therefore fosters connecting in a respectful way sensitive to cultural difference and issues of identity and place. Émilie Monnet (2013) knows this intuitively and applied it after she spent time learning about the Cree teepee pole teachings on FourDirectionsTeachings.com:

> Based on what we learned . . . we were able to form our questions and approach two communities. We chose seven values that we wanted to discuss and met with Anishinaabe individuals and Blackfoot people and Siksika Elders and asked them "What is love? What is respect? What is gratitude?" So we asked these questions, and they provided us with some answers, and we kind of incorporated that into the *Bird Messengers* story.

Indigenous Knowledge online provided Monnet with insights into spiritual and community values. She was then able to approach communities and connect with them based upon her understanding. This ability to connect helped to inspire the *Bird Messengers* story, then shared with larger audiences, both Indigenous and non-Indigenous. Connecting, in this case, was like a pebble dropped in still water: it rippled outward.

Cheryl L'Hirondelle (2014) dropped a pebble into cyberspace when she created what she called a simple database, All My Relations. She built this site because she wanted to list all of her relations, including those adopted: "One day I got an email. The subject header said 'My name is Whispering Wind; do you know who I am?' I was shocked because Whispering Wind was one of my ex's five children." L'Hirondelle helped her ex to raise three of his five children because two of his children had been adopted. She said, "I immediately recognized the name." Whispering Wind had emailed her to ask her if she could help him to connect with his family. He wanted to know to whom he was related. She shared that

> it was just a really beautiful moment for me because, as an artist working in new media, I had to confront a lot of doubt and skepticism at the time in Native communities about the kind of work that I was interested in. So it was just such a beautiful moment for me to realize that this technology could be life affirming, to know that this could be something that connects people and connects families, and I just felt honoured and so grateful that I had made this silly little website that had caught his eye. So I think that's beautiful, that All My Relations brought together all of my relations.

More than ever, being able to connect is crucial for Aboriginal youth and children. Cindy Blackstock, a child advocate and activist, states that "we have never had more First Nations children in child welfare care than we do at this moment." The numbers are staggering. According to Blackstock, 65 percent of the children in care in provinces such as Alberta are from First Nations. In British Columbia, it is 53 percent. "So if you take those two provinces alone, we're talking about 11,000 First Nations children living in foster care," Blackstock says.[20] The ability to reconnect to family through the Internet is potentially a viable strategy for many adoptees today. However, for Indigenous children who have been removed from their families, Indigenous Knowledge online can help them to rebuild those lost connections to who they are and where they come from.

Brenda Dubois (2014), who works in social services with families at risk, specifically uses the Ojibwe and Cree teachings on FourDirectionsTeachings.com to convey Indigenous Knowledge and values: "I know our nations have differences, but we also have commonalities. I like that we can talk about the teepee teachings on the site and then go into the Ojibwe teaching and talk about the seven grandfathers." These teachings affirm the work that Dubois is doing in the parenting class, and the teachings online contribute to learning beyond the classroom: "When I do my parenting class, I tell every-body that you can't get all your learning done in one place. I stress that we all have to accept responsibility for our own individual learning. So projects like FourDirectionsTeachings.com are great because it is something that families can continue to use and share outside of the class." She acknowledges the value of the site for Indigenous families because it reconnects them to Indigenous Knowledge and values and offers them an alternative worldview. She also sees how Indigenous Knowledge sites online can educate and sensitize people in social services:

> I also refer the website to people that we may be working with and have shared it with all of the staff in our office. It's great because they can peruse the site on their own and refer families in their caseload to it. Other online resources that we recommend are the Anxiety page, because we work with youth, and the Aboriginal Portal—this site is now down— and the Aboriginal Healing Foundation Research pages.

Dubois hopes that such sharing, to echo Smith (1999), will ensure that the programming activities connect in humanizing ways with Indigenous communities. She knows first hand that social services need to be sensitive to the impacts of colonization. However, to achieve that cultural sensitivity means to connect through sharing knowledge in a way that establishes good relations. Indigenous Knowledge online provides this opportunity for Indigenous and non-Indigenous communities alike and therefore opens a door onto the pathways Language Is Power and Decolonize Your Diet by pro-viding ways of knowing and relating outside colonialism.

Gendering

> *Colonization is recognized as having had a destructive effect*
> *on indigenous gender relations which reached out across all*

spheres of indigenous society. . . . A key issue for indigenous women in any challenge of contemporary indigenous politics is the restoration to women of what are seen as their traditional roles, rights and responsibilities. (Smith, 1999, 151–52)

It is important to consider Linda Tuhiwai Smith's project on gendering in thinking about how Indigenous women are exploited violently through Western notions of gender and race, as noted by Andrea Smith (2005). Some of the research participants alluded to gender, but the topic was not explored in detail. Monique Mojica (2014) discussed issues of gender with respect to the Sundance Ceremony, but I will discuss her insights later since they relate to the ceremony specifically and not to gender online.

John Borrows (2013) directly addressed perceptions of gender online when discussing his students' responses to certain websites: "I did get some students that were worried about the Nature's Laws website because they thought that gender wasn't well represented and that sometimes women were placed in second-class roles in the way that some of the teachings were being represented and interpreted. Your site doesn't do that; it's very good at working through those kinds of complexities." Borrows relayed that as time went on he relied less on the Nature's Laws site, for he found FourDirectionsTeachings. com more gender friendly and more accessible because of the visuals. His students have an analysis of gender and are critical and cautious of how colonization has shaped the roles and rights of Indigenous women. This critique enables them to look carefully at how gender is being represented online.

In moving forward with Indigenous Knowledge projects online, it will be important for Indigenous communities to carefully consider how gender is presented. This consideration will involve thinking outside destructive colonialist frameworks and regenerating what Taiaiake Alfred calls a "conceptual universe formed through Indigenous languages" (Alfred & Corntassel, 2005, 613). In this way, Indigenous communities can engage with the principle of Naakgonige and plan how they can better represent Indigenous men and women in healthy ways that acknowledge their humanity, strength, and contributions equally.

The Internet and the Next Seven Generations

The research participants have demonstrated in this chapter how they resist colonial agendas by deeply contemplating their plans and responses through Smith's (1999) methodologies of remembering, intervening, connecting, and gendering.

In discussing Naakgonige, Simpson says that,

> rather than blindly accepting the colonizers' truths or acting out of fear, Naakgonige and Naanaagede'enmowin ["the heart must help to guide the mind"] demand presence of mind and heart, engagement, thorough analysis, and a critical evaluation of the long-term impacts of decision making in terms of promoting mino bimaadiziwin ["good life"] and preventing Zhaaganashiiyaadizi ["assimilation"]—which, in my mind, is what resistance is all about. (2011, 58)

It is evident that the research participants are engaged in the principle of Naakgonige in that they consider their actions with all aspects of their being and think about the impacts on and consequences for their present communities and for the next seven generations. They are careful about not acting out of fear or blindly accepting colonizers' truths. They are proactive in recovering ways of Indigenous knowing and sharing these ways of knowing in their work. For this reason, I have included Alfred's pathway Language Is Power with the principle of Naakgonige, because Indigenous languages encode knowledge, and Indigenous Knowledge is implicit in Naakgonige.

In the next chapter, I discuss the principle of Aanjigone, which has great implications for ideas on change. To implement communal change is a huge responsibility and can be contemplated only after a long and deliberate process, which speaks to Simpson's statement that Naakgonige in Indigenous resurgence is critical "as a way of collectivizing, strategizing and making the best decisions possible in any given context" (2011, 147). In the context of change, the principle of Aanjigone is vital to ensuring that we are cautious and responsible for the next seven generations.

CHAPTER 6

AANJIGONE
("NON-INTERFERENCE")

The principle of Aanjigone is important because, according to Leanne Simpson, "it ensures that we tread very carefully" and that we "deliberate to the best of our abilities and that we act out of a tremendous love [and regard] for our lands, our peoples and our culture" (2011, 147). This principle reminds us that healthy change for Indigenous Peoples is possible as long as they promote Nishnaabeg ways of being and prevent *Zhaaganashiiyaadizi* ("assimilation") (54). For Taiaiake Alfred, Indigenous Peoples "must transcend the controlling power of the many and varied fears that colonial powers use to dominate and manipulate us into complacency and cooperation with its authorities" (Alfred & Corntassel, 2005, 613). This statement is located in his third pathway, Freedom Is the Other Side of Fear. Aanjigone reaffirms this mantra by reminding us that change is possible and that we can overcome our fear and build up our confidence by reclaiming the strengths of our communities through the resurgence of Indigenous Knowledge.

In considering the meaning of this principle, I thought about Linda Tuhiwai Smith's (1999) methods of claiming/testimony, returning, networking, protecting, and negotiating—all of which speak to how the research participants negotiate their experiences with Indigenous Knowledge both online and offline. It became apparent in their responses that they are extremely careful in considering how Indigenous Knowledge is represented and transmitted and that ultimately they adhere to Aanjigone while doing the work of deliberation. Aanjigone is a meditative process in which, as I stated earlier, restoration occurs through deep feeling and reasoning. This process is crucial to moving forward and a vital aspect of Indigenous resurgence.

Claiming/Testimony

> Testimonies intersect with claiming because they are a means through which oral evidence is presented to a particular audience. There is a formality to testimonies and a notion that truth is being revealed "under oath." Indigenous testimonies are a way of talking about an extremely painful event or series of events. . . . A testimony is also a form through which the voice of a "witness" is accorded space and protection. It can be constructed as a monologue and as a public performance. (Smith, 1999, 144)

Smith speaks about oral evidence presented to a particular audience in real time and in person. This is important because, with projects such as FourDirectionsTeachings.com, oral teachings, which can also be considered part of oral evidence, are transmitted via audio and images electronically and open to anyone on the Internet who chooses to visit the site. Yet the site resonates on a deep level for Indigenous visitors as a place for claiming/testimony.

For example, Émilie Monnet (2013) thought that the site is really rooted in Indigenous worldviews and that not many sites do this:

> The way it was crafted felt like there was just a lot of respect and protocol taken into consideration, especially with regard to intellectual property. The feeling I got was that

you could really feel the generosity of the speakers. I don't think an Elder would share anything that wasn't genuine. It also feels like the real thing when you can hear the voices of the Elders. They are so generous. To be generous like that, you have to take real ownership over what you are sharing.

Monnet echoed Smith's sentiments on the sense of truth being shared and the significance of the voice of the person sharing it. In really feeling the generosity of the speakers, Monnet was able to connect to the teachings through the experience of claiming/testimony. In this way, she opened herself up to important aspects of values embedded in Aanjigone, in the sense that she deliberated on what she saw and heard through deep feeling and consideration.

Rainey Gaywish (2014), like Monnet, also noted that great care was taken in sharing some of our Indigenous values, worldviews, and teachings. In a sense, both Gaywish and Monnet were practising claiming/testimony because they chose to make strong statements about how they relate to FourDirectionsTeachings.com as a site of Indigenous Knowledge. Their reactions to the work brought the site to life through the practice of claiming/testimony.

Gaywish (2014) noted that students visiting the site can see for themselves the intrinsic values and perspectives across Turtle Island in the ways that different Elders from different nations share their teachings. For Gaywish, the ability to process the diversity of Indigenous Peoples is key because "they also learn that differences between First Nations and their teachings are to be respected. To quote a teacher I respect, Edward Benton Banai, 'all creation stories are true.'" Sharing the site with her students as a place for learning about the diversity of teachings demonstrates that Gaywish actively claims the site as place of Indigenous Knowledge. However, she does not do so lightly: "I am very careful when I find new information that's interesting. I actually review it thoroughly to make sure that what's being shared is something that I see as having legitimacy."

The notion of "legitimacy" here relates again to the practice of claiming/testimony because the person hearing and interacting with the content has to find the truth being conveyed. In this way, Aanjigone comes into play as Gaywish, like Monnet, deeply considers what she is seeing and hearing.

Returning

> This project intersects with that of claiming. It involves the returning of lands, rivers and mountains to their indigenous owners. It involves the repatriation of artefacts, remains and other cultural materials stolen or removed and taken overseas.... Adopted children, for example, are encouraged to seek their birth families and return to their original communities. (Smith, 1999, 155–56)

I frame the notion of returning by that of claiming: that is, how the research participants engage with Indigenous Knowledge online as a way of recovering or returning to cultural knowledge, in the form of teachings historically forbidden from being shared. Monnet (2014) relayed her experience of looking for teachings when she was researching her *Bird Messengers* project. She spoke to Cheryl L'Hirondelle about the teepee pole teachings, and L'Hirondelle referred her to FourDirectionsTeachings.com. On her first visit to the site, Monnet recalled,

> I checked it out and was like wow, this is really inspiring. I remember listening to Cree Elder Mary Lee over and over again on the website, and I was just really thankful to have access to this information—like the time I learned about the Mohawk peacemaker story. I was so moved and really just wanted to hear more! More First Nations Elders sharing from the many more nations that exist. I just wanted more teachings. I remember just feeling really thirsty for more of this kind of knowledge.

Returning for Monnet is about access to more teachings. She stressed her thirst for more Indigenous Knowledge, aware that there are many more teachings and many more First Nations that exist and need to be represented. Monnet is not alone in her longing for the return of Indigenous teachings; many of the research participants expressed the same thirst or desire.

Others, such as Angela Nardozi (2014), were moved to hear that the project followed certain Indigenous protocols: "I remember, when you presented at our conference, saying that tobacco was given and ceremony was initiated for the site. I remember thinking that this means that the site was done in a really good way and that this just wasn't an information website; it was actual teachings, which is a really important distinction." Hearing about the development of the site signified for Nardozi a passage to returning because Indigenous protocols were employed throughout the process. Here returning signifies the picking up of bundles where work and process are considered and deliberated from Indigenous perspectives and values. Returning is integral to the principle of Aanjigone since it promotes Nishnaabeg ways of being and prevents Zhaaganashiiyaadizi and therefore provides a sound method of contemplating the viability of Indigenous Knowledge both online and offline.

For L'Hirondelle (2014), returning is connected to how Indigenous Peoples experience their cultures and take pride in claiming what they find there. She expressed this notion when she described how she watched a young Blackfoot couple spend a couple of hours at a computer terminal engaging with FourDirectionsTeachings.com:

> I remember when I curated it watching people who generally don't go to galleries come in and sit for an hour or two. [They] spent a significant amount of time on the Blackfoot teaching. When they were done, it was so beautiful, because you could see that they were so full of spirit. They were so full of a sense of pride and sense of self. It was like something had shifted from when they first walked in. It may be that they knew the teaching, or were familiar with it, or

recognized aspects of it, but it was like they belonged. They were part of something in this gallery space.

L'Hirondelle did not interview this couple afterward, but it was clear to her that something had shifted for them. In reflecting on this moment, she was reminded of Whispering Wind and his need to return to his birth family. Overcome with a deep sense of humility and empathy, L'Hirondelle shared that,

> when you have moments like that, you just know that the works exist for a reason. It is just so beautiful to witness that somebody you might never get to know has experienced something wonderful. It is the same feeling of connection that I had when Whispering Wind contacted me and I reflected on what would have happened if I hadn't made that site [All My Relations]. How would he have found his relatives? Or the time that I showed a project of mine that translated a story into the Dakota language and my Dakota friend, an adult man, wept when he saw it. He wept because he was so grateful to hear a story in his language and to have all of the work and effort put into it. To be a part of these experiences is such a privilege and so profound because we get to do that for our community.

Over the years, I have had similar experiences and have found, like L'Hirondelle, that Indigenous People are so grateful and moved to find projects online that have had a tremendous amount of effort and time put into them. It is the ultimate sign of respect—not just for the work but also for the heritage itself—because it involves a returning and claiming of knowledge that was once forbidden. It is therefore common that people react emotionally because they "feel" the notion of returning and all that it entails.

Consequently, as we come to experience this returning, we must all be mindful of Aanjigone so that we can give each other the space, respect, and time needed to process all that was stolen or removed.

Aanjigone allows us to experience the realm of emotional upheaval, both good and bad, so that we can experience returning safely. This is how people can really change, by learning and returning, when they are given the freedom to do so in their own ways, from their own hearts.

Networking

> Building networks is about building knowledge and data bases which are based on the principles of relationships and connections. . . . Networking by indigenous peoples is a form of resistance. People are expected to position themselves clearly and state their purposes. Establishing trust is an important feature. . . .
>
> Networking is a process which indigenous peoples have used effectively to build relationships and disseminate knowledge and information. (Smith, 1999, 156–57)

When it comes to discerning Indigenous Knowledge online, networking is an important strategy for validating and authenticating such work. Networking is also used by the research participants to overcome isolation and build up their confidence and trust in sharing Indigenous Knowledge online—all while contributing to their learning processes.

For Monique Mojica (2014), working on Indigenous projects is a form of networking that builds knowledge because she can make connections between past work and present work. For example, she said that FourDirectionsTeachings.com was one of the first projects she worked on that intentionally takes Indigenous Knowledge and creates something accessible on the Internet:

> It wasn't entertainment, and it wasn't a documentary. The project was influential to my way of thinking because of the teepee pole teachings that I narrated. The teepee pole teachings made it very clear to me how we can use Indigenous

structures and apply them, for example, to performance structures. Floyd Favel had talked about this way back, and I didn't get it then, but having to read and understand what Mary Lee was saying in her teaching crystallized for me what Floyd was trying to say so many years prior.

Making connections between her projects and her networks helped Mojica to deeply reflect on the teepee pole teachings and to embrace them as a uniquely Indigenous structure informed by Indigenous Knowledge and values. She was therefore able to revisit prior knowledge and build upon it through her relationships and connections.

For Janetta Soup (2014), being able to recognize Reg Crowshoe on the FourDirectionsTeachings.com site affirmed for her a sense of trust in and regard for the site:

> The level of trust that I had for the site really came from the fact that I recognized Reg Crowshoe. He is one of the Elders from southern Alberta, and he's very well known. That prior connection, and the fact that he validated the work on the site when I was speaking to him about other queries, helped solidify my trust in the site.

Soup based her deliberation on the site through her relationships and community connections. She was able to trust the site as a valid source of knowledge because of her networks. These networks are rooted in the principles of relationships and connections acknowledged and privileged in Indigenous communities. So Soup actively uses the site as a resource for Indigenous content in her work and refers to it whenever somebody is looking for cultural resources.

Many of the research participants rely on their networks when deliberating on Indigenous Knowledge online. For example, Larry Chartrand (2013) said that "one of the reasons I've used FourDirectionsTeachings.com is because the site was referenced by John Borrows." Both men work in the field of Indigenous law in Canada. Chartrand elaborated on this connection: "I trust John's work quite a bit. He is a leading scholar in the field of law, and he's Indigenous him-self. He understands Indigenous teachings and [their] relationship to the law. If he's recommending a website in a text, I am going to give that website a lot of credibility, and won't even necessarily inquire any further, given that endorsement." Here Chartrand identified Borrows as part of his scholarly network. This network is effectively used to disseminate, as Smith (1999) indicates above, knowledge and infor-mation. Chartrand values his database/networks in guiding his work as an Indigenous law professor. As he explained,

> other sites I am a little bit more leery of when surfing the net. I'll look very carefully to see where it's coming from. I'll do background research on the people who've created it to get a degree of comfort with the work or teachings. If it is something that is dramatically new and different, then I will do rigorous research on it.

Online sites that cannot be verified through professional networks or Indigenous community connections and relationships are held at arm's length. The notion of networks, then, is key for Indigenous Peo-ples as they validate online cultural resources.

Both Indigenous and non-Indigenous users of the Internet inter-viewed for this book apply this philosophy of networking. Ultimately, the research participants draw from their personal encounters, which represent their networks. For example, Angela Nardozi (2014) recognized Tom Porter, who shares the Mohawk teaching on FourDirectionsTeachings.com:

> How can you not trust Tom Porter? He's very respected, and I've read his book *And Grandma Says . . . : Iroquois Teachings as Passed Down through the Oral Tradition*, and it really touched me. And I know he has a lot of ancestors behind him and never claims the knowledge belongs to him. So I was really happy after I read his book and then saw that he was on the site as well.

So, like Soup, Nardozi recognized an Elder on the site whom she could verify from her own experience. However, she also had professional referrals to the site, which also greatly affirmed her trust:

> I immediately trusted FourDirectionsTeachings.com when I first visited the site because Dr. Jean Paul Restoule referred it to me. I have a tremendous amount of respect and trust for Dr. Restoule. I also know that he has worked with you. I've also heard you speak about this site and how you put together an advisory committee. I think that's really important—the fact that the Elders on the site have been selected by people from the community—especially when there are people who want to co-opt that position by proclaiming themselves to be Elders.

That Nardozi warmly accepts the advisory committee of FourDirectionsTeachings.com as people knowledgeable and able to vet the Elders on the site demonstrates that she knows that such a network is based upon Indigenous principles of community connections and relationships. She therefore understands that this network can safeguard against self-proclaimed "shamans" and "Elders." Here networking, as Smith (1999) says, is a form of resistance because it helps to establish trust and ensures that people position themselves truthfully.

Moreover, networking is about relating on a personal level. Cheryl L'Hirondelle (2014) shared that, as a musician and an artist, she has travelled around Canada and had the pleasure of visiting many Native communities:

> It was really exciting for me to see people on the website like Reg Crowshoe and Mary Lee, who I recognize from my travels. I know that you went to the source because I know who these people are. Piikani Elders that I have spoken to are always talking about the significance and importance of place. So the fact that you went to those places, you went

and visited the people who are intrinsically dedicated and connected to those places, is very respectful and thorough.

L'Hirondelle extends the notion of networking and connecting to relationships to land and place. For her, seeing the Elders whom she recognizes on the FourDirectionsTeachings.com website is profound because she sees how place and land are integrated and reflected in the teachings on the site. Having visited many of these places, she draws on her life's journey as a way of networking with and connecting to the teachings, Elders, and land.

Networking is a vital strategy for Indigenous Peoples and can be used in a variety of ways, as demonstrated above. Ultimately, it is a personal strategy rooted in one's experience and therefore fits with the process of Aanjigone because it requires that we be respectful of each other's processes and consider carefully and perhaps withdraw quietly from networks that might not be our own. Networking is also extended to how the Internet connects people who might not otherwise meet face to face.

Protecting

> *This project is multifaceted. It is concerned with protecting peoples, communities, languages, customs and beliefs, art and ideas, natural resources and the things indigenous peoples produce. The scale of protecting can be as enormous as the Pacific Ocean ... or as small as an infant. It can be as real as land and as abstract as a belief about the spiritual essence of the land.... The need to protect a way of life, a language and the right to make our own history is a deep need linked to the survival of indigenous peoples. (Smith, 1999, 158)*

Protecting is a huge responsibility and commitment for Indigenous Peoples. It cannot be taken lightly and involves deep contemplation and consideration. Many intuitively practise the principle of Aanjigone when deliberating on the notion of protecting as a safeguard for not being too judgmental or too quick to circulate negative energy lest it come back, as Simpson notes, onto ourselves and our families. When the discussions with the research participants turned to the protection of Indigenous Knowledge, they were careful and passionate about their responses.

Émilie Monnet (2013) made a distinction between information and knowledge sites based upon how protocols and ethics were enacted: "An Indigenous Knowledge site must deal with ownership and respect of the knowledge being presented, whereas an Indigenous information site does not have to address these concerns. FourDirectionsTeachings.com, I feel, is an Indigenous Knowledge site because it gives a voice to Knowledge Keepers and respects the diversity and protocol of the various First Nations." This distinction is important with respect to the notion of protecting because it signifies that, when it comes to Indigenous Knowledge, there are specific cultural protocols and ethics that must be followed. This is in contrast to Indigenous information sites, where adherence to cultural protocols and ethics is not so much of an issue. Monnet noted that, in her observation, there are definitely more Indigenous information sites than Indigenous Knowledge sites. Given the protocols and ethics for Indigenous Knowledge, this is easy to understand. This distinction, then, with respect to protocols and ethics, aptly speaks to why Indigenous Knowledge online should be regarded as different and distinct from Indigenous information online.

Rainey Gaywish (2014) also discussed the cultural validity of Indigenous Knowledge online. For her, protecting means asking the right questions and contemplating the answers carefully: "When I look at a potential resource, I ask the following questions. What does this have to offer? Does it have consistency? Does it have validity? Is it useful? Do I have to spend time explaining it? Is it problematic in any way?" For Gaywish, these questions provide a specific framework for assessing and hence protecting the validity of Indigenous Knowledge resources. She considered the community context for such resources carefully: "The fact that FourDirectionsTeachings.com was put together using well-respected Elders and [Traditional] Teachers who have credibility in their own communities was extremely important. There are a lot of charlatans who don't have the respect of their own communities—or who are not even connected to a community—that try to pass themselves off as respected Elders." Protecting is being vigilant about imposters or "wannabe" Elders/Traditional Teachers who self-proclaim their wisdom, abilities, titles to Clans, and so on without any real community connection or context. This type of cultural appropriation is a huge concern for many people and often is central to discussions on protecting Indigenous Knowledge online.

Donna Bourque (2014) and Priscilla Lepine (2014) also stressed the importance of being able to trust Indigenous Knowledge online. Again, context is vital to ensuring that the people speaking are clearly from the culture and community about which or from which they are speaking. This means for Lepine that "these people were raised [in] or learned at some point in their life about the culture and are obviously not someone from outside of the culture trying to sell it as a means for profit." Prior to her work in corrections, Lepine taught at the college level. She shared how she was adamant about teaching her students how to make distinctions about Indigenous Knowledge online: "As an instructor at the college, I brought students to websites to show them New Age non-Aboriginal people who were selling Aboriginal culture. I did this to teach them how to identify cultural appropriation."

Protecting is multifaceted, as Smith (1999) states. Protecting Indigenous Knowledge is concerned with protecting languages, customs, beliefs, ideas, and natural resources, and to do this Elders and Traditional Teachers who transmit this knowledge need to be identified and authenticated through and within community contexts.

Janetta Soup (2014) articulated the centrality of Elders in the transmission of Indigenous Knowledge: "Elders who provide oral teachings, or guide how the Indigenous Knowledge is being articulated, I would validate as Indigenous Knowledge—because it comes from a particular knowledge source steeped in tradition." This tradition is rooted in an oral transmission that adheres to particular cultural protocols and most often has been transferred via ceremony.

As a result, when asked about the status of sites online, Soup noted that there are more Indigenous information sites than Indigenous Knowledge sites. She distinguished Indigenous information (versus Indigenous Knowledge) as that created by an individual ego (perhaps even a relatively healthy and balanced one): "For example, how do you validate the information and perspective that you are seeing? For me, blogs are not representative of Indigenous Knowledge because they are an individual's point of view, so I would not validate that as Indigenous Knowledge." However, she was careful about making any claim or advocating for more Indigenous Knowledge online:

> I feel that there is definitely a fine line with respect to putting Traditional Knowledge online. I almost don't even feel comfortable answering that because it is such a fine line of "How deep do you go?" You have to be careful not to go too deep, otherwise you may cross a line that will cause disrespect. Even if you have been given the rights, it does not necessarily protect you from making mistakes that could denigrate the knowledge. So I don't even feel comfortable in answering that question, "What kind of cultural sources should be online?" It's a huge question.

Soup was right. Having cultural sources online raises some important questions, and in many ways these questions were the impetus for this study. We need dialogue on what should be offered online across Indigenous communities. Hopefully, some of the ideas presented here will help to frame and start a national discussion rooted in Indigenous perspectives and values.

The research participants demonstrated the importance of protecting by acknowledging how Indigenous Knowledge must connect to community ownership and respect for that knowledge, which includes presenting who the Knowledge Keepers are and how they adhere to the cultural protocols of their communities. As Indigenous Knowledge resources are deliberated and contemplated carefully, they adhere to the principle of Aanjigone.

Negotiating

> *Negotiating is about thinking and acting strategically. It is about recognizing and working towards long-term goals. Patience is a quality which indigenous communities have possessed in abundance. . . . Negotiations are also about respect, self-respect and respect for the opposition. Indigenous rules of negotiation usually contain both rituals of respect and protocols for discussion. The protocols and procedures are integral to the actual negotiation and neglect or failure to acknowledge or take seriously such protocols can be read as a lack of commitment to both the process and the outcome. . . . The continued faith in the process of negotiating is about retaining a faith in the humanity of indigenous beliefs, values and customary practices.* (Smith, 1999, 159–60)

The research participants negotiate their trust and understanding of Indigenous Knowledge both online and offline. Negotiating here describes an internal process rooted in "thinking and acting strategically." So, though I do not discuss actual negotiations between parties, I do focus on a type of negotiation that acknowledges protocols, procedures, and commitment to Indigenous processes, all of which are outlined above in Smith's statement.

Rainey Gaywish (2014) has been following a traditional spiritual path for forty years. When she evaluates a potential Indigenous resource, she not only considers her own knowledge but also assesses the kind of negotiating possible within the parameters of the project. For example, she noted that FourDirectionsTeachings.com clearly presents the Elders and Traditional Teachers from the Mi'kmaq, Ojibwe, Cree, Mohawk, and Blackfoot Nations: "We know exactly who these Elders are and what they are presenting. Their bios also explain their community connections." Gaywish elaborated: "It is obvious that our cultural protocols are being practised on this site and that the people who developed this site have the same kind of values and perspectives. I also looked at who's on the advisory committee and could see that they are also well-respected educators." Here Gaywish noted the cultural protocols with respect to connecting Elders to their communities, but she also indicated the value of Indigenous networks and the fact that the advisory committee is made up of well-respected educators.

Monique Mojica (2014) discussed how, as an Indigenous artist, she must continually negotiate the projects on which she works: "For me, it is always a question of balance. How much do you put out there, and what do you put out there?" Given those questions, I asked her what she thought about working on FourDirectionsTeachings.com. She responded that

> I had an initial comfort level with your project because you explained very clearly that you had the Elders' consent and that you were informed about the parameters that they were comfortable with. So projects that I work on have to be evaluated issue by issue, question by question, project by project, and going in and doing it with non-Indigenous people is probably something that at this time I would say I can't do. I have been burned too many times.

Mojica pointed to the relevance of negotiations with the Elders on FourDirectionsTeachings.com. She also referred to issues that she has experienced working with non-Aboriginals because of a lack of accountability regarding Indigenous protocols and negotiations. In reflecting on her own barometer for negotiating Indigenous projects, Mojica relayed what a dear Clan mother from Onondaga had said: "You don't expose those things that are collectively private." She added that

> what is collectively private to one community might not be as private, or might even be more private, to the next community. I think the Elders that you worked with were very clear about what could and could not be presented. There was a sense that this work could pose a risk—I almost said

with what non-Indigenous people would do with it, but it also concerns Indigenous People who aren't connected to why such knowledge has to be respected. What will they do with it? That's an ongoing bone of contention.

Thinking strategically about cultural privacy is important because it can protect not only against cultural appropriation but also against cultural exploitation. Indigenous Peoples who might not appreciate that "knowledge has to be respected" cannot be accused of cultural appropriation if indeed it is from their own community. However, they can exploit knowledge that they might not really understand or respect. As Mojica stated, this is a "bone of contention" for many Indigenous communities that want to make Indigenous Knowledge available to their communities in ways that demonstrate respect for the protocols and responsibilities for that knowledge. As a result, Mojica explained, "you have to think about the balance and the risks every time, with every project, with every character, with every aspect of the work. It's not like you do it once and you're good forever. You can't be inoculated against exploiting your own culture. It's daily maintenance." Negotiating the exploitation of Indigenous Knowledge is a rigorous job, and I agree with Mojica that it is indeed "daily maintenance" to try to safeguard against the exploitation of your own or another Indigenous culture.

Angela Nardozi (2014) has extended her Indigenous network to social media to get the right information and avoid contributing to the exploitation of Indigenous Knowledge or Indigenous Peoples:

When I look at Indigenous content, I look at where it's coming from. For example, someone might tweet out a resource, and if Taiaiake Alfred says "This is great" then I will look at it. It's amazing to get informed information, because there's no place to get good [accurate] news, so I'm on Twitter all the time. Especially when big things happen, like the conflict in Elsipogtog First Nation around fracking.

I found I was online all the time, literally minute by minute, watching the conflict, as an alternative to mainstream news.

Nardozi noted that, before she went on Twitter, it was hard for her to know what to trust. Now she follows so many people from Indigenous communities across Turtle Island that she is overwhelmed by the quantity of good sources out there. As she explained,

> I also follow Indigenous scholars, Indigenous community members, news groups, Chief[s] and councils, and Indigenous organizations. I check on *Wind Speaker* news, the *Two Row Times*—I use that a lot—and I use the CBC site the 8th Fire, which is amazing. I found that it was really cool and helpful. There's also a lot of blogs; Chelsea Vowel writes one, and so does Dr. Palmater at Ryerson.

Prior to the advent of contemporary social media, Nardozi said, when she was left to her own devices, she would use Internet search engines to find Indigenous content:

> I would use Google and found that there's a lot of crazy stuff out there. Like New Age pink wampum beads that mean love, yellow means happy—very incredible stuff. This type of misinformation must be really intimidating for someone who doesn't know, because when you are on these sites and you read something you don't know who's writing this. Where are they from? You have no idea. So, yeah, there's a lot of weird stuff out there. I don't think a lot of people want to put Indigenous Knowledge on the Internet, and when they do you never know if it's going to be some airy-fairy made-up stuff.

Negotiating what one finds on the Internet is critical to maintaining the integrity of Indigenous Knowledge online. It involves having some basic understanding of Indigenous values, beliefs, and customary practices as a way of recognizing Indigenous protocols. Or, as Nardozi shared, it involves building up one's Indigenous network online in order to access qualified Indigenous resources respectful of Indigenous Knowledge and communities. For Nardozi, websites such as the Deepening Knowledge site are key resources because they have been vetted by people with specific knowledge of Indigenous history, culture, social, political, and educational issues, and current events, all of which are pivotal to protecting and negotiating Indigenous Knowledge online.

Promoting Indigenous Ways of Being Online

In negotiating their use of Indigenous Knowledge online, the research participants practise a form of negotiating rooted in Aanjigone in that they consider deeply and passionately the content under review, key for discerning Indigenous Knowledge online.

As Linda Tuhiwai Smith (1999) indicates, negotiating from an Indigenous perspective involves understanding Indigenous protocols and responsibilities and "thinking and acting strategically," as demonstrated by the research participants. Negotiating entails Aanjigone because it involves a tremendous amount of respect both for one's own understanding and position and for the understanding and position of another person, including the opposition.

In his mantra Freedom Is the Other Side of Fear, Taiaiake Alfred states that the way to confront our fears is head-on through spiritually grounded action: "Contention and direct movement at the source of our fears is the only way to break the chains that bind us to our colonial existences" (Alfred & Corntassel, 2005, 613). Smith's projects provide an ideal framework for "spiritually grounded action" via claiming/testimony, returning, networking, protecting, and negotiating, all of which—as we have seen—are enacted through the principle of Aanjigone, which challenges us to consider all aspects of a decision and, as Leanne Simpson (2011) states, to focus on the concept or decision at hand rather than the individual. In doing so, we avoid divisive colonial strategies based upon jealousy, rivalry, power, and greed, all of which have been used to divide communities.

Aanjigone, then, is an ideal process for ensuring that we help to make changes that promote Indigenous ways of being and prevent assimilation and co-optation by colonial agendas.

CHAPTER 7

DEBWEWIN ("TRUTH AS HEART KNOWLEDGE")

I t can take several years to be able to speak about a particular meaning from within the Indigenous context of Debwewin. Leanne Simpson (2011, 44) explains this when discussing her experiences as a mother and her experiences of Creation stories and ceremonies. She says "it can take many years after hearing a story to know the meaning of that story in one's heart—for it to become a truth—yet the process of it becoming heart-knowledge or Debwewin is the process of integrating that echo into one's experience" (104). Debwewin is what you know intuitively, but it is also what you acquire over the years in coming to understand certain meanings or truths. The meaning of truth in an Anishinaabe context is what you know insofar as you can know it. In this way, Debwewin is your own truth. This concept of truth is distinct from Western concepts of truth. Rather than implying that one or another individual's truth must hold when there is a disagreement, Indigenous understandings of truth generally recognize that no individual human can hold or perceive absolute truth—and that diverse aspects of truth that appear to be incompatible are part of the larger whole (Borrows, 2010).

In talking about strawberries as heart berries, Simpson (2011, 95) refers to the late Anishinaabe Elder Lillian Pitawanakwat's teaching on the FourDirectionsTeachings.com site to explain the significance of working together in a good way and the importance of working through conflict in a manner that doesn't hurt one another: "Odeminan ['heart berries'] remind us of the destructive nature of conflict and of the value of peace. They remind us that the heart is the compass of life and the things that really matter in life are relationships, knowledge and experiences of the heart."

Debwewin is essential to achieving peace and a good life. Without it, we are lost. Simpson writes that heart-based knowledge represents our emotional intelligence, traditionally balanced with physical, intellectual, and spiritual intelligence to create a fully embodied way of being in the world (94). She states that, "if we do not live our stories and our teachings, the echoes become fainter and will eventually disappear. When the land is not being used in a respectful and honourable [way], the power of her teachings are lost. Healers know that plants will disappear if one takes too much, and also if one does not use them at all" (105).

Learning from our stories and teachings is a political strategy for survival because, should we fail to learn, we will lose them entirely. In acquiring Indigenous Knowledge, Debwewin is critical to mobilization because it facilitates the trust and faith to carry on and is therefore integral to Linda Tuhiwai Smith's projects on reading, writing, envisioning, discovering, and sharing. These projects frame how the research participants cultivate a sense of faith and trust in what they know, essential to moving forward. Debwewin provides this foundation, this internal compass, for individuals to negotiate their experiences, relationships, and understandings of knowledge, to the point where they can finally fully embrace that knowledge as their own.

Debwewin is also integral to Taiaiake Alfred's fifth mantra, Change Happens One Warrior at a Time: "Our people must reconstitute the mentoring and learning-teaching relationships that foster real and meaningful human development and community solidarity. The movement toward decolonization and regeneration will emanate from transformation achieved by direct-guided experience in small, personal, groups, and one-on-one mentoring towards a new path" (Alfred & Corntassel, 2005, 613). I will demonstrate his vision here as we observe how the research participants take up the projects of reading, writing, envisioning, discovering, and sharing to impart Indigenous Knowledge as a way of contributing to community building—and ultimately fostering Indigenous resurgence.

Reading and Writing

> *These origin stories are deconstructed accounts of the West, its history through the eyes of indigenous and colonized peoples. The rereading of imperial history by post-colonial and cultural studies scholars provides a different, much more critical approach to history than was previously acceptable. It is no longer the single narrative story of important white imperial figures, adventurers and heroes who fought their way through undiscovered lands to establish imperial rule and bring civilization and salvation to "barbaric savages" who lived in "utter degradation."* (Smith, 1999, 149)

> *Indigenous people are writing. . . . In a localized context, however, writing is employed in a variety of imaginative, critical, and also quite functional ways. . . . The boundaries of poetry, plays, song writing, fiction and non-fiction are blurred as indigenous writers seek to use language in ways which capture the messages, nuances and flavour of indigenous lives.* (Smith, 1999, 149–50)

Here I combine the projects of reading and writing to frame how Indigenous Knowledge online creates opportunities for alternative Indigenous reading and writing. For the research participants, access to this knowledge can be an excellent aid for creating or complementing resources that affirm and speak to Indigenous resurgence.

Janetta Soup (2014) was happy to see FourDirectionsTeachings. com online because it was one of the first resources that she found when she began to research Indigenous Knowledge on the Internet: "We were typing in Google searches on 'First Nations teachings,' or one of those key words, when we came across FourDirectionsTeachings. com. We were so happy when we found it and really just in awe because it represented the diversity of cultures that we needed to express. So finding that there were five diverse cultures presented on the site was amazing." Soup and her team referred to the project in their work on Elder care. She said that it really helped them to define and demonstrate the diversity of First Nations in Canada for health-care workers. She also stated that she appreciated seeing Reg Crowshoe on the site because she was reminded of his teaching on Indigenous diversity, which explains that Indigenous cultures are different but have in common venue, action, language, and song. Soup said that she always keeps this teaching in mind. So, though Crowshoe does not offer this particular teaching online, Soup, in her reading of the site and her consequent translation of and writing about the site for others, demonstrates her prior knowledge, which resonates with a sense of truth—Debwewin—that enables action from an Indigenous perspective.

In reflecting on FourDirectionsTeachings.com, Émilie Monnet (2013) said that "it felt good to be on the site." She then explained her intuitive reaction to it: "From the get-go, the Elders had given their permission and were part of a collaborative process. I don't know this for sure, but I feel that the content was decided with them and that they chose what they would share. I feel this intuitively because I know my process is to work collaboratively with Knowledge Keepers as well." Here it could be argued that she was simply projecting her own artistic process onto the work, but she clarified her reaction:

> Again, it comes back to the work and the success or failure
> of it. A good work comes from a good process. I remember
> all the different uses of the circle, especially in the intro-
> duction and how the visuals and symbols all came together

with the voices of the Elders. It was like listening to an oral teaching, which, given the form, was really inspiring.

Although the oral teaching was online, Monnet nonetheless felt engaged with it and that her reading/response was guided by her heart-based knowledge, in which her emotional intelligence connected to her intellectual and physical sense of being.

Donna Bourque (2014) said that, when she listened to the Elders on the site, she got a sense that they were proud of what they were talking about and that they were speaking with sincerity and confidence. She shared that, when she first started learning about the Cree culture, she heard about the woman being the head of the teepee and about the medicine wheel and the sacredness of children: "When I saw these same teachings on FourDirectionsTeachings.com, they resonated with me on a spiritual level, where I was able to validate what I was seeing and hearing." In speaking about the spiritual level, Bourque evoked the principle of Debwewin as a way of validating what she was seeing and reading.

For Cheryl L'Hirondelle (2014), connecting to Indigenous Knowledge means identifying that knowledge from its source:

> I'm always filtering what I see through what I know about a precontact worldview and what is nation specific. For example, I know of Leroy Little Bear and have heard him speak several times. I have also listened to Elders like Maliseet or Wolastoqiyik Elder Shirley Bear. I have also been exposed to Mi'kmaq Elders, Haudenosaunee Elders, and Anishinaabe Elders. So I filter information based on what I have learned from the Elders and their worldview[s].

In this way, Debwewin circles from Elders to learners, such as L'Hirondelle, who draws on what she has learned from Elders and their worldviews to make those connections to Indigenous Knowledge.

Priscilla Lepine (2014) talked about how Indigenous Knowledge sources that celebrate diversity are healing, especially in the North, where Indigenous communities can be divided. She therefore appreciates how diversity can be celebrated. Like Elder Reg Crowshoe, she also noted that there are similarities among Indigenous Nations:

> It was interesting to see the differences between the Blackfoot, [the] Mohawk, and the Cree and to see the different backgrounds. It's nice to see the different cultural groups and how they are all validated, even though each group applies different meanings but [has] a similar ideology. I found that the people speaking were genuine and that they've learned their culture. It is clear that they understood what they are saying and that it wasn't something that they were just trying to impart.

Lepine acknowledged that she heard truths deeply felt by the people who were speaking. Again, the intuitive understanding of truth was present in her statement. She drew from her internal compass to negotiate Debwewin.

For Larry Chartrand (2013), Indigenous Knowledge online allows him to teach people how to read that knowledge with respect to the legal principles that it embodies: "A lot of Indigenous Peoples reference Indigenous teachings and don't actually identify them as legal principles, but in effect they operate that way. I am trained in the discourse of law. So I am trained to see how legal principles can be derived from legends and stories." Like John Borrows, Chartrand understands the value and meaning of Oral Traditions from a legal perspective and is determined to impart that knowledge to his students: "As a law teacher, I try to bridge the gap between technology and primary law with Indigenous teachings. If I can do that, then I feel I have achieved something worthwhile with my students."

Learning how to read (in the sense of being able to read Indigenous legal principles in various legends or stories) is a strategy for law students interested in Indigenous law. To find the legal principles and values of a community in an oral history requires strategies different from those of the legal principles of a print-based culture. For law students, and any learner interested in Indigenous Knowledge, learning about Indigenous cultural protocols and how to read them in a work is key to validating the work that they are seeing.

For educators such as Angela Nardozi (2014), Indigenous Knowledge online that has been vetted by the community and adheres to cultural protocols is a gift for non-Indigenous teacher candidates:

> Having access to Indigenous Knowledge online demystifies the knowledge. When we discuss Creation stories from diverse First Nations, and demonstrate how to use the smudge, teacher candidates begin to see the commonalities in Indigenous Knowledge and how it makes sense. They begin to understand that it is a philosophy and epistemology for how to live better on the land, and with each other, and how to connect people to the land. Once they start making the connections on their own, you can literally see their faces light up.

Nardozi's reference to "making the connections on their own" demonstrates an act of reading and interpreting by teachers. The teacher candidates learn how to read the symbols, such as use of the smudge, and signifiers presented in the diverse Creation stories and what they mean. In this way, they are introduced to an Indigenous worldview, which, as Nardozi pointed out, demystifies the knowledge for teacher candidates.

FourDirectionsTeachings.com provides an alternative form of writing for Internet users interested in acquiring Indigenous Knowledge. Some of the teachings even represent a deconstructed account of history. For example, Lepine (2014) noted that the Mi'kmaq teaching is more cultural, whereas the Blackfoot teaching gives more information on the Dominion of Canada and distinctions among Indigenous Peoples and is therefore more ideological. For Lepine, the Blackfoot content is less about Traditional Knowledge and more about Aboriginal ideology and Western ideology. In thinking about Indigenous Knowledge online, she referred to sites that offer a rereading of Canadian colonial history, such as those for the Royal Commission on Aboriginal Peoples and the Truth and Reconciliation Commission.

Based upon the research participants' responses, the task of reading is different for everyone. What is gleaned from reading and then transmitted is also different because of individual contexts and needs. So I believe that reading and writing are based upon each individual's process of Debwewin and that what is learned and shared evolves over time. Debwewin respects the fact that we all have our own truths. It is not based upon relativity but upon a profound sense of respect—a belief that each individual is a capable and responsible member of a larger community. Individuals then make contributions to their communities based upon their heart knowledge. Reading and writing are parts of this process, especially in a society now saturated with information, in which we must learn to decipher and integrate what we have perceived into Debwewin, because then we can confidently help one another and our communities to move forward.

Envisioning

> One of the strategies which indigenous peoples have employed effectively to bind people together politically is a strategy which asks that people imagine a future, that they rise above present day situations which are generally depressing, dream a new dream and set a new vision. . . . Similarly, communities who have worked to revitalise their language or build a new economic base or renegotiate arrangements with governments have worked on the basis of a shared vision. The power of indigenous peoples to change their own lives and set new directions despite their impoverished and oppressed conditions speaks to the politics of resistance. (Smith, 1999, 152)

The participants in this study engage in envisioning through the changes that they are making in their work and through their dreams for their respective communities. Many of them envision having more Indigenous Knowledge available online. Given their diverse body of work, they have their own reasons for dreaming new dreams.

For Brenda Dubois (2014), who works in social services, the Internet is a potential gateway for Indigenous youth searching for cultural knowledge and asking questions about who they are and where they come from:

> We have another generation of kids that are coming up. A lot of them are not going to be raised traditionally. For some, the Internet is going to be the only way they're going to get access to some of that cultural information. Youth are dealing with identity issues and don't know who they are. There are some things that they aren't going to be able to learn in a Native studies class, so they will have to do their own learning. Parents can help by showing them where to find the resources.

For parents who are unfamiliar with community resources or have limited resources themselves, access to Elders and Traditional Teachers becomes a daunting task. However, as Dubois noted, some families have computers in their homes, and others have access to computers at drop-in centres: "Knowing that there are resources online like FourDirectionsTeachings.com makes me feel like we're noticed. Our world is being presented, and our values are being affirmed. Our culture is being affirmed!"

Dubois (2014) shared with students in the parenting class that "the only way our culture is lost is if we don't pick it up." For this reason,

> I think it is important that First Nations People have a presence on the Internet because . . . if we're not online we're gone; we're extinct! There would be no trace of us. The genocide would be complete. Even though it still goes on daily. Every time they take one of our children, that's genocide. If we are not on the web, then we are not in the world;

it's like we don't exist. And the reality is that we have to show people that we still do exist, and that we are not all the same, and that we are strong, diverse nations.

Education is central to her work, especially regarding Indigenous diversity and knowledge. Consequently, she stated, "I also never refuse a non–First Nations person admittance into anything as long as they understand my approach is . . . First Nations." For Dubois, education from an Indigenous perspective is key for everyone and not limited to just Indigenous Peoples.

For Angela Nardozi (2014), who trains non-Indigenous teacher candidates, access to more Indigenous Knowledge would enrich the learning experience of everyone, Indigenous and non-Indigenous alike. Yet she is aware that not all Indigenous Knowledge should be posted online:

> I do wish that the FourDirectionsTeachings.com site was much bigger. It would be great to have a teaching for every nation and have each teaching go deeper. Of course, that's very selfish of me, because I know there's a lot of teachings, and some should only be told at certain times of the year and should be told only to certain people depending on their role and Clan and responsibilities. But, because I know this, I understand that we are only scratching the surface and that there is so much more that we could be learning without infringing on the sacred.

I agree with Nardozi and acknowledge that there is a wealth of Indigenous Knowledge that could be introduced online. Doing so would not infringe on the sacred. Indeed, I believe that sometimes people operate from a perspective of scarcity and think that there is only so much Indigenous Knowledge and are therefore afraid to expose it. However, having been exposed to many Elders all over North and South America, I know that the well of knowledge is deep and that much of it is encrypted in Indigenous languages—a form of protection itself because learning the language takes time.

Many of the research participants know the importance of Indigenous languages and articulated how paramount they are to acquiring Indigenous Knowledge because they know that the language encodes the worldview. For this reason, many Indigenous People are eager to learn Indigenous languages in order to embrace their particular heritage, culture, knowledge, and worldview—but it has to be done right. Émilie Monnet (2013) related that,

> ideally, I would like to see more language resources online and more teachings. I can find a lot of stories/teachings online, but checking the source is frustrating. Sometimes I feel it's not really shared by somebody from the culture, and if I am not sure then how can I trust myself to be inspired? So having access to knowledge that I can trust is important. It would be nice if you developed your site to include more teachings and languages. So having more sites like that online would be really awesome.

For Larry Chartrand (2013), there could also be broader perspectives online that demonstrate, for example, the social, political, and legal impacts and recognition of Haudenosaunee law. For him, envisioning Indigenous Knowledge online would change how we view Indigenous relations in Canada: "These perspectives would of course demonstrate a legal framework. For a law professor, that would prove quite useful, especially if that existed for every First Nation and their legal traditions. *You're talking revolutionary reform here!*"

I agree with Chartrand and believe that such work would open up how we think about law, history, citizenship, responsibility, and much more. To think about how Indigenous Knowledge online could function is mind boggling, especially since—as the producer of one of the first Indigenous Knowledge projects online—I could never have imagined its impact. Indeed, I am inspired by the research participants' responses and feel bound, as Smith (1999, 152) says, "to imagine a new future, and rise above present day situations, which are generally depressing, and set a new vision." In this envisioning, I am not alone, for the research participants have challenged me to dream a new dream.

For example, in our discussion, Cheryl L'Hirondelle (2014) reflected on the process of creating FourDirectionsTeachings.com:

> I also really appreciated the fact that you sought those Elders and [Traditional] Teachers out and created lifelong relationships with every single person you interviewed. That exchange is something we know that happens in our communities when we're dealing with cultural and ceremonial knowledge. It's not just knowledge that you take for granted. You don't purchase it and then walk away. It's not a transaction. It's a lifelong commitment.

L'Hirondelle explained that the teachings on the site indicate that you don't just receive these gifts and that's it:

> So this site is your life. It is a part of you for the rest of your life, and you have to be responsible for sharing it with future generations because the knowledge shared on the site is so deeply profound. It will never be "Oh, that old site." Indeed, there may be questions that you might face in the years to come about how to transport and maintain that information for the future. It's a gift that you've been given.

Until this moment in the interview with L'Hirondelle, I hadn't really thought about the site being my life; however, after my interviews with her and the others, I began to realize that FourDirectionsTeachings. com was more than just another website. They taught me that it is a valuable and cherished Indigenous Knowledge site.

L'Hirondelle (2014) posed the question "how does work being done today survive for tomorrow?" After thinking about it for a moment, she shared that

I have a music publishing company for the songs that I'm writing with the women in prison. I told my nephew, because he's a young budding musician, I said, "You know, you're probably going to inherit this company one day." I am also talking to one of my daughters . . . , and I said, "This is going to be something that after I die you're going to have to upkeep. So I'm going to start educating you on music publishing so you can take care of these songs."

L'Hirondelle noted that these young people will have to understand the responsibilities of being lifelong custodians who will pass this knowledge on to their children and then on to the next generation. Coming back to the discussion of Indigenous Knowledge online, she said, "so that's an interesting kind of notion, to consider how work like FourDirectionsTeachings.com is going to be intergenerationally continued, because those stories need to be kept; they don't just end with you. So how's your son going to know that this is the legacy of his parents and that he has to care for it?"

I never thought about being the cultural custodian of this project. However, after listening to L'Hirondelle and the others, I began to understand that FourDirectionsTeachings.com might be the type of project that can be presented as a digital bundle. As the producer of the project, I cannot declare this to be the case. It is really up to the community and Elders and respected Knowledge Keepers to ponder such distinctions. All that I can do is put the idea forward and ask whether FourDirectionsTeachings.com can be considered as a digital bundle and, if so, which ceremonies need to be considered for transferring and maintaining this digital bundle for the future.

Brenda Dubois (2014)—who develops programming and course work for classes on Indigenous Knowledge, cultural values, and approaches to parenting from an Indigenous perspective—also considered the future of this work and noted that the Elders' teachings on FourDirectionsTeachings.com will outlive us: "Their teachings will be immemorial and will go beyond me and will go beyond you. The teachings will be out there long after we're gone. We're going to leave a legacy for another generation of kids that will be raised without access to Traditional Teachers and Elders." For Dubois, being active now about how we approach Indigenous Knowledge online is key to the survival of future generations. For this reason, she stated emphatically that

> what we have to do now is what that old man said: we have to take all their laws, all their words, and use it against them. So a lot of this stuff is legislation based, and, if we don't start changing and incorporating a part of what we want in legislation, they're still going to do it for us. And they're not going to help us in a good way. Not at all!

Indeed, funding does not exist for Indigenous Knowledge projects online. It is not mandated for education, social services, or health services, even though it is evident from this study that Indigenous Knowledge online affects these fields and more. So, like Dubois, I urge our communities to be active and join discussions about how we will move forward and make such projects table worthy; if we don't do it, the government certainly won't. Indeed, the government cannot do this thinking for us because—as noted by L'Hirondelle and others—we have our own cultural protocols and perspectives on these matters. We *need* to have these discussions, and, as L'Hirondelle (2014) pointed out, we need to ask ourselves as a community "where do we want to be in the future?"

Envisioning is a strategy, as Smith (1999) notes, for binding people together politically in having new dreams and setting new directions. By engaging each other, we become the impetus for the transformation that Happens One Warrior at a Time. Indeed, I have been challenged through this book to think not only about how my partner and I are potential custodians of an online digital bundle but also about how such work online requires consideration from Indigenous protocols that privilege acts of reciprocity: how are we bound together through these visions?

Dubois (2014) introduced this notion when relaying experiences working directly with people from the community:

> I did a class the other night with youth, and at the end a young lady asked me if she was supposed to tobacco me. I said, "Well, I'm not an Elder," but for knowledge transfer purposes sometimes people have tobaccoed me, because they've never had this knowledge before, and it's the first time they're hearing it, and it's a way for them to say thank you.

In another class, a young man came up to her and said, "Put out your hand," into which he put tobacco. "It made me feel so humble," Dubois said, thinking that the action was unwarranted but understanding that for the young man it was a way of validating what was shared. "I was worthy. This giving of thanks is the natural way that our community lets us know 'Yep, I got it; I got your information, and that was good for me.' So that good feeling is passed to you when they give thanks. They need to fill you up too, and that's true reciprocity." Regarding FourDirectionsTeachings.com, Dubois noted that,

> when people visit your website, there is no way that they can pay you back, unless you put something on there. Maybe they can fill out something after they're done, so that way they can give you something back for what you have given them. Do you understand what I'm getting at? It's about reciprocity. You are part of the knowledge transfer; it's not for free, you give something for it.

She was talking not about money but about how Indigenous reciprocity is about giving back to each other, acknowledging each other in a kind and good way:

> It would be nice to let the Elders know how people feel about their work online. Send them those good words that people say because it will fill them up too. They gave

us a gift for nothing. You might have gone through ceremony and protocol to do it, but for us out here we forget
that there is that reciprocity exchange and that it doesn't
come for free. You can pay for it in different ways, even if all
you're teaching at the end is to go and offer tobacco for what
you've learned today.

I found it interesting that Dubois assumed that I had gone
through Indigenous ceremony and protocol to access the knowledge on FourDirectionsTeachings.com, because I did not relay this
information. Yet she implicitly understood that I would have done so
in accordance with Indigenous protocols of reciprocity and knowledge exchange. I note this because Indigenous People with cultural
knowledge infer this automatically, whereas for non-Indigenous
people such reflections are generally not considered or important.
For Dubois, acknowledging and practising Indigenous protocols
are extremely relevant and important. She (2014) explained why
even a humble offering of tobacco is important: "Giving tobacco and
offering thanks is the first act of humility that we teach people. When
you offer tobacco, you are accepting responsibility for the things you
have learned."

For Dubois, this need for reciprocity extends to knowledge
acquired online. She envisioned ways that we can bring our cultural
protocols and Indigenous values to the Internet. We must, Dubois
(2014) said, "encourage our community to still follow protocols, even
through the Internet. If you received teachings over the web, go and
offer that tobacco and say thank you."

I was humbled to hear her say this, and I couldn't help but reflect
on how the website resembles a digital bundle for so many people—
and that, in treating it that way, we are inclined to act in ways that
reflect this important cultural distinction, as Dubois noted.

Listening to the visions of the research participants was such a
gift and a humble and valuable learning lesson. It demonstrated for
me that envisioning is indeed a political strategy, as Smith (1999)
notes, because it binds us together in new dreams and new potentials.

To get to this place, the principle of Debwewin is needed, for to dream new dreams is to have faith. And to have faith is to have courage, trust, and belief, which in my mind ultimately strengthen us in order to be Alfred's warriors for change.

Discovering

> *This project is about discovering Western science and technology and making science work for indigenous development. . . . Science has been traditionally hostile to indigenous ways of knowing. Science teaching in schools has also been fraught with hostile attitudes towards indigenous cultures, and the way indigenous students learn. . . . This debate is over the notion of constructivism, and concerns the extent to which knowledge is socially constructed or exists "out there" as a body of knowledge which students simply learn.* (Smith, 1999, 160)

In discussing Linda Tuhiwai Smith's (1999) notion of discovering, we first have to understand that the Internet is a relatively new technology and that it is an invention of the American military for the purpose of defence through a complex communications network that utilizes standardized communications protocol. Here I look at how Indigenous People are using the Internet and making it work for them via access to Indigenous Knowledge online. As demonstrated so far, many of the research participants in this project believe that access to more Indigenous Knowledge online—making this technology work for Indigenous development—would be of great value.

Larry Chartrand (2013) stated that, by increasing access to Indigenous Knowledge online, more teachers would have the resources to meaningfully engage students in learning about First Nations People. He believes that this type of education is necessary and noted that such discussions would gain greater prominence and respect for recognizing Canada as a truly pluralist society that embraces Indigenous Nations and their laws and not just the common law of the English or the civil law of the French. Canada would be a multifarious or multijuridical state where the laws of Indigenous Peoples are equally relevant to contemporary Western law.

Consequently, Chartrand believes that "Indigenous Knowledge resources on the Internet can facilitate that kind of reform and contribute . . . to positive change in Aboriginal-Canadian relations." He sees the value of the Internet for facilitating better political relationships and understandings between settler nations and existing First Nations, and such use of the Internet is discovering in the sense used by Smith (1999): finding ways to use Western science for the advancement of Indigenous communities.

For Angela Nardozi (2014), accessing Indigenous Knowledge on the Internet is also discovering new ways of using Western approaches to advance Indigenous worldviews:

> Teacher candidates generally come with a sense of social justice, of wanting to make the world a better place. Through our presentations, they begin to see how they can teach the next generation of Canadians. They begin to understand how sites like FourDirectionsTeachings.com offer an introductory window to Indigenous Knowledge—and how that type of knowledge then opens a door to discussions on sustainability in a way that is inclusive of everyone.

As Nardozi stated, "in my mind, FourDirectionsTeachings.com stands apart from time. It is not rooted in a specific historical moment. It can be used by anybody." She believes that this is ideal for teacher candidates, and she noted that there is nothing comparable to it in Ontario: "FourDirectionsTeachings.com is *very different* from other websites because it brings together diverse teachings in a comprehensive and coherent way that respects the diversity of each nation represented. I get the sense that the Elders were able to share their teachings inasmuch as they felt comfortable. I don't find that a lot online, I *really, really don't*." Nardozi laments how little exists on the Internet regarding Indigenous Knowledge.

More such sites could contribute in a positive way to both non-Indigenous people and Indigenous People:

> I remember, after we gave a presentation on plants that are indigenous to Ontario and spoke about teachings and knowledge of the land from a First Nations perspective, people responded by saying, "I need to learn more because this is where I live." The land connects people because it is something that we all must take responsibility for in this day and age. The land is a way to unite people and makes it less of an "us and them" thing. It is a way for non-Indigenous people to respect and learn from Indigenous People, which is really positive and healing. (Nardozi, 2014)

For Nardozi, this dialogue between Indigenous People and non-Indigenous people contributes to healthy relations founded upon respect and desire to care for the land on which we all live. Some people might disagree with her since not everyone sees the land in the same way. For some people, land is a commodity to be exploited; for others, particularly those in Indigenous communities, it has being with which we need to cultivate a relationship. Nonetheless, central for Nardozi is that a dialogue begins:

> When we tell the history of how Indigenous Knowledge and ceremonies were outlawed and did not resurface until 1954, when First Nations communities were given the right again to practise their ceremonies after being denied for years, people are literally shocked. In fact, the older they are, the more they're shocked, and they question, "Why has this been kept from us?"

This is the trillion-dollar question that can be answered through the Internet. Indigenous People can initiate discussions with and thereby educate Canadians on responsible Canadian citizenship through Indigenous Knowledge online.

Indeed, Nardozi has witnessed firsthand the potential for dialogue between Canadians and Indigenous People through her many teacher candidate workshops. She indicated that people are eager and willing to learn:

> The result is that teacher candidates begin to say, "Hey, this might be a way forward in terms of responsible and active Canadian citizenship." This change in their thinking is what we are aiming to do with our work. So, rather than just being critical and breaking down their notion of Canada and what it means to be a Canadian citizen, we focus on how to build it back up in a different way, because at the end of the day we are all treaty people in this territory, and therefore we must all take responsibility. This is how we deepen our knowledge. (Nardozi, 2014)

There is still much to be discovered between Indigenous People and non-Indigenous people. Discovering here goes beyond the notion of constructivism and opens up a dialogue that explores the context of knowledge. What is it that we know about Canada? And why do we know it? Exploring these questions within an Indigenous context and a settler context will certainly lead to new insights that will challenge what it means to be a Canadian citizen. Hence, the project of discovering, as Smith (1999) locates it, fits with Debwewin because it entails a cross-cultural confidence, a much deeper sense of truth if you will, in making Western science work for Indigenous development and understanding that knowledge is context specific.

Sharing

> *The final project discussed here is about sharing knowledge between indigenous peoples, around networks and across the world of indigenous peoples. Sharing contains views about knowledge being a collective benefit and knowledge being a form of resistance. Like networking, sharing is a process which is responsive to the marginalized contexts in which indigenous communities exist. . . . For indigenous researchers sharing is about demystifying knowledge and information and speaking in plain terms to the community.* (Smith, 1999, 160–61)

As positioned here, sharing is a political strategy for resistance. It is also a political strategy for resurgence because, by sharing across networks of Indigenous People, we fortify our knowledge, our principles, and our collective abilities. Consequently, Elders and Traditional Teachers are in great demand as their communities seek them out to advise, consult, and teach on a variety of matters. Allies of Indigenous communities such as Angela Nardozi (2014) understand this great demand and responsibility. As she acknowledged,

> teacher candidates are always saying to us "Why isn't there an Elder coming into our classrooms?" They don't really understand what an Elder with a capital E means. It may be that they think that anyone who is elderly and Indigenous is an Elder or, if they do understand what an Elder is, that they have a right to meet with them. I don't think that most people understand that Elders are doing very important work and are not readily available for our classrooms. Elders are needed in their communities and because of Indigenous cultural resurgence are exceptionally busy people.

Consequently, Nardozi acknowledges, the Internet is an ideal way for sharing Indigenous Knowledge in classrooms because it alleviates demands on local Indigenous communities:

> As an Italian Canadian woman, I don't always get to hear teachings, but I have been fortunate over the years to hear some because of the communities I have worked with. So having access to teachings on the Internet is a gift because it provides non-Native teachers with access to cultural teachings that they otherwise would not get. It also circumvents their notion of privilege by discouraging them from making such demands on local Elders and Native people.

Many Indigenous community leaders, activists, Elders, and Traditional Teachers are overworked and stressed out by the responsibilities and demands of their communities. Finding the time to visit schools outside these communities would be tremendously difficult given their workloads. The Internet alleviates this pressure by providing an alternative cultural resource that schools can use. In this way, Indigenous Knowledge online is a gift that goes both ways.

For Cheryl L'Hirondelle (2014), FourDirectionsTeachings.com is a gift of good storytelling and knowledge combined in an enjoyable package. She shared that anyone who has spent time in a Native community learns that some people are considered to be custodians, whereas others are Knowledge Keepers: "The people on the FourDirectionsTeachings.com site are clearly Knowledge Keepers." Being a Knowledge Keeper might sound dry and boring, but it isn't. It involves sharing a good story layered with Indigenous teachings. As an artist, L'Hirondelle is passionate about stories and greatly appreciates the art of good storytelling:

> Everybody needs a good story. Everyone needs to sit back with a cup of good tea and let somebody narrate a good story. It's relaxing, refreshing, and good for the imagination and the soul. I could send anybody to FourDirections-

Teachings.com. You want to know a little bit about gift economies? Check out Four Directions Teachings. You're interested in ecological issues and want to understand why Indigenous People are connected to the land? Look at the site, and then we can talk about why Bear Butte is in the background or why the Piikani always talk about the significance of four things and how one of those things is place. So there are many different levels, and we know that you never finish a good story.

It is evident that L'Hirondelle has spent quality time on the site since she recognizes the subtleties of place such as Bear Butte in Piikani territory. Indeed, much time was spent on graphics and images to capture the subtleties of the knowledge being shared. For L'Hirondelle, the subtleties of image and placement add to the user's experience:

I remember I spent a lot of time just really enjoying and taking my time with FourDirectionsTeachings.com. It was just such a joy to have something on the Internet that was highly informational, robust, and "as all get out," as my mom would say. It was also so multilayered and aesthetically really pleasing as well. The information on the site flows really well from one thing to the other. It's not like a lot of websites where you click a button and all of a sudden you end up on a whole new page and you don't know how to go back to that first page or to get back to where you were. So even the most scatter brained among us can just slow right down. The design is very clean, streamlined, and easy to use. I love that there's an HTML version because I remember seeing someone use it in education as a handout, and I recognized that the pages were from FourDirectionsTeachings.com.

To experience a rich interactive website on Indigenous Knowledge is clearly a gift for many people and one honoured and treasured by communities because of the dignity and respect that it gives to Indigenous content and teachings that were once denied, ridiculed, and outlawed. It is important to understand this because the act of sharing the site between Indigenous users and non-Indigenous users is a gift of dignity and pride.

Like many of the other research participants, John Borrows (2013) wants to see the work developed further. He is dismayed that the site has not been developed since its launch in 2006, which for him represents a gap in knowledge production. As he explained,

> I think that people need to recognize and understand the many uses that a project like this has. I also think that it takes people like myself or other educators coming forward and saying, "Well, what kind of resources do you need to develop another set of modules that would address this gap in production, and how can we work with you, either through SSHRC grants or corporate sponsorship, or whatever it might be, to continue production on something like this?" I believe that this type of work would not only be accessible and beneficial to my class but obviously, because the framework is so broadly accessible, other people might look in and say, "Well, I'm not interested in law, but I'm really interested in X, Y, and Z," and this resource would be available for them and for their purposes as well.

Borrows sees how Indigenous Knowledge online can be shared and networked across Indigenous communities for a variety of tasks and purposes. Sharing knowledge in this way then becomes, as Smith (1999) states, a collective benefit, with knowledge being a form of resistance or resurgence. Consequently, Borrows said,

> I'd like to see what you've done to be taken further, and developed, and deepened, and applied to more nations. I would like to see the content made even better and broader by building and adding to it. For instance, we're trying

to develop an Indigenous law degree at the University of Victoria. I would love to have twenty-six classes of material available there, where we can access Anishinaabe laws, with different Elders from different parts of *Anishinaabe-akiing*, in different ways, with songs and stories and language and visuals.

Hearing what Borrows said, I was deeply humbled that such a project, in his mind, was worth fighting for. Larry Chartrand (2013) also has visions of sharing Indigenous Knowledge online as a way of teaching Indigenous law. To expand FourDirectionsTeachings.com will require a community effort since funding for such projects does not exist. I am therefore humbled and inspired by the visions of these scholars, activists, and community workers who shared with me their desire to see FourDirectionsTeachings.com expanded.

Indeed, Borrows (2013) believed that

> to be able to access a robust and diverse cultural resource like that online would change the way we think about law and authority in the country. It would change the curriculum in Canadian law schools because there are lots of people who don't grow up on reserves, or who are not Native, and they want to learn more about these things too. As someone who is knowledgeable in the field, I can introduce this to them and make it accessible. However, having access to such a robust cultural resource like this can help people in general to start thinking about how they can use the teachings in their own lives.

For Borrows, cultural teachings shared by various Elders can be applied to families, relationships, individuals, and personal struggles. Cultural teachings can help people to deal with addictions and how they have arrived at them or with existing challenges in the law. The opportunities for change and implementation of Indigenous Knowledge online are endless, as Borrows noted:

For example, I could see how this would help me implement our treaty, or deal with the storage of nuclear waste, which we're confronting in our territory now. Having access means we could say here is a teaching that can give us some guidance on how to deal with ecological problems that are happening on the Saugeen Peninsula. Or here is a teaching, for example, that could be applied to personal injuries and property issues or even to the way people do business with one another. It's pretty impressive what that kind of access to Indigenous Knowledge could do for us. *I think it could change the world!*

Excited by his enthusiasm, I couldn't help but think that this is what true sharing is all about: a deepening and widening of community and service to community. The ability to share comes from the principle of Debwewin. When you know and feel something in your heart, it becomes impossible to deny. The enthusiasm of Borrows to share Indigenous Knowledge online comes from his heart-based knowledge. Debwewin is what makes us fearless in the face of adversity or controversy, which can come from within our own communities or from outside them. Thus, sharing in this context embraces Smith's (1999) position that sharing is responsive to diverse contexts in which communities exist, whether they are marginalized or entrenched in power.

A Full Circle

Debwewin is attained after a long journey that begins with Biskaabii-yang. In looking back, we pick up our Traditional Knowledge bundles and begin to unpack them. In unpacking them, we engage in Naak-gonige, considering carefully and reflecting deeply on what we have learned. Taking time to plan is a strategy that embraces Aanjigone, which ensures that we tread carefully by remembering that transformation is possible as long as it promotes Indigenous ways of being and prevents assimilation. By moving through these principles and processes, we then reach Debwewin, in which we have integrated all that we have learned, deliberated, and contemplated through Biskaabiiyang, Naakgonige, and Aanjigone.

It follows that Debwewin is not easily acquired. It is attained over long periods of time, from first-hand experiences, and through what some might call prayer or meditation, in which we engage all aspects of ourselves to better comprehend what we are seeing, hearing, or feeling. However, once acquired, Debwewin becomes a force to be reckoned with because it becomes a part of you. To deny it would be to deny a part of yourself, which is why so many of the people whom I spoke to repeated that knowledge has to become something that you feel and not just think, because then it *becomes* you. Debwewin—your truth, your knowledge—is what makes you a good mentor. It fosters what Alfred calls meaningful human development and community solidarity (Alfred & Corntassel, 2005) by making each individual confident in her or his ability to be Indigenous and to act, as Simpson (2011) notes, from a premise of love for the community.

The pathway Change Happens One Warrior at a Time is enabled by Debwewin. Without it, we would lack faith in our ability to move forward. In this chapter, I have shown how the research participants engaged with the projects of reading, writing, envisioning, discovering, and sharing from the principle of Debwewin, which has made them fearless, passionate, determined, and visionary in their responses to Indigenous Knowledge online.

Finally, Smith (1999) states that sharing is about demystifying information and speaking in plain terms to the community. I hope that I have achieved this goal throughout my analysis of Simpson's (2011) four tenets of Biskaabiiyang, Naakgonige, Aanjigone, and Debwewin.

CHAPTER 8

LIGHTING NEW FIRES
FOR THE INTERNET

I n a podcast lecture on *Networks of Outrage and Hope* in 2013, Manuel Castells surmises that the Internet is a transformative communications network for the elaboration of new forms of social movements that challenge structures of power.[21] In discussing Indigenous Knowledge online as a different kind of social movement, I speak to the assertion (Castells, 2012) that new forms of social movements are taking root because of access to the Internet. I also consider the value of having Indigenous Knowledge take centre stage and how that role requires a cultural shift for Indigenous communities and leaders.

I then juxtapose these reflections with fears in Indigenous communities about cultural appropriation. I illustrate such fears by discussing the controversy over the Sundance Ceremony—a life in two worlds. I conclude by calling Indigenous communities, leaders, and educators to action—to join a dialogue and an effort to take control of the Internet as an Indigenous transformative communications network that speaks to and respects Indigenous Knowledge within Indigenous protocols and paradigms.

Indigenous Knowledge Online as a Different
Kind of Social Movement

In reading *Social Movements* by Suzanne Staggenborg (2011), I was impressed by how the women's movement brought about social change by altering the discourse of rape and domestic violence from private concerns to social concerns. It did so by promoting a collective framework and developing a discourse on the "personal as political." I also appreciated how this work noted the many obstacles to social movements, particularly in the recruitment of Aboriginal People nationally to social causes because of the historical lack of resources and the difficulty of uniting diverse Aboriginal groups into a cohesive movement.

To discuss Indigenous Knowledge online from within an Indigenous research paradigm using Indigenous language and context represents what Staggenborg (2011, 24) would call a "Discursive Opportunity Structure, i.e., [engaging with] factors such as cultural context, and mass media norms, which shape movement discourse." In this sense, my research is engaged with new social movement theory, which Staggenborg defines as a theoretical approach that focuses on new types of social movements that differ from older movements in structure, type of constituent, and ideology.

In writing about the Indigenous movement, Linda Tuhiwai Smith (1999, 110) explains that it is far more complex than simply a politics of self-determination:

> While rhetorically the indigenous movement may be encapsulated within the politics of self-determination it is a much more dynamic and complex movement which incorporates many dimensions, some of which are still unfolding. It involves a revitalization and reformulation of culture and tradition, an increased participation in and articulate rejection of Western institutions, a focus on strategic relations and alliances with non-indigenous groups. The movement has developed a shared international

language or discourse which enables indigenous activists to talk to each other across their cultural differences while maintaining and taking their directions from their own communities or nations.

Smith (1999) and Staggenborg (2011) acknowledge that cultural transformation is a dynamic and complex process that involves an alternative interpretation of issues and events and entails creating new discourses that speak to cultural revitalization and reformulation. In this sense of cultural transformation, Indigenous Knowledge projects online—or what I like to call digital bundles—are on the precipice of new cultural and political openings. These openings can perpetuate Indigenous resurgence and counteract the impact of colonization, which continues to attack Indigenous communities through land appropriation, destroying water and land on which these communities rely. Displacement, disenfranchisement, and discrimination are colonial practices still experienced by Indigenous People today.

These common grievances represent political openings for unifying Indigenous communities around the world, especially with regard to the politics of listening. "Where the broadcast era was characterised by information scarcity, the digital environment opens up the possibilities and challenges of media abundance, raising a range of key questions about listening" (Waller, Dreher, & McCallum, 2015, 63). However, as queried in the article "The Listening Key: Unlocking the Democratic Potential of Indigenous Participatory Media," do the powerful listen to Indigenous-produced media, and does this constitute meaningful participation in the political process? (57). The answers apparently are yes when "the turn to listening puts the onus on opinion leaders and policy-makers to access the interests and claims of communities that have been marginalized" (63). Listening is then achieved by having trusted pundits amplify the needs of Indigenous communities. Yet listening for and by our own communities is also liberatory and necessary for our own sense of community.

The reports of the Royal Commission on Aboriginal Peoples (1996), People for Education (2015), and Truth and Reconciliation

Commission (2015) reiterate the need for public education to address Indigenous education in the curriculum. The Chiefs of Ontario (2015) press release responding to the *People for Education 2015 Annual Report* states that

> the Report includes findings that publicly funded schools are not providing opportunities for students to learn about First Nations peoples and cultures.
>
> "The statistics reported on First Nation language programming in public schools provides stark evidence of the need to implement the recommendations of the Truth and Reconciliation Commission around First Nation languages," said Ontario Regional Chief Beardy. "The Report indicates that although 96% of secondary schools have Aboriginal students enrolled only 11% offer Native language programs."
>
> The 2015 Report also implies that cultural support programs are lacking in Ontario's public schools. Currently, 13% of elementary schools provide cultural support programming even though 92% of schools have Aboriginal students enrolled. Chiefs of Ontario Education Portfolio holder Grand Chief Gordon Peters said, "things are improving in the public education system, but the pace needs to be stepped up. We cannot continue to deprive generation after generation of our children of a culturally-relevant education."

The report also states that teachers need training on Indigenous issues. Only 29 percent of elementary schools and 47 percent of secondary schools offer training on Indigenous issues to teachers, even though, according to the Ontario government, teachers are unprepared for or uncomfortable teaching Indigenous topics (10). Grand Chief Gordon Peters is absolutely correct; we cannot continue to deprive generation after generation of our children of a culturally relevant education. The time has come for Indigenous Knowledge to take centre stage for the benefit of all of our communities.

Taiaiake Alfred states that

> there is no concise neat model of resurgence in this way of
> approaching decolonization or the regeneration of our peo-
> ples. Nor are there clear and definite steps that we can list for
> people to check off as milestones on their march to freedom.
> But there are identifiable directions of movement, patterns
> of thought and action that reflect a shift to an Indigenous
> reality from the colonized places we inhabit today in our
> minds and souls. (Alfred & Corntassel, 2005, 612)

These "colonized places" include not only how we think and talk about
education but also how we articulate research; the need to decolonize research is why I have chosen to express my research findings
through an Indigenous framework while identifying its relationship
to existing scholarship in order to make transparent my approach to
the research. I concur with Smith: "The field of indigenous research
privileges indigenous concerns, indigenous practices and indigenous participation as researchers and researched" (1999, 107). I also
agree with Alfred (Alfred & Corntassel, 2005) that, though there are
no definitive steps to decolonization and resurgence, there are ways
to transform our thinking and our discourse. In *Settlement's Secret*,
Audra Simpson writes that

> Indigeneity—Indigenous difference—is fundamentally
> the condition of "before," of cultural, philosophical, and
> political life that connect[s] to specific territories and of the
> political exigencies of this relatedness in the present. This
> present is defined by the political projects of dispossession
> and settlement, and the difference that is Indigeneity is the
> maintenance of culture, treaty, history, and self within the
> historical and ongoing context of settlement. (2011, 208)

For Simpson, "Indigeneity is quite simply a key to critical analysis, not as a model of an alternative theoretical project or method

(as interesting and valuable as this is) but simply as a case that, when considered robustly, fundamentally interrupts what is received, what is ordered, what is supposed to be settled" (209). I believe that my book has contributed to such critical analysis to some extent and that the combination of theoretical frameworks that I have used "funda-- mentally interrupts what is received, what is ordered, and what is supposed to be settled."

In bringing together the work of Alfred (Alfred & Corntassel, 2005), Simpson (2011), and Smith (1999), I have attempted to create a fluid and holistic Indigenous paradigm for framing the various issues for this research project. I did this by providing Smith's twenty-five projects as a method of analysis or what Staggenborg might call "collective behaviour theory": that is, "a theoretical approach to social movements that focuses on the grievances or strains that are seen as leading to collective behaviours outside of established institutions and politics" (2011, 196). I wanted to frame the issues and grievances using an Indigenous discourse, so I used Simpson's four tenets to create what Staggenborg would call "collective action frames": that is, the "interpretations of issues and events that inspire and legitimate collective action" (23). These frames are Biskaabiiyang ("to look back"), Naakgonige ("to plan"), Aanjigone ("non-interference"), and Debwewin ("heart-based knowledge"). Framing is crucial to mobilization. Staggenborg defines framing as "an important activity [for] movement leaders and organizations. The framing perspective emphasizes the role of movements in constructing cultural meanings, as movement leaders and organizations frame issues in particular ways to identify injustices, attribute blame, propose solutions, and motivate collective action" (23).

The research participants demonstrated that collective action frames have specific functions that contribute to Indigenous resurgence. In my analyses of their responses to Indigenous Knowledge on the Internet, I have shown how Biskaabiiyang is an act of decolonization because in looking back we pick up our political, social, and spiritual bundles—all of which contribute to a psychological grounding in Indigenous Knowledge and worldviews. The process of Naakgonige shows how healing is attainable by treading carefully through the physical, spiritual, psychological, social, and collective restoration of our Indigenous Knowledge and worldviews. To accomplish this healing, we must employ Aanjigone, which grounds us before we leap into transformation to deeply consider the psychological, social, political, and economic impacts of change and what these impacts will be for the next seven generations. Finally, we are inspired to act through Debwewin, the truth and strength required by each of us for mobilization at local, regional, national, and global levels.

I have linked these collective action frames to Alfred's five mantras (Alfred & Corntassel, 2005). In making these connections, I am undertaking what Staggenborg identifies as "frame bridging—the extension of collective action frames to connect together the concerns of different groups or movements" (2011, 197). I have done this because I find the five mantras (Land Is Life, Language Is Power, Freedom Is the Other Side of Fear, Decolonize Your Diet, and Change Happens One Warrior at a Time) very useful as "the mantras of a resurgent Indigenous movement" (Alfred & Corntassel, 2005, 613).

I have connected my analyses of the interviews—which included themes of survival, cultural revitalization, and transformation of education—with Alfred's pathways of Indigenous resurgence (Alfred & Corntassel, 2005). I have utilized Simpson's (2011) four tenets and Smith's (1999) twenty-five projects as ways of contributing to a research perspective that might inspire Indigenous community leaders and policy makers to take note of how Indigenous Knowledge online is contributing in specific ways to Indigenous resurgence. I have attempted to show how the explorations of questions and the conclusions made in this research correspond to the principles expressed through the overlaid perspectives of three leading Indigenous scholars.

In doing this work, I hope that Indigenous communities might consider resource mobilization theory, articulated by Staggenborg as a "theoretical approach focusing on the resources, organization, and opportunities needed for social movement mobilization and collective action" (2011, 147). This task will not be easy: "Social movements have helped to bring about many political and cultural transformations, but they also face numerous challenges in effecting change. Movements typically confront powerful adversaries and long-standing structural arrangements, and they rely on cultural and political openings to afford the possibility of success" (141). Although I hope that the politics of listening will attract pundits to the cause, I have no illusion about trusting them to lead the way. Rather, I call on our own community leaders to come forward and join in dialogue so that we can create our own path for accessing Indigenous Knowledge in a good way.

Indigenous Knowledge at Centre Stage

Mary Lee, the Cree Elder on FourDirectionsTeachings.com, shares in her teaching on the structure of the teepee that each of the poles has a specific meaning. The way that they are tied together also has a meaning. Similarly, Monique Mojica (2014) noted that Guna houses are built with each post representing a cultural principle: "I don't have those teachings, but I know the bamboo walls and palm roofs—the way everything is stitched, woven, and lashed together—all mean something." Reflecting on the teepee pole teaching and Guna houses, Mojica stated emphatically that

> our architecture is more than a building; it is a sequence, a ritual, a practice, all infused within the structure itself. Understanding this conceptually is what I find so exciting about putting Indigenous Knowledges in the centre of my practice, because it offers a worldview and perspective that [are] not fixed but adaptable to the fluidity of culture and the arts. So that's really what I'm interested in: how can we privilege that knowledge and those structures and those shapes and those rhythms?

Mojica's statement captures the excitement as we begin to scratch the surface of Indigenous Knowledge, and it echoes the energy of the many research participants who expressed the significance of Indigenous Knowledge in their work and lives. Indeed, putting Indigenous Knowledge at the centre of their practice is key for the many people involved in this research project, including me.

The challenge is how do we continue to put Indigenous Knowledge at the centre of our practice in a way that is culturally respectful, responsible, and beneficial to all of our communities? To answer this question, we need to look at our changing times—or what some are calling a cultural shift. Early in this book, I stated that our time-keepers tell us that we are entering a new era. I believe this to be true and that this new era entails challenges to long-standing structural arrangements—including how we access Indigenous Knowledge.

The Cultural Shift

During our interview, Rainey Gaywish (2014) discussed how, some years ago, Arvol Looking Horse addressed his concern online about how many non-Native people were participating in the Sundance Ceremony and running their own Sundances. Gaywish recalled that "he cautioned that we need to take more care because non-Native people are distorting our traditions and spiritual teachings." She empathized with Looking Horse:

> Over the years, I have witnessed non-Native people who are so oblivious to their own white privilege and the fact that they project a cultural exoticism onto Indigenous ways and end up exploiting the teachings that were shared with them. These people are often individuals who are very hungry for meaning and sense of self in their own lives. However, because they are not in touch with their own white privilege, I have seen these people, within a very

short period of time, believe that they are more entitled to
a ceremony than the people who taught them.

Gaywish surmised that the problem with the New Age movement is
the propensity to indulge the unrestrained audacity of the human ego.
"New Ageism" in general has little respect or humility as it appropriates aspects of every distinct culture in the world and distorts them,
often on the basis of shallow and selfish preconceptions. She believed
that Looking Horse was trying to warn us that, "if we don't protect
our ceremonial ways, we will lose what we struggled to maintain
through the difficult era of history that made it illegal for us to practise our ceremonies and speak our languages."

Throughout this research, cultural appropriation by the New Age
movement was consistently raised as a concern, along with cultural
exploitation, also raised with respect to how Indigenous People
can exploit their own cultures knowingly or unknowingly. These
fears and concerns are at the core of what it means to put aspects
of Indigenous Knowledge online, and they were uniquely captured
by Gaywish and Mojica when discussing the controversy over the
Sundance Ceremony.

The Sundance Controversy: A Life in Two Worlds

Rainey Gaywish (2014) conveyed that recently there was much controversy among Indigenous People when David Blacksmith, a Cree
Sundance Chief from northern Manitoba, allowed APTN to film
his Sundance for the purpose of streaming it online.[22] Blacksmith
allowed the filming as a way of sharing the spiritual ceremony with
Indigenous People, especially those who might have been struggling.
Gaywish elaborated that,

as Anishinaabe people, it is our rightful inheritance to know
who we are, to know where we come from, and to practise
our teachings and ceremonies. How do we maintain these

rights if we don't teach our ways, if they are not transmitted to the younger generation? The younger generation needs to see the value so that they can pick it up and pass it down to the next generation. So it is about providing access to our youth. It is also about revitalizing the language and ensuring that these ceremonies live on. The fear is how far do we open the door before we begin to endanger the vitality, integrity, and rightful inheritance of our people?

Indeed, Indigenous youth surf the Internet, travel between urban and rural areas, and are bombarded, like all youth, by popular culture everywhere. The fact that they represent the fastest growing population in Canada has created a cultural pyramid in First Nations communities, where the base represents the youth and the pinnacle represents Traditional Teachers and Elders who hold Traditional Knowledge. As a result, as Marlene Brant Castellano (2000, 33) states, "elders are coming together in gatherings such as the annual elders' conference at Birch Island, Ontario, to talk about how to be an elder in a changing environment, and how to adapt old forms of sharing knowledge to ensure that the next generation benefits from the wisdom of our ancestors." The fact that these discussions are occurring indicates a cultural shift among our Knowledge Keepers. Gaywish (2014) shared her understanding of Blacksmith and his reasons for allowing the Sundance to be filmed:

> David says he did this because that's what his vision told him to do. Relating to him as an Elder, I have a lot of respect for that. We have visions, and we have dreams. David is doing what he believes that the spirit told him to do, and he is doing it in the most careful way that he can. He is echoing what all the Elders say, and that is that no one should come to the door of a lodge without knowing what it is that they're entering. So what I think he was saying, I'll show you what a Sundance is, there's no reason to be fearful here.

To be able to "come to the door" is extremely important for Indigenous youth. Yet, as pointed out earlier by Brenda Dubois (2014), sometimes youth feel discouraged if they feel belittled or humiliated because they do not know how to go about the ceremony in a culturally appropriate way.

Gaywish (2014) stated that Indigenous People are in such a vulnerable position because we live in two worlds:

> We live in a Western world where the rules and values are not our own, and we live in our communities where our worldviews and practices are at constant risk of exploitation. . . . We have a proud and strong tradition, and if somebody's watching the Sundance online are they going to feel more empowered, more knowledgeable, to come to the door? Are they going to see or feel its healing potential? Or are they going to take that video and build a Sundance lodge somewhere and start running a Sundance? The truth is that some people might.

That some people might exploit or appropriate the Sundance Ceremony is a huge fear for the Indigenous community and was vehemently expressed through many online posts when APTN first released the Sundance series in 2013:

APPALLED_BY_RELIGIONS
You are not a traditional walking leader, otherwise you would not allow such disrespect towards our Sacred Ceremony!

LADYPHOENIX
How dare you film any part of this sacred ceremony, let alone post it online for all to see? Shameful!

BEN CARNES

I can say that I am very disturbed by this. It is something I would expect from a non-Native news source, but not from one of the very few we have. The sacredness of the ceremony loses its integrity and its intent through the eyes of the viewer. One does not learn or even begin to understand the ceremony without being a part of it. It is not a spectator event, never was. I'm am [*sic*] just very disturbed and saddened by this.

ROSE CHRISTO

You ought to be ashamed of yourself. Ceremony is not supposed to be documented like this. You are stripping it of what makes it sacred, secret and protected. You are commodifying something that has no place being commodified and you are spitting on the memory of the people who died trying to protect our way of life.

GLENDA SUE DEER

It so sacred you put it out there for all to see....hmmm yeaaaaah buhdee.....no wonder we have so many white people stealing Indian ways...if Creator wanted them to know ...he would have given it to them ..but he didn't! This is why mother earth is so off balanced! Sickening..seeing Indians condoning this..sad..this is MY OPINION

RTATUM

Many of our people gave their lives to protect these ways and ceremonies. Posting this publicly is just an invitation to exploitation and abuse.

FRANK BUSCH

The Spiritual Awakening prophesized by the appearance of the White Buffalo is at hand! It is time to reveal the glory of our most sacred ceremony to the 4 Colours of the Earth. No longer will we stay in hiding, no longer will we be ashamed. This is the gift that Creator has given to us. We have been tested, we have been humbled, but we have survived. Any who think our Sundance way off life should remain hidden, has been shamed by the influence of the Church. I will pray for those who are lost that they may find their way out of darkness and into the light of truth, Ekosi.

DISQUS_IU9FUGZZER

This only leads to exploitation and incidents like the sweat-lodge incident where people were killed. People who don't know the true meanings of these ways can really hurt people. Pray for these "Sundance Leaders" and their followers not to cause harm to their own and to other people. There is such a thing as "karma" when you play with the Creator's ceremonies. Pray for the health of our people and for ceremonies to stay alive but with out social media. Take this video down!!

DIANADELILAH

I don't understand why this was recorded and aired. Is nothing sacred anymore? I have no words to express how this saddens me, I can only cry :(

ANGEL YOUNG

Wow...Sad and disrespectful... there are somethings that should be left alone.. next thing you know, ya'll will be making posters and selling t-shirts.. Where is the Humility in this????

DARA FINLAY

If ceremony like this wasn't filmed and shared, then more customs would be lost. Specials like this help bring ceremonies back into people's lives, it's not shameful or disrespectful, it's celebrating a wonderful and rich tradition.

RTATUM DARA FINLAY

Our ceremonies are alive and well, thank you very much. All this does is invite the unscrupulous to exploit and desecrate our ceremonies.[23]

The thread was eventually ended, but the sample here demonstrates the profound outrage and fear from many in the Indigenous community, especially with regard to the notion that ceremony cannot be experienced online. Indeed, as noted above, ceremony is not a spectator sport, and it must be experienced in person to truly participate in its sacredness and integrity. Although I agree with many of these posts and believe that ceremonies must be attended in person, I also believe that there are teachings and Indigenous Knowledge that can be shared online for the benefit of Indigenous youth and communities everywhere.

I am not alone in this thinking. Gaywish (2014) also expressed the need for such connections to be made:

We want to reach out to our people across the country so that they know they are welcome and encouraged to learn and pick up that knowledge again for the next generations to come. This transfer of knowledge is what we want for our children and grandchildren, so that they will be affirmed by their identity as Anishinaabe, whatever First Nation they may be.

The question then becomes "how do we protect and transmit our ceremonies and knowledge in ways that maintain their integrity, for the many young Indigenous People coming up who may not have direct access in their environment to those who hold that knowledge and conduct those ceremonies?" This question is even more poignant after the release in 2015 of the Truth and Reconciliation Commission (TRC) report on Indian residential schools. The report says that the residential schools were set up to *take the Indian out of the child* but that now education is needed to put the Indian back into the child. Having more access to Indigenous Knowledge online would certainly support the accomplishment of this task on a national scale. But to accomplish it definitely requires a shift in our thinking.

In reflecting on her Sundance experience at a different location, also under the guidance of David Blacksmith, Monique Mojica (2014) shared that "there is a shift happening, and I don't think this one Sundance camp is the only place where it's happening." Mojica discussed how women on their moon time (monthly cycle) were granted permission by the Sundance Chief to participate in the ceremony and even to pierce their bodies. She shared that, in her understanding, this had never been done before. She also noted with great unease that an Indigenous film crew was granted access to tape the entire ceremony and that non-Indigenous people were granted permission to participate in it. She mentioned that there were many non-Indigenous people at the ceremony and that "I have never been one to happily enjoy the New Age trend, because cultural appropriation has been rampant for so long." As a result, Mojica felt very conflicted about her experience and shared that "six months later I'm still sifting through what I saw there, because the teachings I have received tell me that what happened there *should never have occurred.*"

Nonetheless, Mojica (2014) also trusted and respected the ceremonial leaders greatly concerned with the epidemic of youth suicide in northern communities:

> They believe that, if we can put the Sundance online and it saves a life, then that justifies doing it, because saving and reaching out to the youth [are] the intent. I don't have a definitive answer for what should be made available online, and I am really glad that I am not the one who has to answer

that. I think that those kinds of questions are things that we have to collectively discuss in order to come to a place where we can all feel comfortable and secure with those decisions. Do I want the Sundance to be able to be watched virtually online? Do I think that a youth who's really in trouble is going to be saved by watching the Sundance online?

Mojica elaborated:

I don't think that's possible. However, if there was someone who didn't know that there were places to go, and that there are people who have dedicated themselves to creating *space for that kind of brokenness*, then it may be that this kind of thing does need to be out there. Our communities and youth are struggling. So if there are people who are reaching out and saying, "Come be part of this," and *that there is something else that's being done, that's going on now*, other than substance abuse, gangs, endless consumerism, or aspiring to endless consumerism, then perhaps this is what we need to be doing.

Ultimately, Mojica (2014) stressed that we are in a critical time. People are dying. With great heaviness, she stated that "we are losing so many of our youth and women that it is truly an epidemic. The new number on missing and murdered women, as of yesterday, has climbed to 824." Reflecting on this crisis, she stated that "I don't think I have a definitive answer. I'm still questioning and feeling out what I am okay with. My suspicion is that we are at a fulcrum, a turning point where, in order for these ceremonies to catch the people who are falling through the cracks, we have to—and they have to—change. Everything has to shift." So, even though she was uneasy about non-Native people participating at the Sundance Ceremony, something shifted for her while she was there:

I will tell you that the epiphany that hit me was this. We've been ranting, we've been praying, we've been marching, we've been walking, we've been doing conferences and panels *up the wazoo* about how critical it is to start treating the Earth differently, and what hit me during that ceremony was that, unless non-Indigenous people start to feel in their bodies that connectedness that is encapsulated in all my relations, unless they feel it in their bodies why the Earth is sacred, why we are related to all of those forces and powers and spirits, then we're doomed.

In that epiphany, Mojica (2014) began to sympathize with the ceremonial leaders, though she still felt uneasy: "My feeling is that there is a shift happening among the Knowledge Keepers. That's what I'm hearing anyway." Yet she emphatically stated that "it's not like they're saying, 'Watching it online is good enough.' You still have to bring your body into the Sweat Lodge. You still have to bring your body into the Longhouse. You still have to bring your body into the [Sundance] Ceremony." Indeed, watching online is not good enough! I wholeheartedly agree that "you still have to bring your body into ceremony." The Sundance controversy captures the tension of a life lived between two worlds and represents the fulcrum, a turning point, where Indigenous Knowledge is perceived to be both at risk and salvation or deliverance from risk. For this reason, Indigenous leaders, communities, and policy makers need to engage in dialogues on how we can ensure that Indigenous Knowledge rekindles our fires in a good way so that we don't choke and become overwhelmed.

The Need for a Digital Bundle

Digital bundles—or Indigenous Knowledge online—can signify a new kind of tool or resource, and hence a new organization (Staggenborg, 2011), and a new opportunity to support Indigenous resurgence that can be legitimate from Indigenous cultural perspectives if undertaken with care. Ultimately, Indigenous Knowledge online reflects an Indigenous social movement for mobilization and collective action through its contribution to the goals of Indigenous resurgence. In thinking about digital bundles or the potential for Indigenous Knowledge online, I am moved by Linda Tuhiwai Smith:

> The strength of the movement is to be found in the examples of how communities have mobilised locally, the grassroots development. It is at the local level that indigenous cultures and the cultures of resistance have been born and nurtured over generations. Successful initiatives have been developed by communities themselves using their own ideas and cultural practices. Considerable reserves of confidence and creativity within many communities have generated a wide range of social, educational, health, and artistic initiatives. (1999, 110–11)

From the onset of production to this final phase of research, I have been inspired and humbled by how Indigenous communities have responded to the idea of Indigenous Knowledge online. Indeed, they have used their own ideas, cultural practices, and knowledge from the outset to challenge me on how to produce, develop, and think about the work that Indigenous Knowledge online is doing. Even now I am being asked to think about the custodianship and eventual transfer of FourDirectionsTeachings.com as a digital bundle for the next seven generations. These concepts had never crossed my mind, and they never would have had I not engaged in this research project.

I am therefore grateful for and humbled by the considerable reserves of confidence and creativity shared with me by the people who have participated in this project from the beginning. I have shared their insights and considerable knowledge as a way of generating a discussion on the potential for Indigenous Knowledge online because I believe, as Smith says above, that "successful initiatives have been developed by communities themselves using their own ideas and cultural practices."

The goals of Indigenous resurgence are focused on reclaiming what Taiaiake Alfred calls our Indigeneity (Alfred & Corntassel, 2005). This work uses Smith's (1999) twenty-five projects to reflect on Indigeneity and the Internet. Using this multifaceted process of reflection demonstrates how Indigenous Knowledge on the Internet contributes specifically to the goals of Indigenous resurgence in myriad ways that relate to Alfred's five mantras.

I have also demonstrated how utilizing Indigenous principles and values for analysis, based upon Leanne Simpson's (2011) four tenets, is ideal for explaining and capturing what I believe is the social movement work that Indigenous Knowledge online is doing. I have distinguished between Indigenous Knowledge and Indigenous information online by qualifying Indigenous teachings as digital bundles because they adhere to, embrace, and reflect Indigenous cultural protocols held by Elders and Knowledge Keepers. In doing all of this, I hope to ignite a conversation with Indigenous leaders, activists, and educators about how we can continue to be present on the Internet in ways that mark digital bundles as respected Indigenous Knowledge sources vetted and supported by Indigenous communities. In so doing, I hope that the cultural appropriation of New Agers and plastic shamans will be thwarted, leaving Indigenous communities and settler allies with access to valuable online resources that can continue to contribute to Indigenous resurgence, education, and community building.

The construction of protective space on the Internet where aspects of Indigenous Knowledge can thrive can accomplish a powerful reassertion of what it means to be Indigenous and support a powerful refusal of and resistance to colonized discourses that seek to obfuscate Indigenous history, languages, political processes, social organization, and the simple dignity of being Indigenous. I see the work of FourDirectionsTeachings.com as being in line with Sandy Grande's work *Red Pedagogy: Native American Social and Political Thought*. Grande writes that "the basis of Red Pedagogy remains distinctive, rooted in Indigenous knowledge and praxis. Though a 'tradition based' revitalization project, Red Pedagogy does not aim to reproduce an essentialist or romanticized view of 'tradition'" (2004, 81).

Indeed, Grande points out that "sovereignty becomes a project organized to defend and sustain the basic right of Indigenous people to
exist in 'wholeness' and to thrive in their relations with other peoples.
Local (tribal) and global aims come together in solidarity around the
shared goal of decolonization" (171).

Throughout this book, we have seen examples of how Indigenous
People from distinct communities relate to the diversity of Indigenous
Knowledge on FourDirectionsTeachings.com and, in so doing, how
they feel connected to other First Nations by recognizing their
shared solidarity as communities involved in the process of decolonization. In addition, I see how the stories of the research participants
relate to what Grande calls "*survivance* narratives": "The survivance
narratives of Indigenous people are those that articulate the active
recovery, reimagination, and reinvestment of Indigenous ways of
being" (2004, 175). Grande states that these narratives form the basis
of Red Pedagogy. These are but some of the many connections that I
see between Grande's articulation of Red Pedagogy and the work of
FourDirectionsTeachings.com.

In continuing to create digital bundles and to come together to
decide on the future of an Indigenous presence on the Internet,
Indigenous communities will control information and thus shape the
minds of their people in ways that support healing and regeneration.
They will be better equipped to counter and resist domination by
educating Canadians on what really occurred in Canada historically.
Significant knowledge of history and treaties, practices of genocide,
tactics of colonization and assimilation, and the ongoing quest to
live with dignity as Indigenous People in this country can all be conveyed to the broader public using the Internet. Our timekeepers have
said that we are entering a new era. Perhaps now is the time to bring
aspects of our knowledge out into the light—in ways defined and supported by our own Knowledge Keepers—so that we can guide our
people and transform the world.

ENDNOTES

1   Linc Kesler, Broadbent Institute, http://www.broadbentinstitute.ca/linckesler.

2   Manuel Castells, "Networks of Outrage and Hope," RSA, May 2, 2013. Retrieved from https://www.youtube.com/watch?v=X-8m66tNPUbo.

3   Ibid.

4   Ibid.

5   Web 2.0 describes Internet websites that emphasize user-generated content and usability as opposed to read-only pages. Facebook, Twitter, and Instagram are all based upon Web 2.0 technology.

6   See the home page of the movement at http://www.idlenomore.ca/.

7   Accessed at www.uottawa.ca/media/experts-details-998156.html (no longer available).

8   "What Is the Deepening Knowledge Project?," Deepening Knowledge: Resources for and about Aboriginal Education, OISE, http://www.oise.utoronto.ca/deepeningknowledge/.

9   "Resources for Elementary and Secondary School Students, *Deepening Knowledge: Resources for and about Aboriginal Education,* OISE. Retrieved from http://www.OISE.utoronto.ca/deepeningknowledge/Elementary_Secondary_Students/index.HTML.

10 "First Nations Community Wellness," *University of Manitoba Extended Education,* https://umextended.ca/access/first-nations-community-wellness-diploma/.

11 The Robina Foundation was created by James H. Binger to fund creative, forward-thinking projects proposed by four institutions—the Law School, Abbott Northwestern Hospital, Yale University, and the Council on Foreign Relations. Funding from the Robina Foundation is intended for the exploration of new ideas and transformative new approaches to complex issues.

12 Accessed at http://www.law.umn.edu/news/borrows-appointment-12-16-2008.HTML (password protected).

13 Originally accessed at http://onishka.org/bird-messengers-en (no longer available). Read more about Bird Messengers on Moe Clark's website at http://moeclark.ca/portfolio/bird-messengers/.

14 Originally accessed at http://onishka.org/en/emilie-monnet/ (no longer available).

15 Accessed at http://www.banffcentre.ca/faculty/faculty-member/1046/cheryl-lhirondelle/.

16 As Soup noted in her email, "our courses are offered to health care providers working within or for First Nation community members. To date, we have over 1000 users set up on our @YourSide Colleague courses and growing."

17 Internet browsers provide a "bookmarks" file also referred to as a favourites list.

18 Marjorie Beaucage and Loretta Todd spearheaded the initiative with the late Ahasiw Maskegon-Iskwew, a sort of technical consultant at the time. Sara Diamond, a Banff Centre director, supported the initiative, which became known by the early 1990s as *Drum Beats to Drum Bytes*.

19 This doctrine refers to acquisition or attainment of that which was previously unknown.

20 "Profile: Cindy Blackstock," *8th Fire: Aboriginal Peoples, Canada, and the Way Forward* (TV series), http://www.cbc.ca/8th-fire/2011/11/cindy-blackstock-1.HTML.

21 Manuel Castells, "Networks of Outrage and Hope," RSA, 2013, https://www.youtube.com/watch?v=X8m66tNPUbo.

22 Shanneen Robinson, "The Sundance Ceremony Part 1," APTN *National News*, August 14, 2013, http://aptn.ca/news/2013/08/14/the-sun-dance-ceremony/.

23 Selected from "19 Responses to 'The Sundance Ceremony Part 1,'" APTN *National News*, August 14, 2013, http://aptn.ca/news/2013/08/14/the-sun-dance-ceremony/.

REFERENCES

Alfred, T. (2009). *Wasase: Indigenous Pathways of Action and Freedom.* Toronto: University of Toronto Press.

Alfred, T., & Corntassel, J. (2005). Being Indigenous: Resurgences against Contemporary Colonialism. *Politics of Identity,* 40, 4: 587–614.

Alia, V. (2010). *The New Media Nation: Indigenous Peoples and Global Communication.* New York: Berghahn Books.

Anderson, D., Chiarotto, L., & Comay, J. (2017). *Natural Curiosity 2nd Edition: A Resource for Educators: The Importance of Indigenous Perspectives in Children's Environmental Inquiry.* Toronto: Laboratory School of the Dr. Eric Jackman Institute of Child Study.

Atleo, R. E. (2005). *Tsawalk: A Nuu-chah-nulth Worldview.* Vancouver: UBC Press.

Bang, M., Ananda, M., Faber, L., & Suzukovich, E. S. (2013). Repatriating Indigenous Technologies in an Urban Indian Community. *Urban Education,* 48, 5: 705–33.

Battiste, M. (2000). *Reclaiming Indigenous Voice and Vision.* Vancouver: UBC Press.

——. (2002). *Indigenous Knowledge and Pedagogy in First Nations Education: A Literature Review with Recommendations.* Ottawa: National Working Group on Education and the Minister of Indian Affairs and Northern Affairs Canada.

Belarde-Lewis, M. (2011). Sharing the Private in Public: Indigenous Cultural Property and Online Media. Paper presented at the iConference, Seattle, February 8–11.

Benkler, Y. (2006). *The Wealth of Networks: How Social Production Transforms Markets and Freedom.* New Haven, ct: Yale University Press. Retrieved from http://benkler.org/Benkler_Wealth_Of_Networks.pdf.

Berners-Lee, T. (2014). Interview with H. Halpin and A. Monnin. In H. Halpin & A. Monnin (Eds.), *Philosophical Engineering: Toward a Philosophy of the Web,* 181–86. Hoboken, NJ: Wiley-Blackwell.

Borrows, J. (2010). *Canada's Indigenous Constitution.* Toronto: University of Toronto Press.

——. (2013). Telephone interview with the author, December 19.

Bourque, D. (2014). Telephone interview with the author, January 29.

Castellano, M. B. (2000). Updating Aboriginal Traditions of Knowledge. In D. Hall and G. Rosenberg (Eds.), *Indigenous Knowledges in Global Contexts*, 21–36. Toronto: University of Toronto Press.

Castells, M. (2004). *The Network Society: A Cross-Cultural Perspective*. Cheltenham, UK: Edward Elgar.

——. (2010). *The Rise of the Network Society*. 2nd ed. Vol. 1 of *The Information Age: Economy, Society, and Culture*. Hoboken, NJ: John Wiley and Sons.

——. (2012). *Networks of Outrage and Hope: Social Movements in the Internet Age*. Malden, MA: Polity. Retrieved from https://www.youtube.com/watch?v=X8m66tNPUbo.

Chartrand, L. (2013). Telephone interview with the author, December 5.

Chiefs of Ontario. (2015, June 8). Chiefs of Ontario Calls for More Cultural Support in Public Schools Following People for Education Report. From Chiefs of Ontario, http://www.chiefs-of-ontario.org/node/1140.

Christen, K. (2012). Does Information Really Want to Be Free? Indigenous Knowledge Systems and the Question of Openness. *International Journal of Communication*, 6: 2870–93.

Corntassel, J., & Spak, S. (2010). Lighting the Eighth Fire: The Liberation, Resurgence, and Protection of Indigenous Nations. *Wicazo Sa Review*, 25, 2: 135–38.

Dei, G. S. (2012). Indigenous Anti-Colonial Knowledge as 'Heritage Knowledge' for Promoting Black/African Education in Diasporic Contexts. *Decolonization: Indigeneity, Education, and Society*, 1, 1: 102–19.

Dei, G. S., Hall, B. L., & Rosenberg, D. G. (2000). *Indigenous Knowledges in Global Contexts: Multiple Readings of Our World*. Toronto: University of Toronto Press.

Dubois, B. (2014). Telephone interview with the author, February 7.

Dyson, L., Hendriks, M., & Grant, S. (Eds). (2007). *Information Technology and Indigenous People*. London: Idea Group.

Foshay, R. (2016). *The Digital Nexus: Identity, Agency, and Political Engagement*. Edmonton: Athabasca University Press.

Freire, P. (1970). *Pedagogy of the Oppressed*. New York: Herder and Herder.

Fuchs, C. (2017). *Social Media: A Critical Introduction*. London: Sage.

Gaywish, R. (2014). Telephone interview with the author, January 13.

Geniusz, W. M. (2009). *Our Knowledge Is Not Primitive: Decolonizing Botanical Anishinaabe Teachings*. Syracuse, NY: Syracuse University Press.

George, P. (2002). The Rainbow Holistic Approach to Aboriginal Literacy. Paper presented at the Light Onwards Living Literacy Text Conference, York University, Toronto, November 14–16.

Grande, S. (2004). *Red Pedagogy: Native American Social and Political Thought*. Lanham, MD: Rowman and Littlefield.

Hall, S. (1996). New Ethnicities. In D. Morley & K. H. Chen (Eds.), *Stuart Hall: Critical Dialogues in Cultural Studies*, 441–64. London: Routledge.

Habermas, J., Lennox, S., & Lennox, F. (1974). The Public Sphere: An Encyclopedia Article (1964). *New German Critique*, 3: 49–55.

Hennessy, K., & Moore, J. (2007). "Language, Identity, and Community Control: The Tagish First Voices Project." In L. E. Dyson, M. Hendricks, & S. Grant (Eds.), *Information Technology and Indigenous People*, 189–91. Hershey, PA: Information Science Publishing.

Hill, D. (1992). *Ethnostress: The Disruption of the Aboriginal Spirit*. Toronto: Ontario Injury Prevention Resource Centre.

——. (2010). Assessment of Learning: A Matter of Cultural Consideration. Deseronto, ON: First Nations Technical Institute. Retrieved from http://fcis.oise.utoronto.ca/~plar/values/first_nations.html.

Idle No More. (n.d.) The Official Idle No More Website. http://www.idlenomore.ca/.

Iseke-Barnes, J., & Danard, D. (2007). Indigenous Knowledges and Worldview: Representations and the Internet. In L. E. Dyson, M. Hendriks, & S. Grant (Eds.), *Information Technology and Indigenous People*, 27–37. Hershey, PA: Information Science Publishing.

Kilpatrick, J. (1999). *Celluloid Indians: Native Americans and Film*. Lincoln: University of Nebraska Press.

LaDuke, W. (1995). The Indigenous Women's Network: Our Future, Our Responsibility. Paper presented at the United Nations First World Conference on Women, Beijing.

Landzelius, K. (2006). Postscript: *Vox Populi* from the Margins? In K. Landzelius (Ed.), *Native on the Net: Indigenous and Diasporic Peoples in the Virtual Age*, 292–301. London: Routledge.

Leach, J., & Wilson, L. (Eds.) (2014). *Subversion, Conversion, Development: Cross-Cultural Knowledge Exchange and the Politics of Design*. Cambridge, MA: MIT Press.

Lepine, P. (2014). Telephone interview with the author, January 29.

L'Hirondelle, C. (2009). *Codetalkers of the Digital Divide (or Why We Didn't Become "Roadkill on the Information Superhighway")* (exhibition catalogue). Toronto: A Space Gallery.

——. (2014). Interview with the author, Toronto, January 21.

Lievrouw, L. A. (2011). *Alternative and Activist New Media*. Malden, MA: Polity Press.

McGregor, D. (2005). Transformation and Re-Creation: Creating Spaces for Indigenous Theorizing in Canadian Aboriginal Studies Programs. *Australian Journal of Indigenous Education*, 34: 67–78.

McMahon, R. (2013). Digital Self-Determination: Aboriginal Peoples and the Network Society in Canada. PhD diss., Simon Fraser University.

Mojica, M. (2008. "Chocolate Woman Dreams the Milky Way." *Canadian Woman Studies*, 26, 3–4: 160–68.

——. 2014. Interview with the author, Toronto, January 25.

Monnet, É. (2013). Telephone interview with the author, December 13.

Nakamura, L. (2006). Cultural Difference, Theory, and Cyberculture Studies: A Case of Mutual Repulsion. In D. Silver & A. Massanari (Eds.), *Critical Cyberculture Studies*, 29–36. New York: New York University Press.

——. (2007). *Digitizing Race: Visual Cultures on the Internet*. Minneapolis: University of Minnesota Press.

Nakata, M. (2002). Indigenous Knowledge and the Cultural Interface: Underlying Issues at the Intersection of Knowledge and Information Systems. *IFLA Journal*, 28, 5–6: 281–91.

Nardozi, A. (2014). Interview with the author, Toronto, January 9.

Noori, M. (2011). Waasechibiiwaabikoonsing Nd'anami'aami, 'Praying through a Wired Window': Using Technology to Teach Anishinaabemowin. *Digital Technologies and Native Literature*, special issue of *Studies in American Indian Literatures*, 23, 2: 3–24.

O'Carroll, A. D. (2013). Maori Identity Construction in SNS. *International Journal of Critical Indigenous Studies*, 6, 2: 2–16.

People for Education. (2015). Ontario's Schools: The Gap between Policy and Reality (Annual Report on Ontario's Publicly Funded Schools 2015). Retrieved from http://www.peopleforeducation.ca/wp-content/uploads/2015/06/P4E-Annual-Report-2015.pdf.

Poster, M. (1995). *Cyber Democracy: Internet and the Public Sphere*. Irvine: University of California Press.

Restoule, J.-P., Archibald, J.-A., Lester-Smith, D., Parent, A., & Smillie, C. A. (2010). "Editorial: Connecting to Spirit in Indigenous Research." *Canadian Journal of Native Education*, 33, 1: 1–8, 154–56.

Royal Commission on Aboriginal Peoples. (1996). *Report of the Royal Commission on Aboriginal Peoples*. Ottawa: Government of Canada.

Simpson, A. (2011). Settlement's Secret. *Cultural Anthropology*, 26, 2: 205–17.

Simpson, L. (2011). *Dancing on Our Turtle's Back: Stories of Nishnaabeg Re-Creation, Resurgence, and a New Emergence*. Winnipeg: Arbeiter Ring.

Sinclair, M., Wilson, M., & Littlechild, W. (2015). *Final Report of the Truth and Reconciliation Commision of Canada Volume One: Summary*. Toronto: Lorimer.

Smith, A. (2005). Spiritual Appropriation as Sexual Violence. *Wicazo Sa Review*, 20, 1: 97–111.

——. (2015). *Conquest: Sexual Violence and American Indian Genocide*. Durham, NC: Duke University Press.

Smith, L. T. (1999). *Decolonizing Methodologies: Research and Indigenous Peoples*. London: Zed Books.

Soup, J. (2014). Telephone interview with the author, February 13.

Staggenborg, S. (2011). *Social Movements*. New York: Oxford University Press.

Stewart-Harawira, M. (2005). *The New Imperial Order: Indigenous Response to Globalization*. London: Zed Books.

Tuck, E., & Yang, W. K. (2012). Decolonization Is Not a Metaphor. *Decolonization: Indigeneity, Education, and Society*, 1, 1: 1–40. Retrieved from http://www.decolonization.org/index.php/des/article/view/18630.

Tuck, E., and K.W. Yang. 2014. "R-Words: Refusing Research" in D. Paris and M.T. Winn (Eds.) *Humanizing Research: Decolonizing Qualitative Inquiry with Youth and Communities*. Thousand Oakes, CA: Sage Publications.

Van Dijck, J. (2013). *The Culture of Connectivity: A Critical History of Social Media*. New York: Oxford University Press.

Vizenor, G. (2008). *Survivance Narratives of Native Presence*. Lincoln: University of Nebraska Press.

Waitoa, J., Scheyvens, R., & Warren, T. R. (2015). E-Whanaungatanga: The Role of Social Media in Maori Political Empowerment. *Alternative*, 11, 1: 45–58.

Waller, L., Dreher, T., & McCallum, K. (2015). The Listening Key: Unlocking the Democratic Potential of Indigenous Participatory Media. *Media International Australia*, 154: 57–66.

Warschauer, M. (2004). *Technology and Social Inclusion: Rethinking the Digital Divide*. Cambridge, MA: MIT Press.

Wemigwans, J. (2008). Indigenous Worldviews: Cultural Expression on the World Wide Web. *Canadian Woman Studies*, 26, 3–4: 31–38.

Wilson, D. D., & Restoule, J.-P. (2010). Tobacco Ties: The Relationship of the Sacred to Research. *Canadian Journal of Native Education*, 33, 1: 29–45.

Wilson, S. (2008). *Research Is Ceremony: Indigenous Research Methods*. Black Point, NS: Fernwood.

INDEX